Prai

MW00582252

THROUGH THE EYES OF LOVE
JOURNEYING WITH PAN, BOOK THREE

"I have just finished Michael's book, *Through the Eyes of Love, Book Three*. I have to say it was incredible . . . it was EXTRAORDINARILY TOUCHING and really resonated with me, (as did *Books One* and *Two*); truly heart expanding and so many WOW moments. . . . I felt expanded, somehow, by reading your book and wanted to say THANK YOU so much . . . it's such a loving connection . . . your book seems to elevate and ground me, expand and deepen me." *–Fiona, UK*

"Michael's new *Book Three* is maybe the most important book ever written for these times. I am recommending it to everyone. If you're ready to see behind the veil of life, then here is the back stage pass." *–G.K., America*

" . . . not to diminish your previous books, but *Book Three* stands head and shoulders above the others. *–B.L., UK*

"The ease and the honesty with which Michael Roads describes his many 'adventures', insights and his own unfolding never ceases to amaze, inspire and touch me." *–M.J. Amazon Review*

"Enriching and enlightening - reminds us of who we really are in essence and of our unlimited potential. Takes us into the world of the Real yet unseen dimensions. Highly recommend!" *–Oneness, Amazon Review*

"Oh Michael, what a brilliant, brilliant book!! I have just bitten my nails, laughed and cried all on one page. God, you're a marvelous bloke!! I love you!! ...now to continue reading...much love to you both." *–C.M., Australia*

THROUGH THE
EYES OF LOVE

ALSO BY MICHAEL J. ROADS

Nonfiction

THROUGH THE EYES OF LOVE, Journeying with Pan, BOOK ONE

THROUGH THE EYES OF LOVE, Journeying with Pan, BOOK TWO

TALKING WITH NATURE—JOURNEY INTO NATURE

JOURNEY INTO ONENESS

INTO A TIMELESS REALM

THE MAGIC FORMULA

MORE THAN MONEY—TRUE PROSPERITY

THE ORACLE

CONSCIOUS GARDENING

A GLIMPSE OF SOMETHING GREATER

Fiction

GETTING THERE

THROUGH THE EYES OF LOVE

~ Journeying with Pan ~

BOOK THREE

Michael J. Roads

SIX DEGREES PUBLISHING GROUP
PORTLAND • OREGON
USA

Published by Six Degrees Publishing Group
5320 Macadam Avenue
Portland, OR 97239 USA

ISBN 978-0-9856048-2-0
Library of Congress Control Number 2013933098

FIRST SIX DEGREES PUBLISHING GROUP PAPERBACK PUBLISHED 2013

ePub ISBN: 978-1476331881

RoadsLight pty ltd Print Edition 2012
RoadsLight pty ltd ISBN: 978-0-9758476-8-8

Michael J Roads books may be purchased by contacting office@michaelroads.com
RoadsLight pty ltd, PO Box 778, Nambour, QLD, 4559, Australia
www.michaelroads.com

Copy Editing by Carol Schrecengost, Brian Longhurst and Theresa Longhurst
Cover Designer: Steve Cook

Published in the United States of America

Printed Simultaneously in the United States of America,
the United Kingdom and Australia

3 5 7 9 10 8 6 4 2

CONTENTS

DEDICATION &
ACKNOWLEDGEMENTS

This book is lovingly dedicated to Carolyn, my beautiful, beloved wife. The other day I was reading some of her outgoing business mail from the office.

"Every letter you write is like a love letter," I said.

She replied, "Isn't that how it should be? After all, we *are* in the business of unconditional Love!"

How could I not Love her? What a precious jewel I have in my life.

To Tracey, my computer literate daughter, my thanks once again for keeping me on track with a patient smile as I continue with my books.

To Carol, my editor in the U.S. who wades into the battlefield of my words, doing the first serious, heavy draft of editing. You do a great job, Carol. Thank you so much. You will be pleased to know I have finally studied the why and when of colons and semicolons.

To Brian and Theresa, my literate English friends and editors who proofread the editing, fine tune it, and make it compatible with the English way of reading and writing, thank you.

Again, to Carolyn, the first person to read my mystical journeys, and the first to make comment. Your regular spoken words, "My genius husband," touch my heart and deeply inspire me. Thank you, my darling. Eagle-eyed Carolyn is also the last person to proofread.

    And she is good!

INTRODUCTION

My gosh, here we are on *Book Three*. It hardly seems possible. I notice that the more metaphysical journeys I experience, then exponentially the more powerfully it affects my expanding consciousness. I like this!

As with my previous books in this series, I **strongly** recommend that you read the two books preceding this, thus enabling you to fully relate to the contents of this book. My journeying is part of an unfolding process, and I am reluctant to write repeatedly of how it began, and what certain metaphysical expressions that I write about actually mean.

I will mention that I do not channel Pan, and that Pan is not a Being, as such. As I expand and grow in consciousness, I realise to an ever greater extent just what an immeasurable state of conscious Intelligence Pan truly is. To borrow part of a phrase from the late Robert Heinlein, I often feel like a 'mote in the eye' of Pan, and yet more and more I feel that the mote-self and the Pan-Self are One—in a way that is impossible for me to intellectually grasp, or explain.

When I focus on Pan, it seems that I connect with a current of energy that is vast beyond words, yet somehow this vastness is able to embrace me without ever reducing itself. With Pan comes a clarity and certainty that have become gifts to me, residing in some metaphysical part of me. I find that mystical cognition grows stronger and brighter, bringing inner illumination into subjects, or interests, that were once a world away from the questing mind.

When Self quests—rather than intellect looking for another bone on which to chew—Self finds that Love and Truth wear many reversible clothes. On one day a certain Truth is revealed, while on another the complete reverse is shown also to be Truth. This is not easy to chew on. It is not at all digestible. All I can do is embrace life's Mystery, knowing that Mystery is multi-faceted, as well as having multiple interpretations. And knowing, finally, that all interpretations through the intellect do no more than reduce Truth. The way through all this—as in so much of life— is to openly embrace within the holistic Self that aspect of Love which already knows and encompasses Mystery.

Pan means panoramic—All. Therefore, as a further introduction to Pan, I can tell you on good authority that Love and Pan are One—a synonymous expression of All/Love. Looking through the eyes of Pan is rather like looking through the eyes of my greatest potential. Looking at—and seeing! We look at so much, but we seldom truly *see*. I cannot do this with Pan. If I am looking through the eyes of Pan/Love, then I am *seeing* through the eyes of Love. There is no halfway, or half place. It is looking and seeing, or nothing. I like that. Sort of 'shape up or ship out' energy. Very clear cut!

As for introducing me—well, if you have read the other two books of this series, you know quite a lot about me. You know that for decades I have walked a rather different path. I share most of my experiences in my books, but, of course there is often a little 'something' that I hold back. I truly do consider myself a simple man. Simple—not stupid! The western world still has a problem with the idea that 'simple' is an expression of power and clarity. It requires an uncomplicated person to see past the complexities of life, seeing into the pure essence of a greater reality. I learned long ago that life is not an intellectual exercise. In fact, as Nature demonstrates, life is the expression of conscious intelligence. Nature is VAST in its expression and diversity, but it is really not complex. It is our intellectual interpretation that creates the needless complexity.

So there you have it. A simple man is able to tap into universal consciousness, while an intellectual person might say, "What is universal consciousness? I don't understand." The joke is—neither do I. But I am able to experience it, because of my willingness to accept it.

'Pondering' is rather a ponderous word, but it does nicely describe the state of sitting by my pond while inner-seeing the mysteries of life reflected in the water's surface. I often do this, aware that all the physical Nature that surrounds me—us—is just such a mirror image. It is a reflection of the vast metaphysical reality of Nature.

We are so very physically based in our relationship with life. I include myself in this assessment, although I am probably considerably less physically based than most people. I am well aware that a physical Nature, just as with a physical body, is the least and lowest of the representations of Nature/Self. I think this is what drives me. I see a world of reality that is basically ignored. It is a far greater reality than our little, physical interpretation of life, but ignoring it does not reduce it; only we are reduced.

When I say the *least and lowest*, I am not in any way making a judgement. I am talking about energy. The physical aspect of Nature and humanity has the least and lowest vibration of all our many aspects. Our physical selves are the dominant factor in our lives, but they are also the aspects of the self which peers through the keyhole at the vastness of life. In this way we reduce the greatness of the view and, unfortunately, the greatness of the viewer.

In my books and writing, I am attempting to redress this. I am attempting to show to the open-minded reader who is heart-connected that we have an inherent greatness which we ignore. I do this by *not* ignoring the greatness of Nature, of life, or Self. I do this by representing a greater reality of life.

Science reveals that the eye of a housefly has around a thousand facets through which it views its surroundings. Makes them difficult to swat! However, my point is that life is like this, especially when you realise that planet Earth has considerably more facets than the eye of a fly. There are facets and realms that go ever deeper into dimensions beyond our knowledge, but not beyond our hidden, long-ignored metaphysical potential.

This is what I do: I remind people of their metaphysical potential.

Okay, now for a few word reminders. Because I am compelled to use the words of a language based in a physical reality, I use capitals on some words in an attempt to give them a greater and more expanded meaning. Most importantly, I capitalise Love to indicate divine Love, or unconditional Love, or absolute Love—not trivialised as in 'I love my car.' Self indicates our immortal spiritual-Self, rather than the mortal identity-self. Also, to expand them and create new meaning: Chaos, the engine that drives—Order, the stability of structure—Balance, the state of greatest potential. I capitalise Mystery as an aspect of life that can *never* be understood. Equally, One is meant to convey a holistic aspect, rather than a term of individuation. I capitalise a holistic Truth, compared with a personal, perceived truth. All life is Nature, whereas the nature of oil is to be slippery! And major Change is not small change. Be aware that wherever I deliberately capitalise the first letter in a word, I am attempting to give it a greater, more expanded meaning.

As always, Oz is Australia!

—*Michael J Roads*

ONE

A SERENE AND STONY SMILE

Some ten years ago a huge gum tree close to our house had to be pruned of a few of its massive lower branches that were stretching out over the house. A few years after that, I bought a large and irresistible Buddha, made of black, volcanic lava, and for a while I pondered where to place it in our quite large garden.

Then I remembered something. When the tree was pruned, I asked the man with the chainsaw if he would cut the lower branch in such a way that it would create a level platform. It was growing at an angle that would facilitate this. Despite being a lower branch, it was still at least five metres above the ground from the base of the tree, but because the tree was slightly downhill from our house, visually it did not appear so high. The next problem was how to get the rather heavy Buddha onto this—the most perfect of resting places.

To this day, when visitors ask me how I got the Buddha up there, I mostly reply, "With a fair degree of difficulty." First, I put an extending ladder in place. When I went up it for a trial run, it bounced and wobbled. I was compelled by the terrain to have the ladder bridging upward from the top of the slope, much too far away from the base of the tree, thus creating the bouncy climb. Looking down, it seemed a long way if I should I fall into the gulley between the tree and ladder. The Buddha weighed around fifteen to twenty kilos. Cradling it in my arms, I began the climb. To my consternation, the added weight now caused the ladder to bounce more alarmingly as, rung by rung, I crept upward. On reaching the top of the ladder, I was well below the flat cut-off branch. This meant that I was unable to hold onto the ladder *and* lift the Buddha the last half-metre to get it onto the platform.

After a few attempts, I began a very shaky retreat, clutching the Buddha while slowly withdrawing down the ladder on wobbly legs. Placing the Buddha on the lawn, I stood for a few minutes, trembling. This, despite the fact I have a good head for heights! I tried to relocate the ladder, making it more upright, but this proved to be impossible. From the top looking down, I was not sure who would land on top if we fell, the Buddha or me. Neither prospect did much for my peace of mind!

A couple of hours later, feeling strong again, I had the sudden idea that if I heaved the Buddha onto my padded shoulder, I could then climb the ladder more easily, and the statue would be at the required height to simply put into place. I went straight into action. Too much thinking about it was not to be recommended. I did make sure that Carolyn would not see me do this—she tends to get a bit upset! One strong heave, and the Buddha was balanced on my right shoulder. Up the ladder I went, bouncing in the most frightening manner. I clung onto the Buddha with my right hand and the ladder with my left, continuing upward in a climb that felt as though it would never end. Finally, the top rung, and my shoulder was at the exact height to gently slide the Buddha into place. It all went perfectly. Then, legs once again a bit shaky, I made my safe and triumphant descent.

From his fitting and lofty perch, the Buddha looks out over the house and some of the garden. Whenever our gazes meet and I see his serene and stony smile, I remember the climb. Odd, that

I was so determined the Buddha should rest there and nowhere else. Meanwhile, over the years, a climbing breadfruit plant, *Monstera deliciosa*, had grown up the trunk of the tree, finally reaching and hiding the Buddha under its huge, deeply divided leaves. Being too difficult to reach, the delicious fruit is eaten by the local possums and parrots.

I decided on a rescue mission so that the Buddha would be fully visible again. Placing the same ladder in the same position — and making sure that Carolyn would not see me — up I went, bouncing more gently to the top where I successfully cut away the enormous leaves, revealing the lava statue in all its Buddhistic glory. Did he give me a special serene and stony smile? It felt like it!

A day or so later while sitting in my study, I was contemplating whether I was stupid to have been so persistent in placing it high in the tree, yet I had the strongest feeling that it was exactly where it should be. Even though I am not a Buddhist, I had the feeling that the Buddha statue is a representation of the Buddha's blessings over our home and garden, and all those who live within. Why I should feel this I had no idea. I knew that the Buddha is not some meaningless entity, but is the spiritual title given to Siddhartha Gautama, a highly enlightened spiritual teacher. Personally, I have never surrounded myself with the effigies of past Masters, but somehow, the Buddha statue sneaked into my life, carrying with him a strong insistence of location.

I focus on my own revered teacher.

"Why the Buddha, Pan? Why should it need to be in my garden, for illogical as it seems, I do feel that it is needed."

I feel the beautiful energy of Pan. *Does there need to be a why? Surely the blessing of such an enlightened soul is enough in itself. Why question it?*

"Well . . . I'm not a Buddhist. So I wondered why the Buddha would be so insistent on being represented in my garden. When I first saw that particular statue, it was clear that I should buy it. Even that is a puzzle, because I have seen many other large impressive Buddha statues, without having any inclination to buy one."

Are you saying then that the Buddha means nothing to you?

"Oh, no. I have nothing but respect for that worthy soul. In fact, now that I think about it, I have several quite small, but beautiful statues of the Buddha. I admire him."

Could you go as far as to say that you Love the Buddha?

Hmm, this is a tricky question. As a matter of fact, I'm beginning to wonder why I started this conversation about the Buddha. "Well, I know already that I can Love someone whom I do not actually know, but I have never applied that to the Buddha. For me, the Buddha is more of a spiritual representation than an actual Being, or person."

The question remains.

I nod my head. "In that case, yes. Just as in my heart I Love the soul-Being we know as the Christ, so also I Love the soul-Being we know as the Buddha."

Good, Michael. In that case, let us go visiting!

After so many years of journeying with Pan, I pride myself on being ready for anything, but this *really* caught me by surprise. "We can't do that! I . . . I don't know anything about him. I'm not even a Buddhist."

Not in this incarnation, but for many lifetimes you were.

"Really? Gosh, such a thing never even occurred to me."

Suppose I told you that you were once quite close acquaintances.

Now I am even more surprised. "Gosh . . . we were friends?"

I did not say friends. I said close acquaintances. There is a difference.

"I hope we were not enemies!"

Acquaintances, Michael. Acquaintances.

"Okay, sorry. I'm a bit taken aback by all this. It seems like the subject you bring up when you didn't bring up a subject . . . if you see what I mean? I feel that I am being manoeuvred into something that is going to teach me another lesson."

I feel Pan's inner-smile. *You mean you do not like learning?*

"Okay, I give up . . . let's go visiting. Making ready!"

Relaxing, my eyes closed, I am smiling. I enjoy a certain repartee with Pan. I have not the faintest idea what his version of *visiting* means or entails, but I will soon find out.

I feel my focus leaving my physical body, while the now familiar waves of time and space are offering a slight resistance to my journey. I have the feeling that something is not quite the way it could be, but I let go of the feeling before it is fully born. I am aware of my Light-body, and the passage of time, although 'time' is not a correct description. I get a revival of the odd feeling that I am making a journey where none is necessary, but it is a feeling I ignore. I am aware of how distraction offers so many tidbits to . . . distract!

You are becoming distracted.

I sigh. "Yes, I'm distracting myself by trying not to be distracted!"

Bring your energy into a focus of clarity. Dismiss all else.

"Okay, Pan. Consider it dismissed."

I become aware of being simultaneously in the past and present. The instant question of how this can be possible begins to surge toward the surface of the mind, but it is as instantly eclipsed by pure clarity: all time occupies the same space. Relaxing more deeply into my experience, it is as though a veil of deceit is drawn away. I am in my usual position, about a hundred metres or so above ground. Beneath me, I see a complex of temples set precariously among the peaks of seemingly endless mountains. How this was built so long ago is a monument to the ingenuity, skills, and commitment of man. Because I am seeing the temple complex from both the past and now, I see that only the deeper colour of weathering stone has changed its appearance from the time it was built.

I also see the remarkable field-of-energy that encompasses the whole complex. It is truly extraordinary. Maybe it is my current way of seeing it, for the field-of-energy of the long ago past, and this present moment, are One.

"Pan, I'm seeing this in a different way than I normally do. Is this under your control, or have I inadvertently caused this? I'm seeing the . . ."

Michael, I know exactly what and how you are seeing.

"Yes, of course you do. Because you sometimes ask me to describe what I am seeing, I tend to forget this. So . . . is this a question you will answer?"

The way you see is under your control, not mine. But please accept that the wider you open your eyes, and yourself, the more you will see as inner-veils are dispersed.

His reply is very pleasing! "So . . . in a way I am seeing beyond time, while mostly I have stayed within the timeframe of my own participating moment."

You could say that. Now . . . observe the temples from this greater reality.

The temple complex is stunningly beautiful, yet the field-of-energy reveals that this was never a purposeful intention, anymore than it was to deny beauty. I have learned that when beauty is within a soul, it will always be revealed through that soul's expression. So it is here. The hundreds of men involved in building this large, multi-layered place of living worship must have been very devoted. There is a huge difference in a building's field-of-energy when the builders build purely for the money involved, as compared with building as an expression of their Love and devotion. Not only that, but the energy of the caretakers of this place expresses the same energy as of those long ago men who built it. On an energetic level, all this is clearly visible and apparent.

As I look from my overview, I notice that there are people, mostly men, moving in a steady, quiet manner about their business. From their robes—and from my prior conversation with Pan—it is apparent that these are Buddhists, and that the temple is home to those whom I see. They are One with this place of devotion and study. I spend a while *being with* the energy, allowing the field-of-energy to reveal its secrets to me. If I were physical, all this subtlety would be lost to me, for I cannot, as yet, perceive the layers of energy that are metaphysically available. Seeing all this in a timeless way is rather challenging, for it needs to be observed in a detached manner rather than trying to interpret the layers of time.

Good, Michael. Knowing will accompany acceptance. Confusion will accompany any attempt at intellectual interpretation. You are using your newfound clarity.

"Thank you for confirming this."

Clarity and certainty have been my companions on many journeys since my conscious expansion triggered their expression. Now, as I sit (I tend to like sitting in the lotus posture, even though it is entirely unnecessary and, for me, physically impossible) high above the Buddhist temples, something else becomes apparent. The long-ago builders of this monastic marvel perched on its eyrie, along with the eagles in the mountains, are the same souls who are now the caretakers. As devout Buddhists, they are bonded to an energy and building that they Love. I look more carefully at these men. Is it really Love, or is it an attachment? Most of these men spent a whole adult lifetime helping to build this monastery in one of the most daunting locations on Earth, along with extremes of weather difficult to imagine. And nor was it built in a single lifetime. I look at the energy-signature, both in the past and the present, of one after the other of the Buddhist monks. With a few exceptions, all are living in a state of grace. The energy-signature of just the occasional monk indicates that these few hold a deep emotional attachment to this monastery. This is based in many lifetimes of involvement with it. None of this is wrong or bad—it is their approach to life and it is in their energy-field.

The human field-of-energy up here in this monastery is like none I have ever encountered in our current earth-frame reality before. Slowly, I begin lowering my Light-body toward the monastery. Immediately, to my surprise, several heads look up directly toward me. Only in this moment do I realise just how aware, how advanced, some of these people actually are. I am hugely impressed. I don't think that I would be able to see me like this! I watch as a small group comes together, staring up at me as though I am some cosmic visitor from the heavens. One walks away with a clear and strong purpose in his energy-field, soon to return with a couple of very elderly monks. Each has a beautiful golden-coloured field-of-energy.

"Gosh, Pan. Those two older monks have an extraordinary energy. I can see their distant past, along with a very extended energy-field of this lifetime. I've never seen anything quite like it. Look at the pure shades of gold in their aura."

No longer descending, I feel slightly like an interloper as I hover just above them. I am not too sure about my reception. I resume my lotus position, watching my watchers!

At this stage, with the brief movement of a hand, one of the two very elderly monks beckons to me. His physical movement is minuscule, but metaphysically his invitation is very open and generous.

Feel free to join them, Michael. You are not an unexpected or unwelcome guest.

I gasp. "Not unexpected! Of course I am. We only decided to come here mere minutes ago. Welcome, I don't doubt, but expected is a whole different issue."

So the student now teaches the teacher?

Suddenly, I feel foolish. Another lesson!

"I'm sorry, Pan. I mean no disrespect. My intellect got in the way."

I feel his delightful inner-smile.

From the moment we began to discuss, nay, from the moment you uncovered the Buddha in the tree, truly connecting with the Buddha's energy for the first time, this moment has been known to these remarkable elders.

In my heart I know this to be Truth.

"I accept this. I know it in my heart. What Michael knows is more limited than Mixael's greater insight and experiences. Michael sometimes does too much thinking, instead of more easily connecting with Mixael's knowing." (Mixael? See *Book Two*. In a way, Michael is the past of me, while Mixael—my walk-in name—is the future of me. Together, they are me—now.)

Continue allowing Michael and Mixael to join in the One dance. It **is** *happening.*

"Yes, it is. Thank you."

Feeling more comfortable in an upright position, I slowly descend toward the temple. Most of the monks' eyes follow my progress. If I had any last doubts, they are all dispersed. I have no idea what to expect—do I ever? Journeying with Pan is always a journey into the unknown. Finally, I feel the Earth beneath my metaphysical feet. Both of the elders come to me, and each gives me a small inclination of the head, their hands clasped before them. I feel their Love and respect. From their energy-fields, I know that this is not a Love or respect for me, the person. It is their Love and respect for life and the living which I represent, and is directed to me. This is a whole different approach to life and people. It is new to me. I find it very refreshing and invigorating.

I bow deeply to them. I *do* feel personal Love and respect for them, as monks and as people. I cannot quite imagine spending my whole life in this one place, even if it does have, possibly, the most spectacular views from any building on Earth. I confess, when Pan suggested *going visiting,* I thought that we were to visit *the* Buddha.

The elderly monks make no attempt to touch me, but I find it very novel that they so easily see and relate to my every move.

I inner-feel the suggestion to 'Please follow.' As they turn slowly away, heading toward the temple from which they emerged, I tag along, pondering on their great age. I see in their energy-fields that they, too, have reincarnated many times to this very temple. In fact, so easily, so seamlessly have they departed their physical bodies at death, to be re-born in nearby villages with such a clear awareness of their destiny that only a few years elapsed between incarnations before they were back in the monastery. In addition to this, I can see that they continued each new physical life seamlessly from where the previous life ended, growing in knowledge, wisdom and awareness. They had the body of child as they grew up, but that body contained a soul of such maturity that they continued as before, bypassing the usual childishness. I am impressed. I learn from their energy-fields that they do not express physical age in the usual way, for in consciousness they *know* they are ageless souls. This *knowing* affects the ageing of the body. It affects the number of years the body can maintain itself, for there is no 'death' within their consciousness. I become aware that they are many decades past a hundred years of age. Paradoxically, for these two monks age does, and does not, exist.

By the time we enter the temple, my respect for them has grown and multiplied. A single glance at me and they are aware of this. Again, the bow of the head toward me, hands clasped, as a mark of respect for my insight. This insight becomes available because I can see the entirety of their fields-of-energy, instead of the usual single lifetime energy-fields.

It helps, Michael, that the elders are aware of their continuity. This affects the expression of their fields-of-energy.

"Is it the same for all Buddhists?"

No. As with Christians, among them are many differing beliefs and viewpoints, thus creating many different expressions of consciousness.

"Yes, I imagine so. It's a shame, inasmuch as it prolongs confusion and fosters conflict."

Just as there are some Christians, who, in consciousness embody the Christ within, so there are the Buddhists, as with these elders, who embody the Buddha within. These are the people who gaze into the eternity of Love.

"I like that. When these two elders look at me, it is obvious that they look through the eyes of Love. I have never seen this before . . . or not in such a profound way. It is unfortunate that most Christians think they are right, and that Buddhism has lost the plot."

So, also, the reverse is true. This is common thinking among many Buddhists.

I realise, even more powerfully, that the form of worship, the belief in a religion, the idealism of 'this is the only way,' all combine to shut us away from the Truth and experience of Love — divine, unconditional Love.

I continue to follow the two elders, along with a retinue of other monks, through this quite dark and austere temple. I notice that all the monks, so far, are dressed in a way that suggests working and being busy, albeit at a leisurely and serene pace.

I follow them along quite a long passage, first going smoothly downward, then easing up and up multiple worn stone steps. We seem to go upward on the very worn steps for a long timeless time before we slowly and reverently enter another temple. As they push open a large, ornate, wooden door to pass through a brilliantly hand-carved entrance, the monks go on bended knees, heads bowed, before arising and fully entering the great room.

I follow, also bowing my Light-body head.

Inside the room, completely dominating it, is a statue of the Buddha. It is not made of gold or silver, or precious stones. It seems to be made of Light. I have never seen anything made by humankind that carries such an energy. Not in any way am I an architect, or carver of wood. What I see seems almost inexplicable. It would appear that many hundreds of small mirrors are embedded in the huge, maybe five metres high, wood statue.

11

Each is embedded in such a way that they mirror the light from the transparent dome above, so that light seems to be continually bouncing from one mirror to another, on and on, endlessly. To me, this is light reflection as a sacred art form.

I stand in awe before this human-made artefact. A field-of-energy is radiating from it that is completely unique.

Say 'hello' to the Buddha.

Pan is right. This is the living Buddha. Maybe I should say that it embodies the Buddha, but you would have to see it to grasp my meaning . . . and I do not mean physically see it. The field-of-energy around the Buddha is incredible. The Love of every Buddhist since Buddhism began is energetically within this statue. How this is possible, I do not know. It is as though the soul-Being, known as the Buddha, decreed that the essence of the true Love of all Buddhists would be contained within this energy-field. With its own vibration of Love and Devotion, the Buddha is one-of-a-kind. This is not just about devotion. This is the epiphany and repository of the highest expression of Buddhist Love and Devotion. It is held in such a way that it is available to all human consciousness that reaches toward the experience of divine Love.

Above and beyond all this, yet intermingled as One, is the energy of the living Buddha: the Being who was once a prince, a man known as Siddhartha Gautama. I have never experienced anything quite like this. Close to tears, I am in overwhelm as just an essence of the Love enters me, lifting me to new heights. In that moment my Love for the great Beings, such as the Buddha and the Christ, reaches a new high, a new clarity. Within me, they are no longer an abstract; no longer a distant figure we read about, a figure that people worship, often in blind devotion. The Buddha has become real and living for me, along with the Christ. I cannot separate them, for unconditional Love is One Love. Love is not aimed this way or that way, or to this person or that person. Love *is* All. All *is* Love. Buddha and Christ—and Pan—express one and the same Love. The avenues of expression are irrelevant, yet it is the Christian and Buddhist avenues with which so many religious people are preoccupied. The avenues have become the religion—not the Love.

The elders are watching me, feeling my awe, my humility, my Love and respect. They know the impact this meeting with the Buddha is having on me. They know of my journeys with Pan—this knowledge is in their energy-field—and they know that metaphysically, I have experienced many wonders. Spiritually, this is another peak experience. It is a pinnacle of human Love in very human terms. Within the area of our physical heart, there is what I term a 'virgin space.' We can live from and within this virgin space. The metaphysical virgin space of my heart has just grown and expanded. For me, this is a monumental meeting with Greatness and Love.

On many of my metaphysical journeys I have felt nourished, but never quite like this. This experience is pure soul-food. I feel such a magnitude of gratitude to Pan, the Buddha, and to these ageless elders who have greeted me. They have opened to me the very pulse and heart of their amazing lives. They have taken me beyond the religion into the very heart of Buddhism. And in this way, the heart of my Christian upbringing has been revealed. The many church ceremonies I had to endure as a boy, the singing of psalms and hymns, all served to turn me off and away from the true Christ of Christianity. All this is dissolved in the splendour of this moment.

I am content. I have received a priceless and unexpected gift. I smile into the Pan energy. "Thank you, Pan. From the soul I am . . . thank you."

I inner-feel his acknowledgement. Around me, the monks are bowing to the Buddha and slowly withdrawing from his temple, for this very special place is undoubtedly where the living Buddha touches the Earth. From here, the Love of Buddha is available to the consciousness of all those who are aware, regardless of their religion. Today, unknowingly and unintended, even as they gain new worshippers, religions close more doors than they open. But, sadly, maybe that is their intention—a form of control.

Under normal circumstances, I would metaphysically view the Buddha from many angles, but here, in full view of the elders, this would seem like sacrilege. Neither do I need to. Taking a last look at the light flowing and bouncing over the statue, thereby illuminating it with Mystery, I follow the two elders out of the temple and, via a different passageway, into a courtyard. Here, I see a gathering consisting of a few elderly female Buddhists, along with maybe fifteen boys ranging from about six years to older teenagers.

The elders, who are Masters—I read this in their energy-fields—are careful not to look in my direction as we join the group. There is a lot of hand-clasping and bowing from the women and children toward the two elders. They, in turn, nod, smiling benignly in acknowledgment.

One of the elders speaks to the group in a precise and deliberate way, neither slow nor fast. I have no idea of his language in words, but his language in energy is very clear—can they see their visitor? Me.

Heads begin to turn, eyes darting all over the place, their expressions serious. Two of them are quickly able to see me. Smiling, I give an exaggerated wave, and another of the younger boys sees me, a huge smile lighting up his face. I notice that one of the women can see me, while another couple are looking very disconcerted because they cannot. I feel a mild concern about this. I do not want to sow the seeds of discord among them. Almost as though he reads my thoughts, an elder looks at me, giving a slight, dismissive movement of his hand. I am again impressed. I am quite sure that very few physical humans can see me as a metaphysical Being, never mind follow or apprehend my every concern.

Having an idea, I deliberately focus on the group with Love and Light, expanding my Light-body so that the whole courtyard is powerfully enveloped within the Love/Light of Self. This has an instant effect. On most faces the seriousness is lost, wide smiles of amazement and wonder taking its place. Both elders nod in appreciation. It is obvious from their energy-fields that the boys are very self-disciplined. They are clearly born with it rather than having it forced upon them. Now, however, they indulge in a low buzz of conversation as they all become aware of my field-of-energy. They have given me a great gift and, however small, I am happy to offer mine.

Not so small a gift, Michael. A visitor such as yourself, and this offering now in this unique way, very seldom happens.

"Yes, I can understand that. Do they get many visitors from the western world?"

Just a few each year . . . and mostly devout Buddhists. This is a very isolated and difficult-to-reach monastery. The weather closes it off for much of the year. It is considered a very sacred place. To acquire permission to visit here would be very difficult; almost unobtainable.

This feels right to me. Some places need to be protected from the invasive/take energy that is common to many tourists. It's all about fields-of-energy—they belong, or they do not.

My Light-body is still expanded, so now I gradually reduce it to my normality. Instantly, all the children and women in the courtyard make small bows in my direction, hands clasped accordingly. Clearly, they all now know my metaphysical location. With a tiny beckoning motion to me, the elders move across to another of the many passageways and staircases that link the multilevelled buildings, one to another. This time it is a less worn staircase, and we are going up it. The elders maintain the same pace going up fairly steep stone steps as when they walk. I get the feeling that despite great age, there is nothing vaguely feeble about them. Instead there is an almost tangible sense of serenity. If anyone I have met personifies serenity, it is these two elders. They have mastered the art of making haste, slowly!

After going up some considerable height, we emerge into another courtyard. This one is tiny—six people, at a squeeze! One elder moves his hand in a sweeping gesture, indicating the view. It is obvious that while metaphysical, I have unparalleled panoramic views . . . I thought! The view of the mountains from this tiny courtyard would probably be unequalled by any other building on Earth. Even I am almost overwhelmed by the view, by the sheer artfulness of the courtyard's placement, by the sheer ingenuity and vision of including this courtyard for no other reason than the view. And yet, if one were ever doubting their relationship with God, a single glance from this courtyard at the vitality of the fresh wildness of an abundant Nature would surely re-establish it.

It seems odd, but it is not so much the view of soaring, white-capped mountains, with plunging ravines and tree-covered slopes reaching to embrace the valleys far below—none of this is the real 'gasp' factor—it is the feeling that you are looking from the eyes of the Buddha. I cannot explain this. Standing in this courtyard, it is as though you are no longer you. In some mystical way, your body/identity—in my case, Light-body—vanishes. You are the Buddha looking through the eyes of God . . . at the scenery of your God-Self.

Tears are trickling down the cheeks of my physical body. I am close to an emotional overload. In my Light-body, I take a very deep breath of fresh, cold air. This air does not enter my metaphysical lungs, but energetically—for all is energy—it has a calming effect. The elders are nodding very slightly to each other. If they had a question regarding how this would affect me, they have their answer. I become aware that to enter this tiny, very special courtyard is an honour, a great privilege.

Sedately, in their calm, quick-unhurried way, we retrace our steps. We bypass the temple of the Buddha, following an open-air walkway to where I initially entered the monastery. Here, with a slight bow, their hands clasped before them, the two elders take their leave. Clearly, they are quite content to leave me to my own devices, and to depart in my own timing. I do not feel dismissed by them, I feel greatly honoured.

I have met the Buddha in a way that I could never have imagined. I have been affected by this experience. My metaphysical virgin heart space has grown. I have been blessed by the Buddha. I have accepted the Christ within. These are my thoughts and feelings as I traverse time and space on my metaphysical journey home—back to my study, and physicality. Again, I have a niggling feeling that I could have done something differently as I journeyed, but when I think about it, I have no idea what the feeling means, or involves. I dismiss it. Whatever it is, timing will deal with it.

Tomorrow, I am going to look again at the serene and stony smile of my Buddha. I am sure that I will see and feel the inner warmth.

TWO

A MYSTERIOUS MOUND AND MOUNTAIN

During one of my visits to America quite a number of years ago, I was taken for a quick visit to the Serpent Mound in Ohio. Prior to this, on three separate occasions, various people had asked me if I had ever visited the Serpent Mound, and I had not. But they certainly engaged my curiosity. Once, ho hum; twice, hmm maybe; but thrice gains my interest. The visit was quick because we were en route to somewhere else when I suddenly noticed a small signpost with the words, 'The Serpent Mound,' pointing down a road at right angles to ours. I asked the driver to stop, and then asked how far it was to the Serpent Mound. About twenty miles, was the reply. Could we go? I asked. I do remember our driver was an amiable woman, and she agreed that a quick visit was possible. Hence quick!

When we arrived at the Serpent Mound, it was drizzling with rain, not a soaker, but light and constant. Happily, it kept other visitors away, suiting me admirably. I walked along the track that encircles the four hundred and twenty metre long serpent, reflecting that it was rather a let-down on what I was expecting. I had no expectations of a rearing rattlesnake, or anything so dramatic, but I had expected to *feel* something. All I felt was wet! Overall, the serpent, with its open mouth, curled tail and undulating body, was a little under two metres high, and several metres wide. Finally, I viewed it from the elevated stand, and then went and read about it in the small museum building nearby.

Here, I read several conjectures of various scholars and people who were interested in the culture of the Adena people of early America. Some said they built the Serpent Mound, others said it predated them, yet others said that it came later. The aspect of the serpent that attracted considerable speculation was its open mouth, with a hillock almost within its jaws. Some wrote that this represented an egg, another that it represented the sun, and some that it was a frog—presumably food! I had an odd, strong feeling that all the theories about the serpent and its gaping jaws were wrong—but it was just a feeling. I waited for inner revelation to hit me, or insight to sweep in with greater knowledge, but nothing happened. I attempted to metaphysically connect, all to no avail. With a sense of mild disappointment, I was ready to leave.

I sat in the back seat of the car, my late wife sitting next to the driver in the front. Just as we drove away, I fell into an instant sleep. I dreamed, and in my dream I was at the creation of the Serpent Mound—most of which I have completely forgotten! The deep sleep and dream lasted no more than two or three minutes, but it left me feeling curious and speculative about the whole Serpent Mound experience.

Despite the passing of about twelve years, I have remained intrigued by it.

Now, with the ability to metaphysically revisit the Ohio Serpent Mound, I decided that it was time. I write Ohio simply because the planet seems to have a fair number of mysterious mounds scattered over it, all of which have generated much interest.

I share my thoughts with Pan, with a question. "These mounds are created in Nature, so do they come under your domain . . . or not . . . because some are man-made?"

I suggest that it is time again for you to look and learn.

"Now why did I expect you to say that?"

Moving into an altered state of consciousness, I concentrate on the Serpent Mound in Ohio. I have not set a time-frame to arrive in, trusting that my enquiry will determine the when.

Relaxing, I focus into my Light-body, moving through the slight resistance of the waves of time and space. Again that faint scratching niggle that this is not quite right, but I disregard it for I am now hovering above the place where I thought the Serpent Mound should be. All I can see are small to medium trees and scrubby plants over a very large area.

"This is unusual. I seem to have missed my target."

Or you have missed the whole point of the exercise.

I'm puzzled by his remark. "What does that mean?"

I feel an inner sigh—it is not mine! Then the penny drops. Ah, this is the right place, but it is before the mound was built.

Taking a position about a hundred metres above the approximate location, I focus toward the time of the building of the mound. Nothing seems to happen. I feel a touch of mild disquiet. Then, with my own sigh, I settle down. In the no-time of timelessness, I see a number of Native American Indians approaching the target area. They are led by five shamans, all of whom seem intent on different aspects of their surroundings. A couple are focused on the land, and with hands extended are gently weaving something in front of them. Closer inspection reveals that one has a dried eagle foot, with claws extended, in one hand, and what I inner-know to be a dried beaver foot in the other. Another shaman has a few cornflowers in one hand, and a fresh hazel twig in the other. A third shaman is staring upwards, his feet carefully stretching toward the soil as he gently and carefully paces along, his whole attention in the sky. In one hand he holds aloft the wing feather of an eagle; in the other, a small rock from the top of a mountain. Yet another shaman, walking slowly and carefully, is shaking a bunch of porcupine quills; this somehow makes a sound like a strong wind in the tops of bare trees. The last shaman I look at is a very old woman. She has nothing in her hands, but is walking with her eyes closed, her head cocked slightly one way as though she is listening to the Earth. Perhaps she is.

The attention the shamans have on what they are doing causes the whole procession to be slow and stately. They reach the area where I know that the Serpent Mound will be built. In the manner of a pointer dog becoming stationary, every part of its body pointing at the game birds to be flushed into flight, so the shamans are now quivering attention, all as one, pointing or facing to the area the mound will one day occupy. This is intriguing. What is it that has their attention? I can see nothing that is any different, or in any way distinctive or special. No large boulder, no stately tree, nothing.

As I, too, give more attention to the area, I feel an energy that is growing stronger with the approach of the shamans. The others in the group, mostly men who look like hunters, stop, while the shamans continue. This is very unexpected. I have never known Earth energy to actually increase in the presence of a few people in this manner. A true gardener and a true farmer—as opposed to a person with a garden or a farm—definitely increase the energy of the land on which they interact, but this is rather different. I have the insight that this land is new to these people, and that they were actually searching for this natural connection.

The shamans walk in large elaborate circles in this area for the next several days, while the hunters and the few women make a light camp in readiness for when this is finished. Eventually, the shamans seem to be fully satisfied that this is the place they were looking for, and one morning they all depart. Several timeless months pass by when I see a whole tribe of these Indians moving into the area. They make a camp that I consider to be semi-permanent: a camp that might be used for several years, but not one that is to be permanent. This is my insight, even though I do not really understand the whys or wherefores of my insight.

Gradually, over several months, the camp site becomes the gathering place for many more of this Indian nation than the single tribe. At one stage there appears to be well over a thousand people here, each tribe making its own nearby campground. They mix easily, with only a minimum of any hostility or confrontations. I am surprised by the number of shamans. I thought that each tribe had only one shaman, and some do, while others have several. And I am surprised at how well the shamans interact with each other. There is the very minimum of ego on display, with maximum unity and efficiency in working as a group. I also get a strong impression that this project is a first, and that this large gathering is a once in a lifetime occurrence. I am impressed.

Hundreds of men and women are now bringing soil from a large area in sling bags carried over their shoulders. Unlike some present day natives of Indonesia where the weight of the bag is supported by the head/neck, these people use their shoulders. Some, especially the women, carry a larger bag between two of them. At the same time, under the eagle eyes and strict supervision of the shaman, other men are digging the shape of the serpent quite deeply into the soil, digging down to some prearranged depth. This digging is being done with great, almost exaggerated care. The workers are quiet and solemn, without chatter. This, compared with the continual chatter and laughter in each camp area, makes it very noticeable. I realise that they are in no hurry. They work with an awareness that is unusual; a solemn intent accompanying their every move while they are on the digging site. Even the soil gathering is done with care, and nor is it all collected from just one place. Areas are selected by the shamans, and to varying degrees each area holds the white light of Balance.

When the shamans who found the site had departed, and before their return, I spent some time looking at the energy of the location. In all the surrounding area, it was the one place with the strongest flickering white light of Balance. Despite my best efforts, I have no idea why this should be so. Now, as the people of the tribe set about their work, the Balance is very slowly intensifying. My respect for the shamans has grown: Balance, the place of greatest potential!

Eventually the base shape of the serpent is ready. The soil has been removed from its foundation, and great heaps of soil that have been carried in are nearby. Now they bring selected stones to the site. These are not just any stones, but stones selected by the shamans. And there are a lot of stones; some from within the soil, some from nearby rivers, some from more distant higher land where they are exposed. Again, I find it difficult to discern how these stones are different from those left behind, for they all have varying degrees of Balance, but the shamans are very certain about which to use and which to discard.

Many months have passed, and a couple of seasons.

Now, as I watch, it is very apparent that something big is about to happen. They are preparing for a ceremony. Watching this metaphysically from more of an energy viewpoint, I see that as the shamans gather, each of the separate talismans held by a shaman are energetically connecting together. In the case of the old woman shaman, still without a talisman, she uses her bony, claw-like left hand. To be clear, each talisman is separate with the shaman who holds it, yet they are energetically One. With continuous chanting, each talisman—as One—points at a certain large stone. This is gently picked up and placed within the dug-out base of the serpent shape in the position that the talisman indicate. One by one, all within ceremony, the thousands of stones are carefully laid that form the base of the serpent. This takes many weeks. It begins each morning as the sun rises, and finishes as the sun sets. It is never hurried, and each shaman and their talisman seem to always be in synchrony with each other.

This is truly amazing. As each stone is laid, so the energy of the area has become increasingly concentrated within the base of the serpent; Balance has significantly intensified. Eventually, the last stone is laid. Interestingly, they began with the tail, ending with the jaws of the head. As the head is finished, so the energy is again amplified. I see that there are a few very small mounds of stone placed around the mound that is almost within the serpent's jaws. They look out of place, but I am sure they know exactly what they are doing. These shamans are aware of ways to move and create energy that have long been lost to us. With less ceremony but equal reverence, a layer of small stones is now laid over the larger stones—and the energy increases. When this is finished, they hold a dancing, chanting, laughing, drinking ceremony/party in which everyone is involved. There is plenty of pairing off between the sexes. And most of them are tipsy on their home brew for the next few days.

Now the real mound building begins. Having laid every stone in its exact position, with ceremony, and covered them all with small stones, they now bring in clay which has been mixed with water to a thick, sticky, clinging consistency. This takes several more weeks, and is laid in a layer about thirty to fifty centimetres thick. When this is finished, it is all covered with tree bark and left to dry. To my surprise, the energy of Balance increases even more.

Eventually, with a new moon and the shamans unanimous that all is ready, the waiting soil is heaped onto the serpent base, giving it a body. This takes months, for again it is unhurried; care, attention, and a sense of great respect for the earth is apparent. As they work, it appears that the serpent being created is considerably bigger than the mound of today. The original is truly impressive. Each layer of soil is deliberately and carefully trodden by feet, and further compacted with wood rammers. Not heavily so, but enough to firmly and strongly compact the mound.

When the formation of the mound within the open jaws is finished, I have a clear and very surprising insight about its meaning. It has become obvious that the serpent is an important spiritual symbol to these people, but when my inner-knowing reveals that the serpent is spitting venom at the mask of deceit— then I am surprised. The mound in the jaws is not a frog, or the sun, or an egg, but the mask of deceit. The serpent reveals that self-deceit is the big enemy of humanity, and that spiritually we are able to overcome its deception. As I see and realise this, I get a flashback to my dream. In those few minutes, I abruptly remember this part of the dream. The mask of deceit was the whole essence of my dream. I wonder why? Suddenly, I know what the tiny mounds around the larger mound represent: they are particles of venom that the serpent is spitting at the mask.

The time comes when the Serpent Mound is finished. From my position, a few more aspects become apparent. The Serpent Mound is connected with the spirit of the Earth and water through clay, soil, rain and stone. It is connected with the spirit of the sky and wind, for the view from above is literally outstanding. And when vegetation grows back on it, so it will connect with the spirits of the plant kingdom. And woven deeply into the serpent is the spirit and consciousness of the Native American builders. I have no idea of their tribal name.

Nearly two years have passed. This was not an undertaking to be rapidly finished; this was a task in which it was an honour to be involved. Just to be at the site was considered a privilege. The tribes are now dispersing back to their home grounds. Finally, the only people left are the original group of hunters, a few women, and the five shamans. It all seems finished, so I wonder what comes next.

The energy of the Serpent Mound is now at a peak. Within the Balance, I can feel it as a radiance of deep, lost wisdom, of a rare and patient spiritual integrity, and of something I cannot identify. This energy radiates in waves from the serpent, as unceasingly as would the fragrance from the flower of an immortal rose. As a group, the shamans are now fasting. They drink water a few times daily, and softly chant, but eat no food as they purify their bodies. They continue this for ten days.

One morning at sunrise, the five shamans position themselves on the Serpent Mound; one at the head, the old woman over the heart, and so on, evenly spaced down the length of the serpent. They squat, and begin a soft, monotone chant, its sound rising and falling in waves of energy. What they intend, I have no idea.

So subtle is their effect that I am with them for three days before I realise what is actually happening: they are singing/chanting the Serpent Mound to sleep. As I become conscious of this, inner-knowing flows into me. They are not dampening or suppressing the energy of the Serpent Mound, they are putting it in suspension. They are holding the energy in abeyance for when the Earth triggers its release—and that will be with the approaching Earth Changes. I am both amazed and deeply impressed. 2012 is many hundreds of years in the future!

"Oh my gosh, Pan, I had no idea that people of this time held such vast inner knowledge. This is incredible. How do they know how to do this?"

Why should people of today have more inner knowledge? Is this not prejudice? How does science know how or why something works? Is this a new skill?

I smile. "Be fair. I only asked one question."

But he is right. I must have been prejudiced in my thinking that we are smarter today. I should know better! The shamanic skills I have witnessed are far deeper and more based in aware conscious intelligence and spirituality than our science of today. Today, science and spirituality have become alienated from each other.

"Yes, of course. It makes me wonder if there are any more human-made artefacts of similar ilk that are awaiting their time."

They exist, and each is different.

I feel deeply touched by what I have seen. I get the feeling that each of these shamans will be on the planet during our present time of Change, probably not knowing that they have created this. Or perhaps they will know. I expect the other human/nature artefacts await their moment to release an uplifting energy. Such wisdom never deserts us, even if we desert our wisdom. I am hugely impressed by the state of consciousness of those shamans. In their own way they are certainly on a par with the two elderly Buddhists, and maybe even greater. But such comparisons are neither appropriate nor necessary.

I now need to see the Serpent Mound as it is today. With this as my focus, I again move through the continuing discord in the folds of time—rather than space—seeming to be unmoving as I appear in our present time.

Strong impressions greet my arrival. The Serpent Mound seems to have shrunk. It is now considerably smaller than the original. The base may be about the same, but the mound has declined. The small venom mounds around the mask mound have been almost obliterated by time, weather and probably people. It is also a modern countryside around the Serpent Mound, bearing little resemblance to the original wilderness.

But the purpose of this visit is to reconnect with the energy of Serpent. Is it still sleeping? Yes. The Serpent is not yet awake, not yet releasing its store of Balance energy. But I *feel* that unique storehouse of patient, latent spiritual energy—just waiting.

With my focus now on home, I again step into the oddly resistant folds of time and space, and with only the slightest effort, I am in my study.

※   ※   ※

While in Japan a few years ago, Carolyn and I were taken to the mountain shrine of Togakushi, where Gods and/or Goddesses of Nature are reputed to abide. On the way there, I remember seeing a rocky, tree-filled mountain ridge from the car window, and playfully saying to Carolyn, "Do you see that big mountain over there? That's where the shrine is." Carolyn gave an exaggerated groan, "Oh, no!" I smiled. "Just joking." But it turned out that I was right! We turned onto a little road snaking through the trees that led us toward the mountain, until finally we were in a cleared area for cars and coaches. Truly, coach loads of Japanese worshippers, following their Shinto faith, visit these remote and scattered shrines of their various Gods and Goddesses. I was impressed.

I was even more impressed as I travelled the track up the mountain. Initially, the passage was wide and smooth, but once on the mountain slope that quickly changed. This was no paved or cared-for path with orderly steps; this was its opposite. The pathway through the trees and up the rocky mountain was made by the sheer numbers of people who walked it. Hundreds of people of all ages either strode easily, or bounded from one rock to another, or laboriously strained and painfully toiled their way over the obstacle of each rock as they grimly endured their pilgrimage to the shrine. It was rough, rugged, and uphill all the way with what served as steps varying in height from easy, or reasonable, to nearly impossible. For some it was simply a good workout, while for others it was quite obviously a painful struggle. Yet I did not see anybody turn back, defeated. I reflected on how many worshippers in our Western world a Christian church built in such an inaccessible place would receive! I concede, however, that lifetimes of indoctrination into religious rituals and religious expectations will drive people to mindlessly continue in what become mindless practices. I would like to think that in this instance this was not the case.

However, beyond all this, I could *feel* the energy of the Gods and Goddesses in the mountains—and this intrigued me. For Carolyn and me the journey was okay. I bounded, while Carolyn steadily walked with our group, but she easily managed the obstacle course. Aries are inclined to bound, when the more steady pace of a Cancer might be smarter!

Even though we have visited quite a number of shrines, Carolyn and I do not really understand them, mainly because we cannot read the language. We are inclined to stand back, keep out of the way, and observe the many worshippers. Generally, they speak rapidly and quite loudly to the God and/or Goddess, clap their hands a few times, offer a few coins—and take it all very seriously. This is just my observation, not a judgement or criticism. On the contrary, I am impressed by their devotion. During this visit, with my *awareness* and *feeling* of Gods and Goddesses being present and spiritually connected with the many worshippers, I decided I would like to view all this from a metaphysical perspective. I have been in, and admired the architecture of many churches and cathedrals, but at this very simple mountain shrine, I felt more of an aware and ethereal energy/presence connecting the worshippers with their shrine than I have felt in any church. Again, this is just an observation. Personally, I have never felt that sacred connection in a church, although I often feel it in Nature.

I discussed my intentions with Pan.

"Will I be able to see Japanese mountain Gods and Goddesses?"

If you are open and receptive, why not?

"I would not go if I wasn't open. I have a concern that at some of the shrines there are hideous monster-type statues or effigies that seem to be the guardians of the shrines. I'm not sure I would want to meet one of them for real . . . not even metaphysically."

Perhaps you are right. After all, this is not for the faint hearted.

"Very clever! Okay, I'm making ready."

Sitting down, relaxing, I focus into my Light-body. Holding my memory of the mountain shrine, I move through the continuing mild resistance of the folds of time. This puzzles me—why the resistance? Letting go of distraction, I zero in on my journey—and am over the mountains in the area where I did my physical leaping and bounding.

I am not surprised to see the constant stream of worshippers struggling and/or walking up the steep mountainside. Does it ever end while there is daylight? I doubt it, even though the tide of people must surely ebb and flow in accordance with the weather.

I am not surprised to find that I am just a touch nervous. The very thought of one of those hideous monsters somehow guarding the shrine from metaphysical invaders is off-putting. But really—they are probably no more than a scary image.

I am wrong.

Coming fast toward me is a creature straight out of a horrific nightmare. It looks like a dog/lion/boar or a boar/lion/dog, not that it matters! It has long flowing fur of an impossible screamingly bright red colour, it is frighteningly huge, and it's rapidly closing on me.

"Yikes! Pan. What do I do?"

This is where I will leave you, Michael. Enjoy!

I have that distinct feeling of Pan departing. "Why do you *do* this to me?" I shout.

Suddenly, I am engulfed in the most incredible creature energy I have ever encountered. Overwhelmingly a garish brilliant red, I can nevertheless see the red of loving Chaos flickering over the living effigy as it cavorts around me. Oh my gosh—it is friendly! It leaps and prances around me in great excitement, as though I am a new toy on the block.

You talk. You speak. You want. You play.

"Er . . . you frightened me. I thought you were a fierce and terrible guard."

Look terrible. Look fierce. Look frightening. Am not.

"No . . . you're . . . rather nice. I like your . . . exuberance."

Good good. You come. Me take. You come.

So saying, the huge creature cavorts ahead of me, leaping in the manner of a puppy. This is absolutely nothing like I expected, although I try to avoid expectations on these journeys. This, however, is way out there! I follow smoothly behind the vast, bounding red creature, a smile in my heart. My earlier nervousness is completely blown away.

We are moving now into the Togakushi Mountain. First there is the long rugged ridge of physical mountain which, like most mountains that do not live in almost permanent snow, are covered in rocks and forest; then there is the metaphysical mountain—and this is something else. A mountain is energy. When I physically bounded up to the shrine without undue fatigue, I was very focused on the energy of the shrine. I asked if it would draw me up to it, to support me within its energy-field—and it did. This was one reason why I am now here metaphysically. I did not really believe it would energise me. I am not a Shinto worshipper!

For the boar/lion/dog creature and the metaphysical me, this physical mountain is not really relevant; it is no more than a nebulous wisp of physicality. We are within the metaphysical mountain, moving into a reality that is breathtakingly beautiful. Great spires and arches of multicoloured light form a vast etheric shrine of surpassing grace and elegance, and into this incredible shrine I am led by my huge and ebullient companion.

You like. You see. We greet. They come.

From out of an archway made of the purest white of Balance, I see a beautiful Japanese lady appear, accompanied by a Japanese man of grace and stature. They do not walk, they glide, yet they choose to approach me in a way that is so very human.

Smiling at the massive boar/lion/dog-like creature, they call out to him using an unintelligible name, and he bounds over to them, his tongue falling over and around his huge protruding lower fangs, his long thick mane trembling in his brilliant red energy of joy.

They here. They greet. They please. You meet.

I bow low to the God and Goddess, for this they clearly are. Beyond this, I am unclear of how I should behave, or what I should say about my intrusion.

They speak telepathically in a way I understand perfectly, yet it is also beyond language. It comes directly from the energy of the heart.

You do not intrude on us. We invited you to visit us in this way when you physically visited us. You are our honoured guest. (They smile). *And you are full of questions; ask.*

"Thank you so much. It is I who am honoured. This may make you laugh, but please, what is the name of your huge, red and . . . somehow utterly beautiful companion?"

You may call him Shishi. It means 'lion'. Shishi is very taken with you.

"Quite honestly, I am very taken with him. His energy-field is pure ebullience."

I like. You like. We like. This good.

I move over to Shishi, and for the first time I dare to hug him. Considering he is about half again bigger and bulkier than an elephant, this requires me to embrace him in my expanded body of Love and Light.

Maybe I lose the plot here, but as I embrace Shishi, I get the impression that I am being engulfed in a pure, red, pulsing Heart of epic proportion.

I Love. You Love. We Love. Are Love.

The Goddess speaks. *You have made a friend and connection that you may call upon any time. Shishi is the guardian of shrines. He determines the hearts of those who worship at the various shrines. He enters the worshippers' hearts, for he is a Heart/Being. He does not judge, but he knows the hearts of the pure and simple who seek nothing for self; he knows all those who follow a mindless ritual of devotion, and those who only call upon us for their own gain. All hearts are open to him.*

"I am deeply honoured to be Loved by Shishi. I Love the Being he is."

*You do not yet realise the import of my words. Shishi **is** the God Being of this mountain shrine. We*—she indicates the God and herself—*are his friends, fellow God and Goddess.*

I am beyond surprise, and yet, when the Heart that is Shishi engulfed me, on a soul level, I knew. "Do the people who come here to worship know of this?"

The God laughs. *You can write nothing in a closed book. You can imprint nothing in a sealed belief. You can remove nothing from an empty container. You can place nothing in a full one. Each worshipper determines their own experience within their own heart. Each worshipper knows and accepts what their beliefs allow them to know and accept, an attitude that promotes a stuck and static state of consciousness. Change is a guest seldom invited.*

Standing next to Shishi in my normal Light-body, I am awed by his huge bulk, while his Love is rather like a beating pulse. I am aware that the whole mountain feels this.

"Why is it that you speak fluently, while Shishi speaks in short syllables?"

Shishi is a God of the heart/space unknown. Words are not his forte. His energy speaks in the language of the heart . . . as you have inner-heard/inner-felt.

I have indeed. The Love radiating from Shishi is palpable.

The God appears as a very virile and handsome Japanese man of an earlier time. I always felt that the male Japanese attire was rather masculine and somehow aggressive in its style and appearance—which is just my feeling/impression—but this God wears a simple kimono style of white clothing that clearly speaks of inner peace.

"When you say 'God of the heart/space unknown,' are you referring to what I call the virgin heart/space of metaphysical reality that the physical heart represents?"

Yes, this is exactly what I mean.

"I'm sorry, but I want to be clear about this. Are you saying that Shishi is the God of that virgin heart/space?"

I am saying that Shishi is a God of that virgin heart/space.

More shock, yet it is a wonderful Love shock. That Gods representing various cultures might occupy the heart/space had never even occurred to me. The thought that I can enter my heart/space and find Shishi within fills me with the deepest joy.

Clearly, Shishi knows the content of my heart.

I find. You find. Joy you. Joy me.

I smile at the enormous radiant face of Shishi. "My honour. My pleasure."

I switch my attention back to the Japanese God.

"May I ask the, er . . . status . . . of your . . . Godship?"

He laughs aloud at my fumbling, word-clumsy manner of asking.

In this culture, I am a God of Integrity.

"Oh . . . I thought that you were a God of Nature."

He nods, and indicates the Goddess. *Yes, we both are.*

I am confused. "But you just said that you are a God of Integrity."

The Goddess smiles at me. *A misunderstanding. I am a Goddess of Beauty, my present companion is a God of Integrity. Within Nature there is integrity and beauty, along with many other qualities. You are inclined to separate Nature from humanity, but to us, they are One. The human qualities of Integrity and Beauty are our focus, but they are also our focus within Nature. All is of Nature/God. This is Shinto . . . and the meaning of my companion.*

"You are right, of course. All the animal, vegetable and mineral kingdoms have their own beauty and integrity simply by growing and developing true to form. I overlooked this."

The God speaks. *It needs to be added that while all Nature expresses its natural beauty and integrity without any hesitation, humanity denies its beauty and violates its integrity.*

I nod sadly. I cannot deny it.

Shishi ambles over to me like a gigantic, screamingly red, utterly fearsome fur-ball.

Heart open. Love open. People open. Fear close. People close.

I know exactly what he means. We are approaching a time when hearts will either open to Love, or they will continue to clutch at old fears and stay closed.

It is easy to see that the Japanese Goddess is a Goddess of Beauty. She is beautiful beyond words in both form and energy. Her clothing is also a simple kimono style, but very bright and colourful. She is the embodiment and personification of ethereal Beauty.

"Thank you for allowing me to visit you. No shrine in Japan will ever be the same for me again. And I will meet with Shishi in the virgin space of my heart often. I am very blessed with such a friendship. However, may I ask one more question?"

They nod a smiling assent.

"I know that in India they have many Gods and Goddess, although I know almost nothing about them. And I have learned since coming to Japan on a regular basis that they, too, have their different Gods and Goddesses. Many other cultures also have their various Gods and Goddesses. I grew up in the Christian faith, being taught that there is but a single God, the Supreme Creator. I find it difficult to reconcile this. It appears the Christian religion is in denial of Gods and Goddesses within other religious beliefs, and I once agreed with that denial. I thought other religions were wrong. Now, I walk in a place of ethereal beauty with two Gods and a Goddess. Please, how do I reconcile this?"

You were once a product of religious dogma, of a limited doctrine. During your spiritual development you have outgrown this. Yes, there is a Supreme Creator, a Supreme God, if you will. But just as the energy of Pan, the great God of Nature, is in your field-of-energy, so there are the many Gods and Goddesses that pour their unrequited Love into the various Truth Principles that express within human life.

"I see. But . . . your Love is not unrequited. You have many worshippers."

They both chuckle. *How many of our worshippers have absolute Love for themselves? Only then can they have Love for us. Humans are the very manifestation of unrequited Love. Rather than come with Love for us, our worshippers come overburdened with countless, endless sorrows and wants. We Love them and accept this, for it is the human way.*

I sigh. "It should not be this way. We have an unrealised greatness in us so long denied. Hopefully, soon, this will change. One last question. Each culture portrays their Gods and Goddesses in different ways, in different appearances. Is this because this is how the Gods and Goddesses present themselves, or is the truth the reverse of this; you are clothed in their own cultural expectations."

As you surmise, the latter is the way of it.

I feel that I should not overstay my welcome. Walking to the nearby Shishi, I again envelop him in my Love/Light body. "You are one of the most incredible Beings it has ever been my honour and privilege to meet, and to know. Thank you sooo much."

We meet. We play. I Love. You Love.

"Indeed, we will meet, and play. We do share Love."

Of all the Beings I have ever met, Shishi is something else again. Looking at his bestial and fearsome face, his massive boar/lion/dog-like body, his prominent fangs, his astonishingly flamboyant vivid red colour, I shake my head at the wonder of it. If there is a living paradox, its name is Shishi—the gentle.

Bidding them all farewell, and blowing a kiss to Shishi, I move into the folds of time and space, pushing through its gentle resistance.

I am home in my study.

❋   ❋   ❋

For the next few weeks, I occasionally reflected on my journey to the Serpent Mound, and the Togakushi mountain shrine. Both the mound and the mountain were powerful places. It occurred to me that a journey to nowhere in particular, but with a focus on relevant Earth power-points or places could be a very interesting experience: relevant to the predicted Earth changes, that is. I had previously made a short list of power places to metaphysically visit, but it felt far too contrived for me to follow through on it. Power-points abound, as do power-drains, although the latter seem to be mostly ignored in all literature. Perhaps power-drains are not so much ignored as unrecognised, or unacknowledged. Maybe power-drains could tell me a lot about power-points via the polarity factor. Hmm, that is definitely worth considering.

While cruising the garden to look at the devastation caused by a very dry period, I remind myself to focus on the positive; "One day closer to the next soaking rain," I mutter, knowing that I need to focus on what I want rather than the opposite. The opposite is blatantly obvious, so I imagine the wilting shrubs and plants glistening with water. "Soon," I promise them.

Your correct focus is as refreshing as the rain.

"That's a matter of opinion," I grumble. "I would have thought that the God of Nature could give us some rain in this overly-dry area. What's the point of being a God?"

I inner-feel the chuckle of Pan. *We have visited the matter of rain, and the when and where you want it, at earlier times. Weather is as weather is!*

I smile. "Yes, I know . . . and I accept that . . . but I don't have to enjoy it!"

Your energy focus has been speculating over power-points and power-drains. Do you really intend to visit a power-drain?

"Yes, actually I do. Whereas the polarity aspect makes sense, I would like to know more about it . . . them. Oh, by the way, why did you leave so abruptly over Togakushi?"

To allow you the opportunity to react or respond entirely on your own terms. I gather that you enjoyed the encounter with the . . . huge red monster.

"Yes. Shishi is utterly beautiful . . . in energy, if not in looks. Even in looks, he is so very huge and scarily ugly that he is . . . beautiful. His sheer size is a challenge. In bulk, he is a fair bit bigger than an elephant, yet he has long fur that feels like filaments of pure silk."

I knew that it would be Love at first contact, if not at first sight.

"You were right . . . as usual."

I suggest you make ready.

Walking into my study, I sit down, close my eyes, and relax. "Readiness made."

I feel Pan's inner-smile as I move my focus of Self away from identity/physical body and into my Light-body. Moving out into the unknown, I push through the waves of space/time quite easily, emerging over a very barren landscape.

"Where are we?"

*As always, this is **your** look and learn.*

"How about a hint?"

Nothing! With a sigh, I focus on the landscape. I have no idea what country this is. I have long been geographically challenged—physically and metaphysically! It would appear to be high country, neither mountains nor an alpine range, but high, wide, dry and cold.

Unsure of what to look for, I focus purely on the energy of the place. Oh! This is different. Energetically, it feels rather like a vast and lazy whirlpool of negative energy. But this negative is not a bad negative, or even a negative negative in the way we think of negative: it is Nature's pure negative polarity of positive. We are inclined to judge negative as bad, because for us it often is. In Nature, it is no different than the polarity of North and South.

I watch for a while as the whirlpool very slowly swirls around, covering an area of maybe fifty kilometres square. It is such a huge whirlpool of energy, and so slow that it is not easy to observe. I cannot *feel* it with any degree of strength, but intuitively I am aware of its vast, yet contained and harnessed power. It is rather like a languishing giant, lazy and gentle, yet with the feeling that when wrathful, it would be awesome in its power.

"Okay, Pan . . . I'm getting a feeling for it. Enough to say I'm very certain that I would not want to be anywhere near here if the sleeping giant woke up. It seems to be a bit like the serpent mound, inasmuch as it is inactive now, but with a promise of awakening."

A fairly succinct summary for such a brief overview.

"So what is the purpose of a negative power-drain?"

I repeat . . . this is your look and learn.

"Okay, then I am going to slowly step back a few thousand years. I want to see what is happening in the world when the vortex is active."

With my words, I begin to focus backward in time. It seems that I have only just started when I am jolted to a halt. The huge whirlpool is now active, swirling strongly as it sweeps around and around and, in the way of whirlpools, carrying 'energy' toward its centre. Without thought, I change my focus toward Chaos and Order. Oh, my gosh! Huge clouds of a vicious and brutal red of negative human Chaos energy are being sucked into the centre of the power-drain. I thought that a power-drain was a bad thing, or undesirable—and it can be extremely negative—but

39

power-drains are clearly of varying functions. This power-drain is literally draining away the very worst of human negativity. It becomes instantly clear that this is the time of the Second World War, when hatred, anger, revenge and human-killing-human were at a peak.

As I observe all this, I realise that the power-drain is removing power of the very worst type; the power of an angry, fearful, hating humanity. Even more surprising is the realisation that the whirlpool of energy is only moving at maybe half of its potential. It is no longer languid as it revolves, but it is a long way from fast and furious. My gosh, if the Second World War did not rate a peak of its ability to drain or remove human negativity from our reality—what would?

On a sudden inspiration, I rise up into the air far above my customary hundred metres. As I relocate high above the Earth, I am aware of maybe a dozen of these massive power-drains scattered over the surface of the planet. A few are immense, maybe five hundred square kilometres, while others are energy-drains of a smaller and very different nature. All the very large ones are reasonably quiescent. I focus on the spiralling energy-drain that started all this, and I see that not only is the negative human energy sucked away into what appears as another reality, but it is also transmuted into a positive energy and returned via an Earth energy-point.

"Thank you for prodding me into action. This is incredible."

You perform very well when you align focus with purpose.

I smile. Unremitting wisdom!

I continue back a very long way into the history of human conflict, and I see this particular power/energy-drain vortex activated many times, but none of the wars or conflicts activate it to a greater extent than in the Second World War. I return to our present time, with the giant vortex in its languishing mode of activity.

"I have a very chilling and intuitive feeling, Pan. I get the impression from the energy of this place that in the very near future this power-drain is going to be fully active. This is what I feel in the field-of-energy below. This suggests one clear scenario . . . not war, but some truly frightening Earth Changes. Something that will trigger so much fear in humanity that all of the negative energy-drains of this type will be activated. This is a chilling thought on a cause level, yet it's reassuring to think of that negative fear-energy being removed."

You will agree that a continuity of more of the same is far more chilling.

I nod. Of that, there is no doubt. To continue with our stupid cycles of human victimising human, of repeating the endless propagation of war, of maintaining our drive for material wealth and power, all continuing as an endless repetition of *more of the same* does not bear thinking about. No matter what it takes — these cycles of repetitive insanity have to end.

The idea of observing this vortex during a future time occurs to me, a time when it is fully active, but I decline. The future is a series of many probabilities, some chilling, and I am not sure that I want to see them at this stage.

I move now to a power-point, a place that feeds positive energy back into the vast field-of-energy in which we live. I could say into the atmosphere, and that would be correct, but energetically it is far more than just atmosphere. This is a power-point that is unknown, in as desolate and deserted a location as the power-drain. Stonehenge, Glastonbury Tor and all of the well-known power-points in Britain and Europe are visited so often by so many different types of people that they are saturated in human energy; worse, they are stained by it. I am not saying this is bad, but the stain is mostly of want, expectation, hope, need, power, manipulation, self-aggrandisement and other imprints of a subtle nature that leave their energetic mark. We cannot avoid leaving energy-imprints. We are walking energy, and we leave our energy-signature in all the places we visit. The longer we physically linger in a place, the longer our energetic imprints metaphysically linger.

I attempt to feel if this remote power-point is more positive or 'better' than the power-drain, but although the energy-field is very different, better or worse is entirely irrelevant. It is as it is. It is the polarity of the energy-drain. I see Chaos and Order are in a kind of Balance, for there are flickers of white Balance to be seen, yet when I take a metaphysical step back to the power-drain, I see almost exactly the same ratio of Chaos and Order.

"Hmm, it's interesting the way my metaphysical approach to positive and negative is still so logical and rational. I have two simple truisms for life: *It is as it is . . . Choose Love.* To the best of my ability, this is what I live by. Right now, *it is as it is!* Yet here I am applying logic to something as metaphysical as power-points and power-drains."

I feel an inner ripple of Pan laughter. *You are as you are.*

I feel happy about this. Let Change happen as it may, but I will not change myself based on self-judgement or self-criticism. I have done my share of this in the past, and I can vouch for the fact that it does not work. Quite the reverse. Self-acceptance is the path, with huge dollops of self-appreciation and Love.

You have learned that comparisons do not apply in the natural world . . . nor in the field of human endeavour.

"Thank you, Pan. I'm going home."

THREE

ACCOMPANYING TRANSITION

I have been wondering if I am a bit too flippant in my attitude to Pan! After some thought on the matter, I decided that playful is a much better description! We like humour.

A few days later, while sitting in my study, I was thinking about people dying. I have reached an age where friends can be with you one day, gone the next! Not so easy to be flippant about this! I had a couple of cards recently, sharing the passing of old friends from my past. And it is a *passing*, not The End as the word *death* implies. Thinking about them, it occurred to me that I would like to follow different types of people at death. I would like to see what happens to a person both during and following their transition, while they are deeply embedded in the human illusion. In other words, a person who believes that they are nothing more than a body. Following that, I would like to be with a soul-aware person during and following *their* transition. Without a doubt, there must surely be a great contrast.

"Would you agree, Pan?"

Of course. Each type of person lives very different realities.

"Does this mean that they will experience different realities at death?"

I expect it means 'look and learn' time!

I agree. Nicely relaxed, I decide the time is right.

"Okay, Pan. I'm making ready if you are!" See . . . playful!

Again that familiar inner-smile. *Making ready.*

I focus on transition as the primer for my journey. I feel strong inner-movement in my Light-body. This time the waves of resistance are also stronger, more defined than usual. I again wonder why this is. Once more I feel a vague unease.

To my surprise, I am in a large hospital ward. Why should I be surprised? This is where the Grim Reaper makes his daily rounds, looking for more volunteers! The beds are all occupied with very sick, ailing men. This must be a ward for terminally ill men with life-threatening ailments. Oddly, there are two distinctly contrasting energies here. There are men who are resigned to death and have come to terms with it, and men who are quietly terrified of death and in strong denial of it. Interestingly, I see that most of the former group has a clearly defined, religious belief. The others are mostly men who believe that when you are dead it's . . . The End. That would have to be scary!

"Hmm, this makes it just a bit more complicated. One group has an energy suggesting that, hopefully, God will bail me out, while the others feel that death is The End. Okay, Pan. How about I begin with one from the first group of men. One with a strong religious conviction about life after death? Then I'll go with the dead-is-dead type!"

However you choose it, Michael.

For me, no time passes in the hospital. But a day or so later a man named Henry, who has strong but somewhat scattered religious beliefs of Christianity, loses what he has described to his weeping family as his 'fight for life.' What an illusion! As an immortal soul you cannot lose your life. You can lose your physical body, yes, but not life! For a while, Henry-soul lies in his bed after his body has died. It is obvious Henry-soul is not yet acquainted with the *real* facts of life. However, a buzzer that went off when his heart failed has brought the life-support team hurrying in. After a brief discussion, resuscitation is discarded for his heart is too diseased to continue supporting life. The curtains are drawn around the bed, and his family is notified.

By now Henry is aware that his physical tenure is at an end. I am not keen on offering help because I want to be an uninvolved observer. Maybe I should have kept further back, more out of sight, but Henry sees me. In a rather energetically-weak Light-body, he calls out to me. "Hello! Are you an angel? I think I'm dead. What do I do now? Where do I go?"

So much for my uninvolved observation!

"Do you believe in God?" I ask.

"Oh . . . yes. Very much so."

"Then call to God. Or pray to Him. Maybe He will come."

"Er . . . thank you. But what about you? Can you help me?"

I sigh. One good idea . . . kaput! "Okay, I'll help you. Focus on the Light."

"Oh, good. Er . . . what Light?"

"You are surrounded by Light. Look for it. Feel it. You are no longer in a physical body. You can move. You now have a Light-body. Look for the Light."

So saying, I fill the room with my Love/Light.

Still lying rigid in his bed, Henry gazes around hopefully. **"Oh God! I can see it. I can see the Light! I can see God!"**

"Okay. You don't have to shout. And that Light is not God . . . as such. Now, move your focus of self into the Light and ask for help."

"What do you mean . . . move my focus of self? How do I do that?"

Another sigh. So much for religious education! "Just *imagine* that you are in the Light."

"Oh, right." So saying Henry-soul shakily rises from the bed, moving into the Light. "I did it. I did it. **I'm in the Light.**"

At that moment a feminine angel of Light appears in the room. I smile at her with genuine sympathy. "I wouldn't want your job. You must be the angel of patience!"

She smiles at me. *We have heard of you. Thank you for helping.*

I feel that I should explain my presence. "Attempting to be an uninvolved observer, I'm interested to know what happens to a religious believer during their transition . . . and after. I'm not doing too well. I keep getting involved. Do you mind if I accompany you? This time I plan to stay out of his sight."

She gives me a radiant smile. *If you can stay with us, you are very welcome to do so.*

"Oh, I'm fairly sure I can. Tell me, do you know Lady Gold?"

Of course I do. We all know her. It was she who told us about you.

"Well, well. As below, so above!"

I feel puzzlement from the angel—and a laughing frown from Pan.

"Human gossip . . . angelic gossip! Get it? Sorry, just my sense of humour!"

The Light containing one lost and bewildered soul, and one smiling, indulgent angel gets ever brighter. As it becomes brilliant, I step into it . . . and we are elsewhere. This time, I am not surprised that we are in another hospital, albeit a more heavenly one.

"I take it that Henry is now in a halfway-hospital?"

The angel nods. *Yes, for a while. This soul needs to come to terms with the physical death of his body. After a while enveloped in Love and care, he will be ready to move on.*

"Do you attempt to surgically remove religious beliefs and false illusions from your patients? Or do they get to keep them?"

She chuckles. *You take transition very lightly. No, of course not. We leave all ideas and beliefs strictly alone, although we communicate with Love and Truth if we are questioned about being here, or about life.*

"Okay, but to be serious. If a belief is literally terminal, do you still leave it in place?"

Of course. It's their creation. It is each person's right to believe what they will.

"Even if it's dangerous to their health?"

Yes. You know this. An immortal Being can take as long as is needed to learn that beliefs can be liberating or lethal. As I said, all questions are answered with Love and Truth.

"Okay. So right questions get right answers?"

That is a fair way of describing it, yes.

Henry quickly moves from confusion back into his religious certainty. In quite a short timeless/time he is recovered enough to move on. As the energy-field of his Light-body becomes brighter and stronger, so there comes the moment when he slowly becomes transparent, shifting frequencies. I am easily able to accompany him as he is enveloped in Light . . . re-emerging into a room in a house, quite close to what appears to be a busy town.

Taking much more care, I remain invisible to him.

His immediate family is there to greet him; his wife and two daughters. It seems not to occur to him that he recently died and left them behind. Perhaps he has forgotten!

"Okay, now I'm a bit confused, Pan. Is this his creation? I'll continue to 'look and learn', but I'm not sure how Henry's wife and daughters can be in both his non-physical reality, and their own physical reality."

Fair enough. Yes, the family you see is his creation. He continues to create his own reality by clinging to the reality that he is most familiar and comfortable with.

"Is this because of his emotional attachments?"

Yes. It is now up to him how long he takes to 'let go.' Gradually he will notice that all is not quite as it was, that his life does not 'add up,' as it were.

I stay with Henry. For him, days pass by and weeks become months, but they are all part of his illusion. It becomes obvious

47

that he has forgotten that he physically died. He is not going to work because he believes he is slowly recovering from his heart disease. Otherwise he would create his workplace and all the other staff. One thing he is noticing, however, is that everybody in his life has strong, inflexible religious convictions that match his own. Unrealised, he is in a religious cluster. (Cluster? See *Book One* and *Book Two.*) This is neither good nor bad, nor right nor wrong—we each create our own reality. And so it continues. So-called death makes not the slightest difference to our unwitting creativity. Henry continues to go to his church each Sunday, but he is noticing that his wife is not with him. She is his creation, and he is forgetting to create her at church. This, and many other discrepancies keep creeping in to his reality, gradually and surely undermining it.

A couple of years pass by for Henry, but still he does not go to work. Clearly he did not enjoy his work, so his subconscious avoidance—yes, this continues—is avoiding recreating it. By now he is very aware that something is seriously amiss. He has called on angels for help, and they have come to him. This, in itself, surprises him, for it is a new phenomenon in his life. Despite believing in angels for most of his life, they were something he never saw, nor did he ever meet people who saw them. Now, angels are almost an everyday occurrence. He has asked several round-about questions, but he is afraid to ask the question that will reveal the truth; what is actually happening in my life right now?

Finally, his room blazing with the Light of his own slow, but definite growth, Henry asks the questions. "Please tell me the truth. Did I die? Am I in some sort of heaven? Where is God?"

So he again learns that he is no longer physically alive. He learns that everything in his current life is his re-creation, all based in his emotional attachments. He learns that he is not in heaven. He learns that heaven is not a place, but a state of consciousness. He learns that he is in a reality that he has long been clinging to, and that he is constantly re-creating it. And he learns that God is in all Life, although he is not yet ready to believe or relate to this. He learns that once he is ready to truly 'let go' of his tightly-held beliefs and emotional attachments, then his situation will change again. He will again be in the most perfect position for his continued growth.

Another of Henry's months passes by while he digests this. It is clear that the 'letting go' process is a bit of a mystery to him. He discusses it with a rather masculine angel. Perhaps I should say here that while angels do not have obvious genders in the way we do, they do have a definite masculine or feminine energy.

"What am I supposed to actually let go of?"

This is entirely up to you. However, people create collective beliefs and, because many people accept them as real, they become their reality. Your God belief is an example.

"Are you suggesting that a religious belief is not real?"

I am saying that God is a definite reality, but not necessarily in the way that people construct God from their collective beliefs.

"Does this mean that the God of my religion is not necessarily the way that God is?"

Fundamentally, yes.

"Should I let go of all my beliefs about God, and life? Just . . . be open to however God and life present themselves to me? Does this apply to my wife, and daughters? Do I just let them go, knowing that all will be perfect? Is that it?"

Unseen by Henry, I am nodding enthusiastically.

The angel glances at me and smiles. *You have stated it very well.*

It takes another month of Henry's time before he gets the full picture. "Oh, my God. I'm actually creating my own time here! I'm creating everything; even day and night because I am so used to it. Oh heavens . . . even my wife and daughters!"

Henry has finally figured it out. I decide it is okay for me to reappear again.

"Hello, Henry. Remember me? I'm proud of you. Well done. You have travelled from being stuck-in-a-bog of religious beliefs, to becoming considerably more free and open. That's quite a journey."

Henry stares at me. "Yes, I remember you from a long time ago . . . when I died."

With a sigh, I shake my head.

"Ah! Right. You were there when I thought I had died. Now . . . I have learned that death only happens to the physical body. But . . . who are you?"

"Very good, Henry. Me, I'm just a student of life on a metaphysical journey."

"And . . . metaphysical is?"

"You and me, Henry. It means beyond the physical. You are no longer physical at all, whereas I have a physical body to which I will return. So . . . are you ready to move on?"

Henry is shrewd. "Student. Is that why you're hanging around?"

I nod. "That . . . and I'm truly interested in your welfare."

"How would you suggest I do this? Moving on, I mean."

"Just focus on Love, Henry, and step into the Light."

By now Henry is familiar with the Light. Around him the Light becomes brighter and lighter, easily enveloping both of us. Just as everything is lost in the Light, so a new reality is emerging into view around us.

"Where are we?" Henry asks.

"The end of the journey for me, Henry, and a whole new beginning for you. This is a University of Holistic Life. Here you will have the opportunity to move to a whole new level of life and learning. Congratulations. You have done really well."

Henry looks very pleased. "Well, I still do not know who you are, but thank you for your help. Will you at least tell me your name?"

"My name is Mixael," I say, using my soul name for probably the first time.

"Well . . . thank you again, Mixael."

Focussing into Love, I feel myself moving back through the layers of reality.

"Hmm. That was interesting, Pan. Henry did far better than I expected. This now leaves me with a man who is a non-believer. A fearful, dead is The End, type."

I suggest you first take a break.

"I think that's a very good suggestion."

❋   ❋   ❋

A few days later, I let Pan know that I am again making ready.

Relaxing in my study, I move into my Light-body focus, quickly moving through the folds of so-called time and space. Again, there is an odd, quite firm and puzzling resistance.

Nevertheless, I am back in the familiar hospital ward of terminally ill men. Moving between the beds of sick men, I look for a man whose energy-signature shows his fear of death. One thing they all have in common; they know this is the last hospital ward for them. Among them, it is quietly and jokingly called the Ward of Lost Hope, although nobody is laughing. In truth, they all have a fear of death, but for those who believe death is The End, the red Chaos of suppressed fear holds an awful finality in its energy. Despite their fear of death, the 'believers' hope to see their deceased loved ones on the 'other side.' The signature-energy of 'non-believers' reveals no hope of any sort. They fear the conceptual, horrific emptiness of total annihilation.

Feeling compassion for these frightened men, I decide to offer them my Love/Light. I know that Love/Light will make a meaningful connection with each man, even if it is only the soul-self who feels it. Standing in the middle of the ward, I allow the Love/Light of Self to fill the room, shining with a non-visible intensity into the physical bodies of everyone in the ward. This includes a number of visitors.

One of these is a slight, fragile-looking woman who is whispering to her husband, Jim. She clearly feels the shift in energy. I see her stand up sharply, looking around the room.

I hear her whispering to her husband. "Jim. There's an angel in the ward. I can feel it. I'm tingling. I've always told you you're wrong about death, and there's an angel here to prove it."

Jim, who is only a few breaths away from his expiry date, feels nothing at all of my Love/Light. He makes a brief and momentary rally. Ever the pessimist, he whispers, "It's just the devil come to take his own."

"Oh, Jim, you shouldn't say things like that. **Jim** . . . oh God . . . **JIM**."

Jim is no longer listening. Unsurprisingly, his soul-self felt the Love/Light, releasing the sick and failing physical body in a quick release of energy. Jim, the sceptical non-believer, is now facing his worst nightmare . . . The End.

He and I are now in his reality, just the two of us. As Jim dies, his awareness of self is slipping into a dense, grey fog. In actuality, Jim-soul is lying unmoving in/on his physical corpse. I watch in fascination, but I am not without compassion. I will probably step in at some stage to help him, but I am here to witness his creation. The creation of a man who truly believes that there is no longer 'him' available to create. He stays with the body when it is picked up and wheeled away to the mortuary, and remains with it in its refrigerated state.

Linear time marches on, and Jim's body is duly cremated, his family going through their various emotions during the short service. Having been a morose and pessimistic man, Jim had not inspired great love and admiration in his family, so there was a lot of laughter and more than a few jokes at the wake following his funeral.

Meanwhile, Jim-soul is being forced to make some movement. He stays with his body when it is placed in his coffin, and throughout his cremation service. He stays with it as it slides out of sight, and he stays with it until, some time later, it eventually enters the incinerator. At this point, for Jim-soul all 'hell' breaks loose, as he and his body are engulfed in flames.

With a great shriek of utter fear, Jim-soul is elsewhere. Now he is lying in the dense fog of nothingness away from his physical body, still in denial that he is experiencing a reality.

A month of linear time passes in our timeless place of grey-fog nothingness. Jim stirs, a thought emerges. "What the hell is going on? What happened to the flames? How the hell can I possibly be thinking? I'm dead!"

It takes another couple of months of timelessness before other thoughts emerge. "Fog! Endless bloody fog. I hate fog. Where the hell am I? Oh . . . perhaps this is hell."

An interesting hate . . . fog! Unwittingly, he has attracted what he hates.

Another month in the timeless realm of dense grey fog . . . and Jim gets to his feet in his dull, shadowy Light-body. "Christ almighty! How can I be dead and yet think and now walk around? What in the hell is going on? Dead is bloody dead . . . ain't it?"

Maybe another linear month slides past. Jim is now impatient and aggressive. He has shouted his anger out aloud, but nothing/nobody responds. The dense fog persists.

"Help!" he finally shouts. "HELP!"

"Hello there." The voice that answers him takes *me* by surprise.

A man who is as alive in his physical reality as I am appears in the fog. He is in his astral-body. The grey fog shrinks away from him.

"Who are you?" asks Jim.

"Well, for what it's worth, my name is Clive. "I'm here to help you to move on."

"What do you mean, move on? I'm dead aren't I?"

"Your body is dead," Clive corrects him, "but you are very much alive. I heard you call out for help. So I answered your call. Are you ready to be helped?"

"How can you help me if I'm dead?" Jim asks.

Clive is all business. "Do you want to wait another month or so while you decide whether you are dead or alive, or do you want help now? Just say so. There are more than enough lost souls to keep me busy."

"Good for you," I murmur.

Clive is suddenly staring at me. "I thought there was somebody else here, but I couldn't quite see you. I still can't, but I'm aware of you." He frowns. "This is unusual. You seem to have a much higher, lighter frequency than me . . . yet you're in this place."

"To be honest, I've been with Jim," I indicate the lost soul, "for several linear months. But of course, it's no-time here. I've been observing him. I'm interested to see what happens to a person who believes that death is The End."

Clive laughs. "Well, you're a curious sod, you are. Here I am working my butt off rescuing just a few of the many lost souls, and here you are just *observing*." For some reason this seemed to really annoy him.

"Oh . . . I would have helped him soon enough."

"Just who the hell are you talking to, er . . . Clive? I'm here and you're here, but there isn't anyone else. Are you talking to yourself?" Jim groans. "Oh God! Are you a nutter?"

I laugh, then look questioningly to Clive. "Go ahead, answer him."

Clive stares hard at me, takes a deep breath and releases it. "Okay, my apologies. I came on a bit strong. Maybe you can tell me who you are? I've never run into anyone quite like you."

"Apology accepted. Like you, I have a physical body. I explore different reality-frames in my body-of-Light. Jim is a case study. Be aware that for him no time has passed. I take it that in your astral-body you are rescuing people like Jim from the lower astral realms in which they get lost. I think you call it soul-retrieval, helping lost souls move on. What you do is very needed, very worthwhile work. I applaud you and others like you."

Looking mollified and rather pleased, Clive asks me, "Why can't I see you more clearly? Is it because you have too high a vibration?"

"Actually, yes."

"Gee! You must be a master. I can normally easily see anyone travelling who still has their physical body. I'm impressed."

"To be honest Clive, I'm impressed by you. Do you actually do this rescue work on a regular basis? Do you have others to help you?"

"Yes, to both. We usually work in teams, but I like operating solo as well. When we are in the lower astral realms, most of us like to work with a reliable back-up team. Makes sense."

I nod. "Very good sense. Although if you centre yourself in Love, you have nothing to fear. Unfortunately, that's easier said than done."

"Yeah, especially with a few of the unpleasant apparitions we have seen."

"Hey," says Jim loudly. "What is going on? You're obviously talking with someone I can neither see nor hear." He suddenly sobs. "God, I'm scared shitless. Please get me out of here."

I nod at Clive. "Enough is enough. I have my answers. Will you take him, or shall I?"

"Personally, I would like to see a master at work. He's all yours."

While I do not have a clue how Clive would handle this, I know what works for me. I step close to Jim, holding him within my Light-body. Focussing in the Love/Light of Self, I allow my Love/Light to radiate forth, erasing the fog and gloom instantly. There is a sensation of pulsing movement . . . and we are in the familiar half-way hospital.

Clive is next to us, a look of comic amazement on his face. "Bloody hell! How did you do that? It takes me three stages to get anywhere near this far. Oops, can't stay, gotta go . . !"

To be honest, he did amazingly well to accompany me. His few moments indicate to me that Clive is rapidly growing in consciousness. (If you read this Clive, my congratulations.)

Jim is now staring around. "Whoa! I've never seen a place like this before. Where am I?"

He stares at me wonderingly, for in this reality I allow him to see me.

"First things first, Jim. Do you accept that despite physical death you continue to live?"

He hesitates. "Well . . . yeah. I don't have much bloody choice, do I? I was wrong. I'm definitely alive. So . . . I suppose this must be heaven."

I laugh. "No. This is a type of hospital, Jim. It caters to healing the illusions that helped damage your physical health, while also opening your psyche to a greater reality."

"What illusions?"

"Your whole physical life was lived in an illusion. You lived all the conditioning and beliefs that have been with you for many lifetimes. You reduced your life from the potential of magnificence to an expression of the mundane. That's not bad or wrong, but you can do better."

He looks at me thoughtfully. "You know what? You're right. I've been real closed-minded, pig-headed and stubborn all my life. Got me nothing but pain and misery. Christ, my poor old Millie . . . the wife. She got on at me often enough. 'You gotta change your ways, Jim, you're a right old misery.' God . . . the times she said that! God! I'm rapt that I'm still alive. You know what? I'm ready to change."

There are nurses of a higher order in the room now, waiting for Jim to notice them. I point toward them. "Okay, Jim, you're in the best hands possible. Learn, grow, and keep an open mind about everything. Just remember, life goes on . . . and on. How you live it is your choice. My recommendation; choose Love."

Jim nods. "Thanks. I don't know who you are or what you're about, but thanks."

The nurses recognise me and are waving. I must be getting a bit of a reputation!

With a wave, I step into the energy of . . . Between . . . ! Gosh! This is the first time this has ever happened. What did I do? How is this possible? Where am I? It seems to be a place of Light. Where did I step to? How did I get here?

"Pan . . . what happened? I made a different move, but I don't know why or how I did it. I don't even know where I am! And please don't say look and learn."

You did well with Jim.

"Thank you. But . . . where am I?"

Where would you like to be?

"Pan . . . is this a joke?"

Suddenly, with the intensity of the rising sun, clarity and certainty burst forth within me. I know exactly what happened. "No, it isn't a joke. I can be any-where or any-when in a single step, can't I? I have been travelling in my previous way because I still held a sense of time and space. I held it emotionally, so I kept re-creating it. In this moment, spontaneously, I moved beyond that habit.When I moved Jim from a lower astral realm to the halfway hospital, I did it directly, even though I was not fully aware of it. Now . . . I have fully engaged that awareness. Now I can do it at will. **Yes!**"

Congratulations, Michael. I wondered how long it would take you to figure this out. You have surprised me once again. Very pleasantly so.

"Thank you, Pan. But why didn't you tell me how to do this?"

*Because I want you **self**-empowered.*

" I bow to your wisdom. I noticed on my last few journeys that the waves of time and space seemed more resistant. I had the odd feeling that something was askew, but I let it go. I figured that in perfect timing it would sort itself out. And it has!"

Where to now?

"Okay. I would like to be back in my study."

So do it.

Without hesitation, I step out of . . . Between . . . directly into my study.

"Oh my gosh! This is so simple."

It always was. You only had to find the way.

"Thank you for being so patient with me. Now I'm ready to look for and observe the transition of someone who is spiritually aware. Not someone who *thinks* they are—there are many such people—but someone who *actually is*."

Deciding to experiment, I step into the energy of . . . Between . . . and out to the jungle of devastated rain forest that I had recently over-lighted in my Love/Light.

I step back into . . . Between . . . stepping out into my garden. Gosh! This is wonderful. Not really knowing where to go, I focus on a dying person who is very spiritually aware. I step into . . . Between . . . and step out into the back garden of a large house.

Looking around, I can see the rear of the house. An elderly golden retriever, who seems to have noticed me, is slowly wagging his tail. Dogs and cats mostly see or sense me, humans never. I am in a beautiful large garden, very well cared for. Energetically, it is obvious that a true gardener lives here. I can also see a big sturdy, homemade set of wooden swings. Two swings are moving back and forth in steady arcs. On one seat is a slim, athletic-looking lady, somewhere in her sixties. On the other is a young man, maybe in his mid-twenties. They are chatting to each other as they swing, and laughing at whatever they are saying.

I cannot help but wonder who is about to die here. They both seem to be in perfect health. I watch as they continue swinging, oblivious to my presence. Not so the dog, his tail wagging as he watches me. I walk over and scratch his head, and he clearly feels it; he is twitching, with a big silly grin on his face. The people on the swings are both facing my direction, and the woman notices that the dog appears to be receiving attention.

"Look at Bruno. He is twitching, like someone is scratching his head."

Despite the fact that the swings are moving back and forth quite vigorously, the young man slips off the swing landing nimbly on his feet, and runs toward the dog. I step smartly back, keeping well away from them. On reaching Bruno, the young man holds his head, looking the dog in the eyes. "Who is here?"

An odd question for a dog! Bruno gives a soft bark, then ambles over to me, sitting well within my Light-body. I stay still as the young man follows him, inevitably entering my field-of-energy. Abruptly, with a soft expulsion of exhaled air, he slowly, gently, and almost gracefully, crumples to the ground.

"Oh, my God! Pan, what have I done?"

Stay calm, Michael.

The woman slows her swing, jumps off, and runs toward us. Kneeling down, she pulls back an eyelid from his closed eyes. "Oh . . . Ben! Oh, dear!" Quite calmly, she checks the pulse in his neck. Then, looking very sad, she hurries into the house to phone for an ambulance.

Meanwhile, the soul of the young man is now standing close to me, staring at my field-of-energy. He has both a surprised and pleased expression in his energy-field.

Hello! You really are something special. Have you come for me?

I am so startled, I take a step back. "No, I didn't come for you. But I did know that someone very spiritually aware was about to die . . . here. I didn't expect it to be you."

No, I suppose not. It's strange, living while knowing that you can die at any moment. I had an inoperable aneurism in my brain. Short of a miracle, it was just a matter of when.

"I really am very sorry. I wish I could have helped."

He laughs. *You did help, actually. When I stepped into your incredible field-of-energy . . . wow . . . the soul I am just stepped away from my physical. I no longer needed to wait for the aneurism to burst.*

"I hope I didn't do anything amiss."

Oh no, nothing like that. On a soul level, I have felt very close to transition for a week or so. You simply provided the higher energy stimulus for me to let go of the body. Actually, it was a very uplifting experience. I owe you my thanks.

"Personally, I'm surprised that I failed to see your readiness to depart the body. I guess my focus was more on your . . . er, mother?"

Yes, she is my mother.

"She is very calm. Obviously she knew about your condition".

Yes, my mother is a remarkable woman. You said you are here because a spiritually aware person was about to physically die. I have been raised with a great awareness of life. I know that I am a soul on a journey, and that the journey continues. This is the way I was raised. That is why none of this is a shock, nor does it frighten me.

"I heard your mother call you Ben. My soul name is Mixael. In case you are wondering, I am a person who travels a metaphysical multiverse, learning about life."

With a very unusual and powerful travelling companion!

I smile. "You mean Pan. I think perhaps I am more his companion than the reverse. Pan is an enigma. Tell me, how do you know he is with me?"

Although in our reality no time has passed, Ben's body, having been declared dead, is being gently lifted onto a stretcher. His distraught mother is accompanying the body.

As Ben and I watch, he turns to me. *Do you mind if we go along with my mother? She will be comforted by my soul presence . . . and yours.*

"Not at all. You're right. She must be very aware to be able to feel your soul in her distress. Even though she knew of your condition, the moment of parting is very painful."

As we move smoothly alongside the ambulance, Ben answers my question. *I feel Pan's energy as a wild and ethereal Nature in your field-of-energy. It does not interfere with your energy in any way, almost the opposite. It is as though it empowers your freedom, while enhancing you energetically.*

"You have obviously learned about the human field-of-energy. Not many people have."

My mother was . . . is, an unusual person. He smiles. *It is I who am now a 'was!'*

"I came here to accompany a soul-aware person during their transition. To be honest, I have been with a religious man at his death, and with a man who believed that death is The End. Quite an education! You are my last case study . . . and by far the most enlightening. What do you want to do now? You have clear choices; they had only reactions."

I would like to stay with my mother for about a week. She will know I am with her. Then we can go to . . . wherever it is that I should go.

"Yes, that's a nice idea. She'll be comforted by you being close."

For a week we stay with Sybil, Ben's mother. She weeps a few times, and I watch Ben hold her in his arms at these moments. She often whispers, "Oh Ben, I can feel you, but I am going to miss you so much. You were such a gentle and beautiful soul."

Ben soothes her brow as he holds her. *I still am, Mother. As you are also.*

The week passes, but we stay an extra day for the funeral. Ben has no trouble at all in standing in the small local church, gazing over the tearful faces of his family and many friends. Sybil is embraced within the family love, and her younger sister arranges to stay with her for a while.

It is a shame that this is such a sad occasion for most of my friends and family. Most of my friends think that I am dead. I used to tell them that death is a fraudster, but they really did not understand. They thought that I had found religion! I used to say, 'I have found truth, not religion.' I am glad now that I was not yet ready to get married.

Another day passes while Ben satisfies himself that his mother is okay. He is very concerned for her. Ben is a wise soul. He knows that despite her being intellectually prepared for his death, this is not the same as being emotionally prepared. Now she is making the emotional adjustments . . . and gradually letting go.

Before we leave, Ben tries an experiment. While his mother is sleeping, he enters her dreams. He meets her in the familiar back garden, discovering that for a while he can hold her dream in a place of his choosing. He shows her how radiant he is, letting her know that he is alive and well. He tells her that he Loves her, and that they will eventually be reunited. He tells her to live her life fully, and not to enter a long grieving period for him. This is only a temporary parting, not an ending.

Interestingly, I am able to witness this dream. It is as though I am looking through a window into another reality. The reality is only a reality for as long as the dream lasts, then it is gone. In that instant, I have an overwhelming insight. Oh, my gosh! All our lives are no more than this dream. It is a reality for only as long as we are in the moment of it. Because we have nightly dreams within our dream, we think that we wake up each day, but in reality the dream-moment continues. Until the moment that we truly *awaken.* Not even death interferes with this dream, because death is simply part of our dream. Life is real because we put substance into our dream; the substance of a dream-reality. And the final paradox, it is all an illusion! I know that this insight will change me in ways that will slowly change the fabric of my dream, my reality, my life.

When Ben's mother and her sister, his aunt, are settled in together, and Ben knows that she will be visiting her family, he is finally ready to continue his journey.

He looks at me. *Okay, Mixael. Where to now?*

I laugh. "I'm here to accompany you, not the other way around. This is my 'look and learn,' not yours! However, it would seem that this is mutual learning! Pretend that I'm not here. Where would you go? What would you do?"

Hmm. I think I would call an angel to assist me.

"Then that's what you should do. I don't want you to be influenced by me."

How do I call an angel? He laughs, answering his own question. *Out loud! But do I just call out . . . angel? That feels ridiculous. Any ideas?*

"I'm an observer, remember!" I sigh. "Okay, focus on Love and Light."

Ah, of course. Good idea. Ben stands up straight, his face open and glowing, the radiance from his soul-self growing ever brighter. Lighter and brighter, growing rapidly and powerfully. I am impressed. I have seldom seen a regular person radiate so much Light. But, of course, Ben is not really a regular person; he is far more aware and conscious.

I join my Love/Light with his. Again there is that pulsing energy. Everything fades—then then our surroundings become strongly visible. Ben looks around. *This is good. Wherever we are, I like it.*

We have come a long way. Ben is a *very* powerful person. I have reached about as far as I can go. Anywhere beyond this field-of-energy and I would lose the tether of my physical body. I am not yet ready for this. I have things to do. Besides, I am too busy loving my life with my beloved Clarion! Ben and I are standing in an outdoor courtyard area in what appears as a huge botanical garden. I can see throughout the whole area of gardens simply by applying my scope of metaphysical vision. The range and diversity of plant life is absolutely breathtaking. I could spend a happy lifetime or three in here!

However, in the courtyard there is a Being. Who this is I have no idea, but the magnitude of radiance coming from this Being is immense. So great is the radiance that I cannot truly see the Being. I can see the Light, but only feel the Loving presence. I pale in comparison.

Not so. I feel a strong silent communication. *Your presence here is testament to the soul that you are. Very rarely does a person with a living, physical body stand where you now are. Although you are not alone, the Pan energy within you is not responsible for your being here. The credit is yours. You have returned one of our dear brothers to us, and for this you have my deep gratitude.*

"But . . . but . . . I didn't do anything. Ben did it himself."

I am fully aware of what took place. The Ben-soul drew inner fortitude and strength from you, allowing him to reaffirm his place in life. That you were able to accompany him is to your credit. I can only assume now that your last 'case study' is complete!

I feel much laughter and humour in this last statement.

"Yes. I have finished this stage of 'look and learn.' I would just like to say goodbye to Ben, and I will be on my way. Er, would I be allowed a walk in your beautiful garden?"

More laughter. *Quite a privilege. Yes, you may visit the garden. Ben can accompany you.*

I feel waves of amusement. I confess, I *love* Beings with a good sense of humour.

The garden I walk through is far beyond my ability to describe. Landscaping, that in my physicality would be impossible, is quite normal here. Cliff faces filled with bromelaids and orchids of every description tower into the air, with droplets of water cascading artfully among them. Where a cliff abruptly terminates, a rock garden appears, all festooned with rock and alpine plants. Then, with subtle ease, I am entering caves which are filled with light and a bewildering array of ferns. These areas alone cover many hectares of land. I see tropical plants of amazing growth and vitality growing within metres of a changed landscape displaying species of plants that endure extreme cold and hardship. The impossibility of them growing so closely together is challenging. Thus it continues as we walk through just a tiny part of the garden. I am stunned by the extravagant beauty and impossible plant associations.

I smile at Ben. "This garden gives a whole new meaning to impossible. I think I'll need to readjust my dream-garden when I get home."

Ben smiles at me warmly, and hugs me. *Thank you, Mixael. It is an honour to know you. Thank you for everything. We must meet again.*

"Thank you for being so patient with me. I would think that some people could be very offended by being a case study at death. In fact, I'm glad that you were my last case study. You have been an unforgettable highlight."

So saying, I step into . . . Between . . . stepping out into my study.

Time to relax . . . and reflect on dreams!

FOUR

THE BLESSING OF BALANCE

A week or so later I am ready once more, eager to use my new method of journeying. I am also pleased that it signifies my increasing ability.

Deciding to do this without Pan, I physically relax, focusing into my Light-body.

Metaphysically, I step into the energy of . . . Between . . . stepping out into the air high above New York City.

Looking down at New York, I wonder why I chose here. Very odd! It certainly was not an intellectual choice. Was I the chooser? Ah well, nothing by accident, nothing by chance.

I decide not to ask Pan why I am here. It's my soul choice, I think! As far as I am concerned this is my own self-created 'look and learn' time!

My focus will be people with the energy of Balance. I will make it a general observation rather than personalise it with individual people.

Standing high above New York City, I look down on the overall energy of haste and hurry, of push and shove; all the many people expressing a barely restrained impatience. The energy-signature of the crowd has the unpleasant stain of a debilitating and draining red of Chaos. This is deeply etched and intermingled throughout their emotional bodies. And when they go home this will continue—it is their own self-made life-energy. If they are not the most numerous of the city people, they certainly make up a large percentage of them. The whole city is stained with their signature-trails. It is thick on the walkways, and no less so on every road and street.

Within this, and affected by it, are the people who are basically drifting through each day, not centered in themselves; people who feel themselves as victims of the escalating and out of control circumstances of their lives. Impatience is not their problem. They are the victims of self-pity. Unknowingly, such people are badly affected by the negative energy-stains of impatience and intolerance. It sucks at their strength while feeding their self-pity. In turn, these people also add their own brand of negative energy to the negative stain of agitation.

It is even worse for the drop-outs; the homeless street people. The energy-stain is almost literally their home, their patrolled beat as they scavenge for food and money. For them, the unseen, negative energy-stain feeds their apathy, while draining and denying any new incentive. These people are lost souls. Their energy of lethargic hopelessness is an extra drain on the overall human energy in any city. They too add their stain of self-pity, despair and hopelessness to the negative energies of the city.

There are also all the people who are upbeat and happy with their lives. Even though they are usually a minority, they nevertheless offer a large, if unwitting, contribution to the human consciousness in any city. And it is always very much needed. These are the contributors. Their contribution is both on a personal level, with their family and friends, and impersonal with the people of the city as a whole. All unrealised. These people lighten the negative stain created by those people who are less aware. Not always less aware in life, but less aware in their personal relationships with themselves. Seldom is it realised that your relationship with yourself is the substance of your relationship with life.

Then, as always, there are the fewer blessed people who bring the Chaos and Order to Balance within themselves. They are the real cohesion of a city. These are the people who, all unknowingly, hold the confusion of human energy from exploding into utter city Chaos. These people live closer to unconditional Love than the regular people of the city. Where these people walk, the energies of impatience, negativity and despair are erased. Their energy-fields clean the city like flowing streams of Light. Their energy-trails erase the red anger of Chaos. Although there are never enough of these people, I am pleasantly surprised by how many there are in New York City. They are easily seen, each with an energy-field that stands out rather like a beacon on a dark night.

None of my observations are a criticism or judgement on any type of people. All of us are souls on a journey. Far too many are lost in transit. Most have lost all connection with their soul intent. Soul intent is the purpose and intention you had when you took on this incarnation, then completely forgot when you were physically born. Soul intent is always based in the growth of that soul. People who live with Balance in their lives are those most connected with their soul purpose. Balance is the place of greatest potential for our soul's growth. When a person believes success is measured by their amassing of money, then that person is mostly at odds with their soul intent. The soul's intent is to experience and live within unconditional Love, and to grow in wisdom. And you get to keep it!

Among the many millions of people who inhabit New York City, the people of Balance number in their thousands. Personally, I admire them. They certainly give credibility to the old adage, 'Serenity is not shelter from the storm, but peace within it.' And New York City surely is a storm of humanity! Serenity and peace go hand in hand with Balance.

Having decided not to investigate their personal lives, I watch the people of Balance as they go about their day. Not yet sure why I am here, I can only assume that there is something to observe, and thus learn. Watching to see if anything unexpected happens to these people, I wait patiently. All seems to be well. The day passes. Evening draws in and expires. By now it is almost midnight, and I wonder what it is that I am waiting for. Then it happens.

I see the astral bodies of the sleeping people of Balance emerging from their homes. To my surprise, these people in their astral bodies are coming directly toward me. This is a bit disconcerting. I did not call them. Despite this, I am soon surrounded by several dozen people in their astral bodies. An astral body is, in essence, the same as a body-of-Light, although the Light intensity varies a great deal according to the awareness and consciousness of the person involved. Everyone has an astral body, and everyone's astral body leaves the sleeping physical body at night. However, some people learn to keep their conscious awareness with the astral body, so while they are physically asleep, they are consciously aware and experiencing a non-physical, astral realm. As with Clive! My journeys with Pan are not in my astral body while sleeping; they are in my Light-body while conscious, awake, and aware.

However, these people have intense and spirited Light in their astral bodies. They are very clear and certain about what they are doing. Apparently, *they* are investigating *me!*

With more and more people continually arriving in their astral bodies, I attempt to telepathically communicate with them in the way that I do all my Light-body communication.

Not sure what to say, I call out, "Hello people. What's the attraction?"

Dozens of telepathic voices reach me together. *You are the attraction. On a personality/ physical level we were not aware of you, but as souls, we have been aware of you for several hours. We are curious as to who you are and what you want from us.*

Completely taken aback, I am almost speechless—almost! "Me! I am merely a person learning about metaphysical realities. I have been looking for, and observing people who live with a greater Balance in their lives."

Are we those people? How did you find us?

"Well . . . I have learned to metaphysically read the energy-signatures of Nature and people. From my position over the city, I looked for the energy-signature of the people of Balance in New York City. You are some of those people. You are the people who, mostly unrealised, hold the energy of the city inhabitants together. You are the cohesion of the people of the city."

Why do you describe us as people of Balance?

"Because this is your primary energy. We are each and every one of us a field-of-energy. You could say that we all fall into an energy category. This is a huge subject, so I'll be brief. All life is subject to the energy law of torsion. On one end is Chaos—the engine that drives, and on the other end is Order—the stability of structure. Determined by the torsion between them, both Chaos and Order have a huge range of expression. The perfect equilibrium within this torsion is the point of Balance—the place of greatest potential. To one degree or another, you are all people of Balance."

How do you know this?

I smile. Perhaps I am receiving a touch of what I give Pan! "I know this because the energy of Balance produces an intense flickering white light over the people who have it." I laugh. "And you do. Your energy-field actually does make you outstanding people."

An astral woman asks, *Why have we been drawn to you? This was not my conscious choice; it has come from a much deeper inner-place.* Her words precipitate a chorus of *We have the same question. The same happened to us.*

"I suspect this is soul attraction to the energy I represent. You have already taught me that being Balanced does not necessarily mean being soul aware, but neither does it exclude it. You will notice that despite the fact that all the sleeping people of the city are in their astral bodies, none are here with us except for you . . . the people of Balance."

If you are as human as us, how have you reached this advanced state of awareness? Can you teach us how to achieve this?

"Oh my gosh! I'm a student, not a teacher. Although that's not entirely true. I'm a metaphysical student when I'm with Pan, and a metaphysical teacher in the physical world."

Who is Pan?

"Whoa! This is escalating too fast. Briefly, Pan is the Spirit of Nature. Pan is pure Conscious Intelligence . . . with a capitol C and I. Just accept that he is my teacher. And please don't ask me how. As for me teaching you while we are in an astral realm, that is very unlikely. However, I would like to try an experiment. A completely harmless one, I might add. I'm going to expand my Love/Light to include all of you. I will immerse you all in the Love and Light of Self. When you return to your bodies, I would ask you to focus on remembering our meeting. I want you to ask the soul-self you are why you were attracted to me. You reach the soul you are by asking the question into your heart with full focus and intensity, then simply relax . . . and trust. I will be here on the third night from now to hear what you have learned."

So saying, I focus on the Love/Light that I am, expanding out my field-of-energy to easily encompass all the Balanced astral people from the ever-busy city of New York. As I do so, I inner-feel a welcome from so many of the souls these people are, souls that are fully aware of what is taking place. "Please communicate with your persona," I silently suggest.

Holding the Love/Light for quite a while, I gradually let it go.

Stepping into the energy of . . . Between . . . I step out into my study at home.

71

"Yes," I shout, elated. "I like this! Well . . . that was unexpected, Pan."

Are you going anywhere with this? Do you have a direction?

"At first I was not sure, but I am now. Yes, I *am* going somewhere with it. I'm going to see what unfolds. I have no exact plan, but I have a feeling that this will be to the mutual advantage of those Balanced souls and myself. And this is my direction . . . the unexpected . . . leading perhaps to a greater insight into the human state of Balance. After all, that's what started this! I'll just see how it all pans out!"

An inner-chuckle. *Fair enough.*

✻　　　✻　　　✻

This is the first date I have ever had with a bunch of astral souls high above New York City around midnight! Sounds more like the theme for a Twilight movie!

Moving into my Light-body, I am unconcerned about the time. Only an hour or so has passed since my return, yet I am off on a date at a linear time that has not yet arrived. I smile. I can step into any-where or any-when I choose.

"Are you with me, Pan?"

Yes. This should prove to be interesting.

Stepping into the energy of . . . Between . . . I step out above New York City around midnight, the appointed time of our meeting. Neat, huh!

To my surprise there are a lot of Balanced astral people already there. Many more than I expected, a lot more than previously.

"Gosh, Pan. So many! What have I started?"

Aware souls do communicate with other aware souls. Or had you forgotten that?

His energy is teasing. "I think I overlooked it."

I will withdraw and leave this to you. You always prove to be very capable.

"Please don't go too far. I may need some insight."

A chuckle. *I am sure you will be able to provide it.*

I literally feel Pan withdraw his energy from me.

Okay, solo again! And a different type of diving deep! By now I am surrounded by a crowd of astral-bodies. I scan over them, noticing quite a number of soul people who are not truly Balanced, but nevertheless are fairly aware.

A *very* Balanced and aware soul lady comes forward. Her astral-body is not just Light. I can clearly see that she is an energetically strong, middle-aged woman with a brisk energy. All astral bodies reveal an image of the physical person they are, and most of them only see themselves this way when in an astral reality. This soul lady holds the glow of unconditional Love within her aura, and I suspect she is their appointed spokesperson.

My name is Angela. It would help if we knew your name.

"My soul name is Mixael. In the physical world, I am Michael."

We will call you Mixael. Most of us are aware of a mass communication taking place between us. This has never happened before. Do you have any explanation for this?

"Intuition suggests that this could be a result of the Love/ Light. I did not do that with any expectations, but interesting things often take place when people are in the Love/Light."

Interesting things?

I laugh. "Please don't misunderstand me, but I have seen everything from people leaving their physical bodies in death, to killing everyone in sight, to manifesting greater Love in their lives. And a whole lot more. You could describe the Love/Light as a very powerful catalyst. Anyway, this is not important."

Maybe not, but as you said, interesting. I will assume it is always positive.

"Always. So do you have an answer to the question I suggested?"

The question was why were we so strongly attracted to you in our astral bodies? The answer that most of us either dreamed, intuited, or inner-felt was that we are approaching a time of great change. Indeed, we are in a time of great change. We all agree that we were attracted to you because on a soul level we feel a very deep connection with you. We feel that you can give us some guidance on how to act during these times.

"How to act?"

Let me explain. We are aware of a growing confusion, anger, and apprehension among the people in the city. We see it in both friends and strangers. How do we avoid this in ourselves, and help other people through it?"

"Hmm. I take it that you are open to what I might say?"

Yes, I'm fairly sure we are open.

"You will need to be very sure. I have no intention of arguing, or even trying to convince you people of its truth. You can agree or disagree, act or not act. That is up to each person. All I ask for is your collective trust and attention."

Angela smiles. *We would hardly be here if we did not trust you on a soul level.*

"Point taken. Although you are the spokesperson, can all of you hear me telepathically?"

Yes. As I said, we seem to have developed a mutual form of communication among all of us at this astral level. But it's gone when we are physically awake.

"First of all, I think that your new communication is an aspect of Earth changes. In your state of consciousness, you reach the necessary level of energy for telepathy while in your astral bodies. Okay. You will remember earlier I briefly mentioned the torsion between Chaos and Order. We are now in a period when Chaos is rising. In effect, Balance will be more difficult to achieve, but easier to maintain.

Excuse me, but could you define what you mean by torsion?

"Torsion is two equal forces moving in opposing directions: wringing out a wet towel is a good example. The energy of torsion applies to all life. Let me give you two extremes. In a rock, Order is dominant. In a wildfire, it is Chaos. The torsion in people is created and affected by their own relationship with themselves. In effect, Balance occurs in a person when the torsion of Chaos and Order reaches equilibrium in their energy-field."

I think I understand.

"For those who manage it, Balance is becoming a more powerful state of consciousness. More difficult to achieve, but paradoxically easier to maintain. Sorry for the paradox, but that's the way it is. There is a reason for all this. As you probably know, life is not random chance. It never has been. Physical life is the manifestation of metaphysical expression."

I don't understand.

I sigh. "Probably not, but you can ponder it later. As Chaos rises, it will break down ever more of the stability of structure— Order. This is already to be seen in an increase of earthquakes, floods, volcanoes, tsunamis, and in climate warming. But more importantly, the rising Chaos will gradually break down the stability of human belief systems. We are living lives of prolonged insanity. We destroy our own lives by self-attack. We believe that all life forms are separate. We actually believe that we can fight for peace! Few people have any real idea of the Oneness of All Life. We plunder the forests. We kill and murder. We cheat and steal. And we worship at the altar of money and the intellect. We are becoming increasingly insane. Hopefully, rising Chaos will tear all this apart. We are entering a period of de-structuring— we call it destruction. Only after the de-structuring can the re-structuring begin. It will begin when we have released the beliefs that bind us into mere pygmies of our true selves. It will begin when we realise that we are immortal souls, here to learn the Laws of Creation. It will begin when Intelligence and Wisdom re-emerge as the creative factors in humanity, and unconditional Love reigns supreme as our natural self-expression. It will emerge when we actually know that we, each one of us, are the creators of our own lives. Then we will emerge as our giant selves."

Angela stares at me, visibly shaken. *Well, I did ask!*

"Yes, you did. Walk into some of your New York hospitals and you will see that they are full of sick people. Of diseased people. Of suffering people. Of accident victims. Of people dying from their own self-destructive creations, all without a clue that they have created it. This is repeated in every hospital all over the world. Every courthouse of the world is over-packed with people blaming and suing other people to right the so-called wrongs of their lives. All this is false! It is all illusion. Each person creates their own reality. Blame is a human creation, an illusion. Huge pharmaceutical companies destroy the lives of hundreds of thousands of people annually, all in the name of health and medication . . . and the Great God of Money. Our agriculture is now increasingly based in the genetic manipulation of Nature. Personally, I think Nature may object! And the rising Chaos in the Earth is entirely of Nature. We are becoming an increasingly insane race of people. Unless Chaos tears down the very structure of our society and the structure of our stupid and erroneous beliefs, we are also a doomed people. We are not homo sapiens: we are homo stupidus! We march, no, we race toward extinction. Theoretical and research anthropologists know it, and anyone who uses their conscious intelligence knows it.

"But, to add truth and balance to my words, we are also children of eternity. We are also magnificent, metaphysical, multidimensional Beings of Love and Light . . . in denial. We are truly beautiful children in the kindergarten of Earth . . . thinking that we are adults. We are newborn expressions of unconditional Love, learning how to experience our divinity."

By now there is a large crowd of astral people all around me. *Has everybody heard what Mixael has just shared with us?* Angela asks.

She turns to me. *We have all heard you. Many of us are shocked .*

. . and touched. I know

I am. Can we ask you some questions?

"No. You can spend the next weeks and months trying to prove me wrong if you wish. That should easily clarify what I have said. A bit of research. A chat with a few true spiritual teachers. Read a few of the better books. Inquire and investigate, and really listen to the inner-voice of your heart. The soul whom you are will speak to you from your heart—the spiritual seat of the soul.

"However, I will come back after a period of you doing your own investigations. You will know when I return, just as you knew the last time. One midnight, I'll be here for you."

Without waiting for a reply, I step into the energy of . . . Between . . . stepping out directly into my study.

I sigh. "So . . . how did I do, Pan?"

A beautiful inner smile. *You have all the subtlety of a swinging hammer, but what you said, and the way you said it, should shatter any resistant apathy or complacency. And you ended rather agreeably!*

"So you agree with what I said?"

I agree that this is the way you see life. I do not have a human viewpoint. Your viewpoint is based in time because, no matter how soul-focused you become, linear time is a reality that you physically live in. However, borrowing a human perspective, I agree about the urgency of change, and fundamentally, I agree with what you said and implied.

"So was the way I said it a bit too intense?"

*Michael, you **are** intense. It is a personality trait in you that I enjoy. Intense holds hands with passion. Passion and Love and relaxed intensity feed each other.*

"Relaxed intensity. That's a new one! Another oxymoron. But it makes sense. I admit, when I get passionate about something, I do get a bit intense."

Get some rest.

"Right. Goodnight . . . er . . . that's ridiculous. You don't experience night or day, do you. You live in a timeless realm. Am I correct?"

Is this you at rest?

"No, but saying 'goodnight' to you suddenly seems trite . . . even ridiculous! In all honesty, do you ever even experience night . . . or day, in the way that we do?"

My experience is the eternal moment of infinity, never a moment. The 'goodnight' term may well be meaningless for me, but your Love within it is very meaningful.

"Oh. Good . . . night!"

❋   ❋   ❋

A few days of working in the garden pass by, intermingled with a bit of shopping. I often think about the people of Balance in New York City. It makes me wonder if I were to visit a few other cities, if the same scenario would repeat itself? I suspect it would. Do I want that? Having made a commitment to return to the astral people of Balance in New York City, I am not sure that I want a string of cities involved in wanting me as an after-hours, late night, non-physical, spiritual teacher-cum-consultant. On the other hand—I can easily leave when I'm ready! No physical transport required. No need for trains, planes or automobiles! Okay, I think I will try this in one more city, just to see what happens.

"Pan. I'm considering visiting London. I'm curious about Balance in London."

Was it not curiosity that did something rather unpleasant to the cat?

I chuckle. Pan humour! I like it. "I'm a different type of cat! I must say I like not having to do all the 'make ready' preparations any more. I really enjoy this new way."

Maybe so, but if your consciousness is not at the right level, stepping Between will be no more than stepping into unpreparedness and disillusionment.

"Point taken. Making ready."

I know that Pan is correct. There is a state of consciousness involved in all that I do, and as playful—never flippant!—as I so often am, that state of consciousness must always be my reality. I am happy that the required state of consciousness is pretty much my regular, permanent way of living and loving these days.

In my Light-body, I step into the energy of . . . Between . . . and out over the city of London. Metaphysically, I am aware that it is around noon, so I decide—unlike in New York—to venture into the city in a close-up and meta-personal way. I am already aware of the similar human energies in the people of the city. The many who typify the worst of human impatience and frustration. The human energies of apathy. The physical and spiritual poverty of lost human souls. The upbeat and happy people. The souls lost-in-wealth types. And the fewer souls rich-in-wealth-and-awareness. In addition to these all-sorts, there are those I am seeking: the people of Balance. And, I happily admit, many more than I expected.

I see all these and more in a single, all-embracing, metaphysical glance.

Walking the streets, non-physical and unseen, is a strange experience. Quite honestly, it is one I usually avoid. There is something deeply disconcerting about walking metaphysically in a city that is as ancient as London. Physically, we see life as it is only in the linear moment. But when metaphysical, there is so much more. True, I can screen it out of my vision, but this is a choice that I need to consciously continue to reassert. Now, as I walk along, I see the physical living people (embodied) of this time, and I see the non-physical living people (disembodied) who are either lost souls, emotionally attached souls, or angry souls. To summarise, they are all negative lost souls. The angry ones— and there are many—constantly shout their anger at an unaware embodied public. Emotional attachment is so common that large numbers of non-physical people cling to the known and the familiar of their lives. Those who shout their anger are constantly feeding and recharging it.

All this is not so much spooky as *very* disconcerting. And accompanying all these people are their energy-signatures, along with their almost indelible energy-trails. It adds up to such a bewildering mishmash of negative energy in almost every human expression and variation possible that I tune most of it out. I do not want to see such confusion. It is just too much!

Lifting into the air, I look for the Light of a physically living, Balanced person. Easily finding one, I come down to the street quite close to the middle-aged woman. She is in no hurry—living without undue haste and hurry is common in Balanced people— simply window shopping as she strolls along. My interest is in whether or not her field-of-energy affects the many non-physical people who throng the streets. I think that it will. It really is interesting to observe. As she walks along, the disembodied people seem to avoid any close proximity to her. They do this as easily and casually as physical people would avoid walking into each other. Watching, I become aware that her field-of-Balanced-energy, which is strong, clear and Light, is literally a no-go zone for them. Feeling a bit mischievous, I try pushing a disembodied person into her field-of-energy. As I suddenly step close and push, the disembodied person screams at my very touch. Gosh! Talk about making me jump! My touch must be anathema for ghosts.

Okay. So I am an untouchable! This opens a whole new field of speculation. Am I 'scream material' to all these left-over human relics? Although embodied people cannot hear the scream, the disembodied certainly can. Having a new thought, I relocate myself into an area which is clearly an older part of the city. As I suspected, I now find several more generations of disembodied people going back quite a few centuries. I notice that the further back in linear time these lost folk belong, the more faintly they appear. Some are no more than mere ghostly shadows, difficult to see or perceive even for me. All these wayward souls live in a no-time zone. None are aware that linear time is passing for they no longer experience it. Such a thing is difficult to comprehend. It is probably just as well that physically we cannot see our non-physical surroundings. If we could see it, most city people would have to live with the visual company of ghosts. Ugh!

To be fair, some of these disembodied people still hold the shape and appearance they had while physically alive. Some are quite beguiling. There are a few, however, who epitomise all that is evil and degenerate. These were murderers, thugs, the dregs of the city. And yet, the paradox; these too are Light Beings in total denial of their greater Truth.

Despite the new buildings and the new renovations to old buildings, the older of the disembodied people see and relate to the buildings as they were in their lifetimes. I can see a few people going up stairs that no longer exist in our present day reality; but they are not present day people. I can only imagine people sleeping in their modern bedrooms where an old corridor used to be. I have no doubt that the disembodied people walk right through the bed and its occupant while they are sleeping—and dreaming! Most of the disembodied people are as unaware of the physically living, as the physically living are unaware of the . . . ghosts! I have noticed that the disembodied people, as much as is possible, automatically avoid walking into, or through, normal physical people. It is as though the two differing fields-of-energy automatically repel each other. The energies of the disembodied strongly avoid the energy-fields of the people of Balance. I think the reason is obvious. Balance in a human is dynamic; a very strong flickering white Light-energy. The energy of a Balanced person would give a disembodied person such a charge of energy that it would be a bit like an electric shock. Which, on reflection, is probably why the disembodied person I pushed, screamed. They were shocked—me also! I smile. I wonder if I could shock a few

81

of them into an awareness of their situation.

Hmm! That's a thought.

Looking around, I see a disembodied couple who appear to be husband and wife. They must be from at least a century back in time. How does this happen? They are aware of me, and doing their best to avoid me in this very narrow lane of their reality. They are carrying an old wicker basket full of shopping, mostly vegetables. This is amazing! I will have to look deeper into this. It is as though there is another whole layer of non-physical society beneath the fabric of the present day society of a physical London. However, despite so many appetising distractions, I decide to pursue my intent of convincing this couple of their reality status.

Waiting until they are both sure that they are safely past me, I relocate, appearing in the entrance to a shop a little way ahead of them. As they stroll along, I notice that the lane of their reality is off to one side and parallel with the actual narrow street of today. So the folk of the past, and the modern people, do not always share the same space. Mind you, this is just in this place. It is not all like this. As the couple gets close to me, almost within reach, the woman gives a sudden high-pitched screech. In fact, she makes me jump—again! With her scream, both turn tail and run like they are being pursued by the devil. Me! So much for my attempt at kindness. I had wondered why Clive and his soul-retrieval team, or at least others like them, were not operating here—now I know. The disembodied residents are very tuned-in to the higher energies that threaten them. Strange, that they should see threat in that which could offer redemption or freedom. But then, surely this is a physical, everyday normality also!

It is understandable. These quirky lost souls of a bygone era are living in an astral reality of quite a low energy. Low—not bad or wrong; it can get considerably lower than this. The thugs, murderers, and suchlike have a significantly lower energy than the merely emotionally attached ones, and these types live in an even lower astral realm. Quite nasty! For all these disembodied people, anything of a higher energy is deemed as much a threat as their lower astral energy would be perceived as a threat by us. In effect, although they appear to live in the same space in London, they are actually living in a very different realm of energy. Their energy realm of non-physical reality, and the modern energy realm of physicality are rather like oil and water—they stay apart. This, despite occupying the same space! Fascinating.

I still intend to see if I can get a disembodied person to accept their reality of physical death, but catching a disembodied person is obviously going to be tricky. I notice that there are quite a lot of disembodied children, so choosing a teenage boy, I stalk him. To be accurate, I attempt to stalk him. He is a skinny adolescent, very skinny, skinny to the point of complete emaciation. He must have died of starvation or some debilitating illness. The more I attempt a stalking technique, the more obvious it is that I might as well be waving a flag. I am never really aware of my own Light. After all, it is me! But I realise that my Light-body is a warning beacon to these canny, disembodied residents of London. Changing strategy, I lift myself a half metre off the ground and rush at the teenager, intending to catch him by sheer speed. Aware that I have changed tactics, he runs like the wind, far faster than could be physically possible. To no avail! My speed is beyond the wind, and in mere moments I grab him. Only to let him go like a red-hot coal. As I grab him, he screams. Oh my gosh! The two previous screams were nothing compared to this. His is a lower-astral scream, like the demented, piercing screech of a manic banshee— or how I imagine a banshee would screech! It goes through me like a cold/hot pain of anti-Light. Any desire to continue my attempts to do good is shocked and shaken out of me. I had no idea that anything like this could be possible. I shudder.

"Pan . . . are you anywhere in the vicinity?"

Everywhere Nature is, I am.

"Yes, I'm sure . . . but that's not quite what I mean. I'm

wondering if you have been following my, er . . . adventures?"

Misadventures would be a more appropriate term.

"Be fair. I mean well."

I have no doubt, but if this could be called a 'look and learn,' what exactly have you learned? That is, apart from 'touch and shock.'

I smile. "Ha ha, very funny. It *is* a look and learn; one of my own devising. I've relearned an old lesson. Change what you can, but leave well alone what you cannot."

That sums it up rather well. In every older city you will find a similar situation. As with all humanity, these people are immortal. People of infinity. Just as you jokingly enjoy reminding other people, let me remind you . . . infinity is a very long time. Life has a way of dealing with recalcitrant souls all in perfect timing. Meaning well does not always add up to well done.

I sigh. "Yes. I think that is the main lesson I have learned here. My rescue attempt was *not* well done. Leave well enough alone. Don't meddle. Look before you leap. I think I must have been relearning some of the basic things I thought I knew. Sort of . . . lessons in disguise."

Then I smile. "Nevertheless, I'm having fun."

Of that, there is no doubt. Perhaps you could have fun while leaving the non-physical citizens slightly less stressed.

"You're right, Pan. I'll do my best to behave. I had no idea that a scream could go through me like . . . like . . . anti-Light. Both freezing cold and scorching hot simultaneously. That's what it felt like. It . . . sort of . . . hurt."

The pain you inflicted with your grab was exactly the same for the boy.

"Oh! Yes, of course. That makes sense. I had no idea."

Michael, please. Look and learn with a little more care.

"Okay, Pan. Lesson learned. I'll leave the untouchables well alone."

I inner-feel a deep inner-sigh. Pan . . .?

For a period of no-time, I stroll the city. Investigation reveals that there is, indeed, a whole non-physical shopping area used by the denizens of a disembodied reality. I wander the ancient market stalls, basically frightening the living daylights out of all the citizens of long ago as I walk along. I am curious and amazed to see the array of food, clothing, and the various weird miscellaneous articles for sale. I feel a bit of remorse for the scare I am causing, but short of not visiting, it seems unavoidable. On the other hand, I guess some of the disembodied folk get fun from scaring the physical people from time to time, as must occasionally happen. I guess I am, sort of, the inevitable reversal that eventually had to happen. A metaphysical version of what goes around, comes around! I'm the *comes around*. I chuckle. Sounds good to me, anyway. The metaphysical haunter of ghosts!

As I wander and observe the long-deceased people reacting to my presence, I realise that 'deceased' is not really an appropriate word. These ancient people are not truly deceased. They have only ceased *physically*. On an astral level they continue to function as before. These are the people who are deeply attached to sameness. They are so attached that even physical death cannot shake loose their attachments. I find this rather sad. I would far rather leave the physical reality, so filled with strife and struggle, and enjoy the playing fields of a greater reality—not a lesser one.

Promising myself that I will return to this fascinating playground—one that I had no idea even existed—I lift up to my former position high over the city. There I remain, waiting until midnight. As it was above New York City, so, perhaps, it will be above London. Of course, in my timeless reality waiting is a meaningless term. In no-time at all it is midnight.

Once again, I am surrounded by the astral bodies of both Balanced and consciously aware people. While their physical bodies repose in sleep, these people are consciously active. When they wake up in the morning, memory of this event is entirely another matter! As before, there is a crowd of these astral people.

I see one person who is clearly enlightened, a woman who has a considerably brighter, stronger, astral-body than those around her. Her field-of-Balanced-energy is a statement of her state of consciousness.

I'm glad to see that you are up to no mischief, she says sternly.

Hmm, this is a strange way for her to begin communication with me!

"I assume that just as I am reading your astral energy, so you are trying to read mine?"

Trying, yes. I can see that you have skills far beyond mine. I had concerns about what I would do, or could do if you should prove to be troublesome. To my relief, I can see that my concerns were clearly unnecessary.

She now has my complete attention. "Why would you even think such a thing?"

Her energy-field is apologetic. *I'm sorry, but in the older parts of the city there are some very degenerate human energies. To me . . . it is a haunted city. And rather frightening.*

"Ah . . . I understand."

*Do you . . . I'm so glad. I sometimes think that I'm too sensitive. Most people think I have a crazy imagination, but I cannot help but be aware of some **very** negative energies.*

I had already perceived a sensitive vulnerability in her energy-field. "I spent the afternoon in the older section of the city . . . in my Light-body. I observed many past generations of physically deceased people, living and working as in their bygone years. I became aware that a few of them are violent, were probably murderers, and they now occupy a lower astral realm than most of the others. They have a very nasty energy-field."

Oh . . . thank you. You have no idea what a relief it is to hear you telling me this.

I move toward her, embracing her in my field-of-energy. "If you will accept some advice from me, I suggest that you leave those decaying entities well alone. Don't feel that you have to save them, or help them just because you are aware of them. They have created their negative reality, and they will eventually have to uncreate it. There is a timing to everything, particularly when it comes to seriously disturbed and dangerous entities."

I have tried. She shuddered. *With very unpleasant results.*

"What happened?"

There are now two . . . violent entities that seem to take turns in haunting me. Even though I know they cannot truly harm me . . . it is extremely distressing and . . . offensive.

"So what do you do? Do you attempt to defend yourself?"

Oh yes. I put a shield of white Light around me. It's a good defence.

Disengaging from our close proximity, I shake my head, smiling at her. "Wrong. The energy of defence is a clear invitation to the energy of attack."

She stares at me in astonishment, then in quickly dawning comprehension.

Oh . . . golly. You're right. This is exactly what happens.

"These are two very angry lost souls. The souls are probably young, lost in the fear, hate and anger of their strong personalities. This happens. While the acts and expressions of the personalities are violent and murderous, the souls are simply lost and confused. If you can, ignore all the antics of astral aggression and offence. Take away your defence and, as much as possible, consciously Love them."

She smiles, tremulously. *How do I do that?*

"I just embraced you in my field-of-energy. What did you feel?"

I felt Love . . . strength and clarity . . . and . . . safe and protected.

"Your energy-field has an abundance of Love and compassion. When these lost souls come near again, just as I did with you, so you do with them. Open your auric field-of-Balanced-energy to them, just focussing on Love. No stray thoughts of saving them, or helping them, or defending yourself from them. Just focus on divine Love. They will leave you so fast you'll probably hear a rush of astral wind."

Oh . . . thank you so very much. It . . . feels so right, so perfect!

During our conversation, most of the Balanced astral people have been listening. I always forget about directing my communication to a single person, or Being. As I have been told on numerous occasions, I broadcast. Maybe one day I'll remember, but I'm okay with it.

At this stage, a literal chorus of thanks and gratitude came pouring my way. It seems that my enlightened friend was not the only person troubled by hostile ghosts. I smile. If anything, my method of broadcast communication has a lot of advantages!

The astral lady and I turn toward each other. "What is your name?" we both ask simultaneously.

I laugh. "My soul name is Mixael. My physical name is Michael."

Hello, Mixael . . . I like your name. I'm Anne . . . just Anne.

"I'm happy to make your acquaintance, Just Anne."

No . . . just . . . Anne!

"I know. I find it difficult to be serious for too long. I like to play . . . just . . . Anne!"

She has a beautiful smile, which I suspect has not been used enough.

Where do you come from? Even metaphysically you don't seem like a Londoner.

"Oh, just a step away . . . Australia."

Australia . . . golly. That's the other side of the world.

"It's one metaphysical step away."

You're very different. We're all here in our astral bodies . . . but it seems you're not?

"No, I'm not. Your physical bodies are sleeping, mine is relaxed in my study at home in Oz. I can sit and relax with my eyes open, aware and awake to my surroundings. It is all to do with focus. I focus away from my physical body/reality and into a greater metaphysical reality."

But . . . both at the same time?

"Ah, that takes practice."

But . . . there is something very different about you. You are not a . . . regular person. I don't mean that in any offensive way, she said hurriedly, *but you add up to something different!*

"You're perceptive. As Mixael, I'm a walk-in. Michael is my personal name."

Oh . . . I don't know what to say! I've heard of walk-ins, but I was not sure about it. And anyway, I don't know much about them.

"We are just people who are spiritually advanced and prefer to avoid nappies (diapers)."

What? I don't understand. Are you joking?

I chuckle. "Just a bit. A walk-in has a prior soul agreement with a soul who has an intention to walk-out. In my case it was when Michael's mission was completed. He walked-out, I walked-in. But I didn't come here to talk about such things, it's not important.

"I recently visited New York City at midnight, and the Balanced people came in droves to connect with me, without knowing why they were doing this. I came to see if the same would happen here . . . and it has."

What do you mean by balanced people?

I swallow a groan. Then, knowing I have no choice, I explain all about the energies of Chaos, Order, and Balance, and how Chaos is rising, precipitating Earth changes.

By the time I have shared all this, I am in the midst of a dense crowd of astral bodies. Odd, really—a tightly-packed crowd without being crowded!

I feel/receive a mass of communication. It all adds up to the same scenario as over New York City. Everyone felt a strong compulsion to come to me in this place. Some of them felt it before they went to bed, fully intending to be here; others felt the compulsion when they fell asleep. Yet others are fully conscious of being on an astral journey. For some, it feels like they are in a powerful dream.

I made the same suggestion to these aware Londoners that I made to the New Yorkers—that they focus on remembering this meeting. And that we will meet again. They will feel my energy-field when I arrive, so we set no dates.

I sigh. Am I nuts? Do I really want to do this?

This time I decide not to embrace them in my energy-field. I am interested to learn if it makes any difference to their continuing process.

With a smile and a wave, I step . . . Between . . . and back into my study.

The Lone Ranger returns!

FIVE

CHANGELESS CHANGE

Weather-wise, January 2011 has produced a month of almost ceaseless heavy rain. The soil is absolutely saturated. As a result of this, we have had massive wide-scale flooding, with fully three-quarters of Queensland inundated: a H-U-G-E area, as big as France and Germany combined! Then we got hit by Cyclone Yasi, a monster of a cyclone. With a diameter of about seven hundred kilometres on the ground, it was reported to be the biggest cyclone to hit Queensland since white settlement. This, combined with the floods, created huge overall damage to people's lives, homes and housing, city/town/business infrastructures, farms and livestock to mention but a few. Thousands of families were affected; a few by the spectre of death. The families not touched by flood or cyclone were affected by the emotional impact of being so close to the devastation—witness to the human tragedy. Carolyn and I were in the more fortunate group. The cyclone was far to the north of us, while the floods, although not far away, were minimal in our area on the Sunshine Coast.

So often in Oz, the extremes of Nature and climate affect and impact the farmers and country communities. This happened again, but this time it included Brisbane, the capitol city of Queensland. For the first time since their great flood of 1974, the city was awash, as suburb after suburb succumbed to the flood waters. I will not attempt a description. Enough to say that many houses were washed away, while hundreds of others were completely submerged. However, in several of the Queensland outback country towns, it was far worse, with people drowned and families ripped apart as, uninvited, Change dropped in. The overall infrastructures of several towns were almost completely destroyed. Amazingly, one town was literally smashed and almost demolished by a small, but savage inland tsunami as a huge wall of water from the catchment area in the nearby hills swept down and trashed the valley town.

I listened as the television reporters used very colourful language to describe the scenes to which they had been sent. An overall impression would suggest that Nature was some type of unrelenting and archetypal monster, unjustly and uncaringly punishing the innocent people of Queensland for crimes not committed. It probably felt like that! The first impact of such flooding heralds the death of untold numbers of creatures in the affected areas. But as the floodwaters slowly crept toward the south—in a typical Oz slow flood—spreading over much of the country, and connecting with other floods in other states, so it regenerated and, literally saved thousands of dying wetlands, victims to over a decade of relentless drought. This means resurgence and new life to countless birds and animals. It suggests that you cannot have a re-structuring without a prior de-structuring. Life and death hold hands, walking the same path. Nature knows nothing of death, taking no part in the monumental death-illusion that ensnares humanity.

Like so many other people, I watched quite a lot of television coverage of the floods, particularly regarding its impact on people. It was very emotional. I was blinking tears from my eyes quite often. It was all to easy too identify to with the numbing loss and pain of so many hurting people. While I was watching, I decided that when the city and flood victims were settling back to some sort of normality, I would over-view the scene from a metaphysical viewpoint. If you truly accept 'nothing by accident, nothing by chance', then you become aware that this flood could, possibly, be a forerunner of major Change for Oz.

On being interviewed, one flood victim spoke the words that very succinctly described the feelings of all the victims, "We just want our old lives back." Old lives back! Yet the very act of destruction is to remove the old, making way for the new. This reveals conflict. Most people cling to more of the same, yet our human consciousness is crying out for newness—for Change and growth. Hence, conflict. And conflict always invokes the unrelenting power of Change—in whatever form it may appear.

When the floods receded, they left thick mud in their wake. This was not the 'mud, mud, glorious mud' of the funny song: this was sticky and stinking. Without being judgemental or critical, and speaking in general terms, when mud invades cities, towns and homes, it indicates the 'stuck-in-the-mud' sameness of so very many lives. It reveals our human resistance to the unwelcome disruption of change; it reveals how sameness clusters. I experienced the inner turmoil of Change when my late wife passed. I, too, have had to cope with the numbing loss of the same and familiar. Hence, my heart went out to these unfortunates, as did the hearts of many thousands of other people—many of whom put their heart-feelings into action. Over the next few weeks in Brisbane, thousands of people turned up every day with brooms and shovels to clean up the mud in homes, shops, and streets. When the chips are down, people rise. The Mud Army, as they were affectionately dubbed, did an incredible job. And all from their own, heart-felt human compassion. Tradesmen were giving their time to 'gut' the flooded houses, ripping all the plaster-board off the walls and ceilings so they could dry out, ready for internal rebuilding. Sadly, on the opposite end of the scale, there were the usual sick and sad looters that emerged like scavengers, to feed off the victims of disaster.

A few weeks passed. Just as Brisbane was reaching some sort of normality, suddenly there was another disaster as an earthquake ripped through Christchurch, New Zealand. As I write this, a week after the quake, it seems obvious that the death toll will rise; there are still a hundred or so people missing, believed dead. I reflect on how, in the southern hemisphere, Change is hitting hard. Perversely, with flooding over much of Oz—not just Queensland—there was high heat and wild fires in the west, destroying homes and lives. It even touched the outer suburbs of Perth, the capital city of Western Australia.

It would seem that, both metaphysically and physically, a lot is happening!

A few days later I am in my study, getting ready for metaphysical journeying.

"In view of all our recent disasters, Pan, what is actually going on?"

It would seem that it is 'look and learn' time again.

"Can you give me a hint?"

Hint . . . it is time for you look at the bigger picture.

With his words, I feel a mild inner disturbance.

"Why do I feel uneasy all of a sudden?"

Why not step Between and find out?

I sigh. I have a feeling that I am not going to like the bigger picture.

Bringing my focus into my Light-body, I step . . . Between . . . coming out into a scene that is totally mind-boggling. This is *not* the expected Queensland floods!

Far beneath my elevated viewing place where I sit in the lotus position, the planet surface is seething with metaphysical activity. I see the energy-field of the planet from a timeless perspective, as I did with the Buddhist monastery. This shows me what is relevant now, and how the past relates to this moment and the whole. On this metaphysical plane of reality, past and future are One with the moment. I describe it as spherical time, where all time occupies the same space.

I am not sure whether I have developed a new skill, or if Pan has changed my focus as I look through his eyes of Love, but it seems that I am seeing the planet involved in biological creation. My attention is held by the energy-fields of untold numbers of living creatures. My impression is that this dates back maybe five hundred million years. A very l-o-n-g time! Concurrently, I am able to see the energy-fields of all the creatures of our present day reality. At the same time as all this, I am seeing the rise and fall of all the creatures in the vast span of time contained in this stunning, all-encompassing vision.

I stare in awe, trying to take it all in. It is impossible for me to encompass and assimilate all this. It is just *too much*.

Relax, Michael. There is no hurry. Observe, look and learn. Where you have a question, allow your own inner knowing to come to the fore.

I am aware of my physical body taking a deep, involuntary breath. A feeling of being out of my depth comes fluttering to the surface of my awareness, then sinks — as I drown it. For too many years I struggled to accept my greatness; I will not, now, let this mind-boggling vision in any way reduce me. In my body-of-Light, I also take deep breaths. This is no more than a way of relaxing, refocusing, and reorienting myself. I accept that I will probably only achieve a fairly minimal interpretation and assimilation of all that I am seeing, but it will have to suffice. And possibly it may act as a catalyst to deeper insight.

I am calm, accepting. I feel an inner-sense of approval from Pan. Even the magnificent realm of dragons was not quite as challenging as this, albeit in a very different way. The sheer scale of linear time is overwhelmingly confronting. Although well versed in timelessness, I have never before gazed at the scales of linear time in any way that is close to this. Going back in time is simple—you are there with it. But this—this truly is *all time occupying the same space*. And even though this could cover as much as five hundred million years, I realise that it is only a snippet of linear time on the grand scale of planet Earth.

Even though my metaphysical senses can handle this in a timeless way, my everyday, normal, time-oriented senses are also present. These senses require that I look for a sequential progression with which I can connect, observe, and encompass what I perceive as I gaze over the metaphysical spectacle of an energetic Earth. In the way that a novel contains both a beginning and an ending, I am required to read from the start of the book in order to fully understand the flow of the contents. I need to do this with what I am seeing now. It is the only way that I can encompass and, however sketchily, comprehend it.

While in no way denying the full energetic spectrum of many millions of years of life on Earth, I nevertheless focus on the earlier periods. I am looking at the energy-signatures of creatures that were alive on this planet around five hundred million years ago. In a physical reality, these energy-signatures would have long, long ago faded away to nothing, but in the world of energy, they are here for as long as the planet lives. As I watch, I see that the torsion of Chaos and Order is extremely active and very powerful, almost as though it was more powerful then, than now—but this could simply be my perspective. It is tricky when *then* and *now* occupy the same moment! For a vast time period, life flourishes and proliferates. I watch as Chaos begins to rise, becoming ever more dominant. With this, Earth Changes become apparent. Huge, fiery volcanic upheavals occur causing dramatic climatic change. Oceans and deserts change places, and complete planetary mayhem is taking place in the flicker of a few tens of thousands of years. The great mass of animal energy-signatures are mostly erased from the physical planet—the physical extinction of vast numbers of physical species, both animal and vegetable. Over the next few million years, life once more creeps back over the face of the Earth. I am just now realising that what I thought to be fog over the Earth, persisting through all that I am seeing, is the energy-signature of—microbes! Oh, my gosh! Their energy-signatures are so infinitesimally tiny, and so utterly immeasurably numerous, they literally appear as a swirling fog. As with the energy-fields of all life on Earth, they are now congregating in the greatest density in different locations from the earlier periods, but the microbes continue, undeterred!

Let me simply say that on a linear level of time on Earth, it would seem I am watching five Great Cycles of what I would call mass-extinctions of most plant and animal life, followed each time by a powerful and dynamic resurgence of life on Earth. Each time the locations of the Earth plates are different. The Poles vary from green and verdant forests to sheer ice. The equator changes from desert to ocean to jungle and back time after time. Several times the Earth is hit by asteroids and meteorites, causing its axis to tip, completely changing the location of the Poles. You can only imagine such catastrophe! Sometimes the driving force of a cycle is an ice age; other times fiery volcanic eruptions and earthquakes. I find it interesting that when the change is driven by an ice age, it is Order that becomes the dominant factor, slowing the engines of Chaos to a comparative crawl. This whole scenario I am witnessing seems to happen in an overall period of around five hundred million years! It is difficult to be sure of linear time in all this immensity. I am making no attempt to claim accuracy time-wise, because time does not come into my awareness as fixed and certain. On this scale, linear time is so irrelevant as to be meaningless. In all eternity, time only has the scale and value we give it for our three-dimensional benefit! In a greater reality—in which we metaphysically live—time and space are not the way that we physically experience them. One factor is very clear and constant; we live on a planet of perpetual change. As immortal, metaphysical Beings, we deliberately incarnate into mortal physical bodies for the very factor of conscious, spiritual growth.

We cannot change and remain the same, obviously! The fact that we physically incarnate onto a planet of powerful Change, aware that all Nature is ever-changing, and yet remain so resistant to change in our personal lives is surely the greatest paradox of humanity.

Just as Nature is the expression of the vast diversity of the animal, plant and mineral kingdoms, so also Nature is the expression of planetary change. Nature is the life *of* planet Earth, as well as the life *on* Earth. We are of Nature. As I see the upheavals beneath me, I am aware that in every major Earth Change there is no death. There is only the release of the physical body, followed by transformation; change! I get the energetic impression that as soon as a species becomes super-successful, unsuccessful, stagnant, redundant, over-abundant, in decline, or whatever—its very energy-field invokes Change. As a species, we also do this. We invoke Change. We stagnate by resisting change. We stagnate in so-called failure. We stagnate in so-called success. Stagnation invokes change. Nature is not looking for a success story. The very nature of Nature is to keep the consciousness that is expressing through all life in dynamic growth. Not the growth of physical form, but of spirit, of consciousness. This seems to require periods of total Change. Change which is so complete that it literally empties the cooking pot—ready for fresh ingredients to become another simmering stew!

Michael, remember to allow room for the probability factor.

"Oh! Yes . . . thank you, Pan."

Relaxing and letting go, rather than trying more, I gaze at the holographic, holistic Earth beneath me. Okay—a recap. I see the five great cycles of enormous Change on the planet. Each of these Great Cycles covers a hundred million or so years. These are the times when life begins again—which it does, albeit slowly. Nevertheless, as soon as the foundations of new life are laid, Nature speeds up the process, quickly enveloping the land.

Okay—this all seems in order. Now, where does the probability factor fit into all this?

Everything in life runs along the lines of the probability factor. In human terms, this means it is most probable that your current lifetime will be a fairly close repeat of your previous incarnation. And that your next incarnation will follow the same pattern of habits and beliefs as in this lifetime. As these habits and patterns become more deeply ingrained in each lifetime, so the probability of more-of-the-same is increasingly fortified. The growth of our intellectual ability does not change this. I repeat— life is not an intellectual expression. Each of our lives can be very different, but the probability factor applies to *us*, not our lives. It is most probable that the daily stress in this life will have the same, or a similar, effect on you as it did in your last life. The probability is that no matter what life throws at us—we actually throw it at ourselves!—we will continue with the same habitual reactions. The probability factor follows the path of our habits, our subconscious beliefs, and our more-of-the-sameness! It is the cohesion of this fixed and stuck probability factor that Nature disrupts and obliterates with each major Earth Change. The nature of expansion and growth in Earth-based consciousness demands it.

We embrace major Change by non-attachment to anyone or anything. Not easy, when this includes family and friends. Non-attachment is not a lack of Love; it is that most rare expression of *absolute* Love. By living consciously, we break most of the subconscious habits and patterns. Living consciously with unconditional Love breaks the negatives within the probability factor. Simple—but not easy! As stated, being conscious goes hand-in-hand with unconditional Love.

This is the probability factor I am now looking for in the major Earth changes unfolding within my metaphysical vision. It is a bit like looking into a library for a certain book, although I am familiar with the library in which my perception roams.

With this in my consciousness, I look again at the first of the massive Earth changes. Ah, yes! I missed this completely. I now see a type of crystallisation in the energy-signature of a great number of the life-forms—rather like a decline in their resilience. When major Change took place and life re-emerged once again, very clearly their resilience had been reinstated, with a new toughened and restored flexibility. This applied to the vegetable kingdom, as well as to the animals.

As I look closely at the major Changes, I bring my observation closer to our present time. Paradoxically, there is so much time in this vast timelessness that I am getting lost in it! Ah, this is what I am looking for—humanity. We humans are only recent players in the overall act of Nature. I see a few million years of tiny trickle-traces of humanity as they wax and wane. The energy-imprint becomes stronger and more apparent somewhere around two to three hundred thousand years ago. Ah—I think I follow this sequence!

Within the last of the five Great one hundred million year cycles of Nature, there are five cycles that begin with the real emergence of humanity. So—five human cycles of around fifty thousand years, all within the last of the Great Cycles of major Change. Oh—and even more interesting—the ending of the fifth of the Great Cycles, and the ending of the fifth of the human cycles both converge around our present time! Oh my gosh! The closing of the last of the hundred million year Great Cycles of Earth change and the ending of the last fifty thousand years of human cycles both converging in our present time!

"I take it this is what I was missing?"

Some of it. Now observe these human cycles to get the bigger human picture.

I notice now that each of these five human cycles follows a similar pattern. Over the first twenty-five thousand or so years, the energy of humanity seems to be uplifted, then, over the next twenty-five thousand or so years, it goes into a decline. Cycles within cycles!

This theme continues through each of these human cycles of time. It is rather like I am witnessing the probability factor growing and building its own adverse strength. I also see a correlation between the ice ages and the human resistance to change. The crystallisation of ice is an excellent representation of the energetic crystallisation that takes place in us as we subconsciously resist personal inner Change. We modify ourselves, but this is not Change. It is our unrealised subconscious attempt to avoid Change. I comprehend now that the ever changing climatic conditions of Nature are designed to be a prompt toward new and more appropriate ways of life and living. While it is Nature's prompt for a step forward, our probability factor is inclined to step us back into an old, safe, repeat pattern. Hence, a crystallisation of expression. In effect, safe is no longer safe!

There are other energies involved with the early emergence or appearance of humanity. As I look at the energetic-signatures, I see nothing that suggests that we evolved from the apes. Our earliest energetic-signatures have nothing of the energy-signature of the ape in them. As I observe the holographic Earth beneath me, one moment there is no humanity, then we are here. I notice that Earth is visited several times by other human-type Beings. It would seem that the visits came from other parts of our galaxy, or beyond, to colonise Earth. The visitors clearly had the capacity to leave colonists behind because the energy-signature of their craft indicates that they were massive; big enough to contain one of our largest cities. The energy-signatures of the craft's many inhabitants suggest an advanced human consciousness. These are the energy-imprints of very aware, highly developed humans! I see that the first visit appears to be many millions of years before mankind is theoretically supposed to have come on the scene. I think that as many as several hundred thousand colonists were left here. It appears that they flourished into a huge and thriving civilisation, far in advance of us, but then came violent Earth upheavals and Change, and they and their civilisations were practically wiped out, apart from a thousand or so desperate survivors. Utter disaster! After a period of struggle and loss, it is as though they gave in to the inevitable, and mated with some of the early primitive humans, people indigenous to Earth. Our human energy-field imprint is a trickle for a very long time as the two species interbreed. I will try for more clarity on this.

As I focus on the human thread of life, I see something that really surprises me. From my view of the energy-fields, I get the impression that the airspace of our planet was a battlefield for other visitors to our Earth. There are huge areas where the land was so super-heated from their energy beams as they fought each other that it became glass-like. These battling visitors were reptilian-humans of a violent and aggressive disposition. Their energy-fields are very different from advanced-human or primitive-human, yet I get the sense that the crashed and abandoned survivors also, at some point, merged with us. I do not have the knowledge to understand this, but strange and unlikely as it may seem, our energy-fields seem to blend advanced-humans with primitive-humans with reptilian-humans. This is what the energy-signatures indicate. All this seems to be many millions of years ago. It's all a bit confusing, because there is only a trickle-trace of this merged complex of humanity until comparatively recently. The more I learn about our human beginnings, the more complex it becomes, and the bigger the picture grows. If, as it appears, advanced-humans did colonise Earth, they had a very long period of peaceful, stable and consistent development, building their hi-tech and sophisticated civilisations in jungle and forest areas over much of Earth. Then came the upheaval event; a major Earth Change which destroyed their whole civilisation, thus the few survivors had to learn new skills if they were to continue as a species. They were now forced onto open grass and scrub land. Suddenly they were a prey species! This is when they apparently blended and mated with the early primitive-humans. It was quite a time after this early blending that the alien battle took place in the skies over Earth, and its subsequent reptilian-human energy appears in the human line of evolution. From then, despite the great numbers of humans today, it seems to have been a progressive struggle right up to our present time.

"Gosh, Pan. There is *far too much* for me to assimilate. I am way out of my depth."

Actually, you are doing surprisingly well.

I also notice that from the time after the first advanced human colonisation was almost erased, and we emerged from a struggling trickle-trace to a definite established humanity, we seemed to go into these unfortunate cycles of ascending in a thriving, nurturing way—pause—then descending into a decline of more barbaric behaviour. These cycles are long in relation to our own lifetimes. As I said, around twenty-five thousand years of progression and development in the human psyche, followed by a similar time period as we sink back into a more aggressive decline. During these cycles, it is the mass consciousness that engenders the energy uplifting humanity, and it is the mass consciousness that foments the human decline. However, throughout all this, many individuals are able to maintain the inner-growth of their consciousness. It is interesting to see the energy-fields of all animals indicate an overall consistency in the evolution of each species. In the energy-field of collective human consciousness, there are also increasingly more people whose energy-fields contain conscious growth during each uplifting and progressive cycle.

This brings us to our present cycle. As I said, we are at the end of a period of decline and aggression. We long ago had the twenty-five thousand or so uplifting years, and now we are at the end of a similar period of decline. The end! Finally. Hooray! As Chaos rises, it is breaking and shattering the negative templates of our beliefs and behaviour. This indicates that we are at a pivotal point. People who are Loving, who are open to newness, who are flexible, and who are able to let go—literally, let go—will not be shattered for there is no resistance to shatter. The people who are attached to sameness, who are inflexible, very restrictive and fearful, who aggressively hang on, will find that life at a crux point is, indeed, shattering.

"Pan . . . I'm going to take a break. I feel as though I have taken in so much . . . time . . . that I'll burst from five hundred million undigested years."

So saying, I step . . . Between . . . and out into my study.

An hour later, refreshed by a cup of coffee and a down-to-earth walk around my garden, and stroking our cats, I am ready. Relaxed once more in my study, and bringing my focus to my body-of-Light, I step . . . Between . . . and out into a place above the Earth. I seem to be standing in a small bubble of—calm. Calm! Why do I need calmness? This is alarming!

"Pan . . . am I in the same place as before?"

All is as it should be.

"Pan, please don't go all ambiguous on me. I'm in a bubble of . . . what I can only describe as . . . *calm*. I'm fully prepared to look and learn, but this is a strange place from which to continue my journey. It wasn't here before."

Michael . . . just look at the Earth beneath you. Describe what you see.

Just realising that I am now very much closer to Earth than previously, I try moving a small distance and the bubble of calm stays with me. Questions compete with uneasiness. Why do I need this bubble? Suddenly—there is no bubble. Instantly I feel vast, diverse, and disruptive energies all around me, pulling, pushing, pounding. I feel like a mote of dust in a maelstrom. Then, abruptly, all is calm once more. Okay, bubble, now I know! Thanks.

Lesson learned. Good. Now look down on Earth and describe what you see and feel on all energetic levels.

When in bed on a cold night, I like having the blankets snug around me. Now I make sure that the deeply appreciated bubble of calm is snugly in place as I assume my lotus position! Using metaphysical vision, I look, feel, open to the Earth below. Even in the bubble of calm, I sense and touch the roiling energies rippling over the planet far beneath. I can see the plates of Earth in violent upheaval, shifting and grinding, one against another. I was aware that the plates are always on the move, causing our earthquakes and earth-upheavals, but I had no idea that they could be this violent and unstable.

Obviously this is a period of major Earth disruption. Focus.

With full attention, I take my vision in closer, looking and feeling for something else. It seems that the entire surface of the planet is in turmoil, as though something bad and terrible is happening, yet energetically it does not *feel* that way. Chaos and Order seem to be involved in a battle raging over the surface of Earth, the vast energies of torsion tearing it apart, but the energy imprint of Nature shows no indication that this is a disaster. It feels more like a rebirth. The flaming, disruptive, yet creative red of Chaos is totally dominant on the crust of the planet, but despite this, within the energy of Nature being destroyed, the energy of the black of Order is strong. It is resilient and creative. Although a glance suggests that Chaos is completely out of control, destroying everything, once I look long and closely I see that Order is powerfully holding the blueprint of an abundant Nature in creation. While I had learned that the torsion between Chaos and Order is the dynamic of creation, I am now witness to a far higher level of this. My earlier intellectual understanding is being replaced by the deeper conscious imprint of the actual reality.

I realise that what I am witnessing is not the beginning of creation. It is a period of creative de-structuring and re-structuring during the continuity of creation. Just as we, on a very small scale, are continually destroying and simultaneously recreating aspects of our personal lives, so this is happening on a far grander scale to the planet Earth. I feel myself being affected, as old hidden concepts and expressions of belief collapse before the disruptive power of Earth's transformation. In my considerably closer position above the Earth, I am aware that the changes affecting planet Earth are reaching far out into our section of the galaxy. The energies buffeting around me are so powerful that even in the bubble, I, too, feel the effects of Chaos and Order, albeit in a more subdued way.

Gazing into the energies beneath me, I bring my awareness to the unmistakeable imprint of human energy in all that is happening. Whether the way I see it is for my eyes only, for my benefit, my lesson, I am not sure, but I see the human energies of people as though they are bricks being tossed into a vast cosmic crusher. Strange that we powerful immortal Beings should have such frail and mortal bodies. Is it the frailty of our bodies that causes so many of us to live such protected lives?

Behold . . . this is Earth Change.

I gasp. As I gaze beneath me into energies so very powerful that, even metaphysically, I need protection, everything on Earth is going through Change. Yet I know, historically, that we of humanity will continue to cling to sameness. What we need is Change that will affect human consciousness as powerfully as it affects the material world. We need Change that will once and for all destroy our addiction to more-of-the-same.

What you see beneath you failed to achieve human Change.

It appears that I am seeing one of the early cycles of humanity at the end of a twenty-five thousand year cycle. Let me clarify this: since humanity has been involved, each of the five fifty thousand year cycles is split into two twenty-five-thousand-year cycles by an upheaval event. During the first twenty-five thousand years people are nomadic hunter/gatherers. Interestingly, I see this as an ascending cycle in the growth of human consciousness. As the hunter/gatherer consciousness develops over the cycles, it remains nomadic, yet they also become a thriving and expansive civilisation within this frame of expression. Their commerce is aimed toward meeting the needs of the people, rather than for profiteering. The people are peaceful and content. Then comes an event, and humanity moves into an agricultural cycle for the next twenty-five thousand years. In terms of human spiritual consciousness, these appear to be descending cycles. In these cycles the people develop agriculture and grazing, along with their accompanying villages. Towns and cities flourish, with commerce aimed toward the accumulation of wealth and material gain. Profiteering is the main focus. The people become aggressive and more inclined to fight.

What I am seeing now is the ending of an early agricultural cycle; one of increasing attachments and overall decline. It seems as though Nature would like to obliterate the energy-imprint, but the Change event is not a major Change.

"You're right. I can read it in the energy imprint of a partially destroyed humanity. I see in the human consciousness that our terrible addiction to the illusory safety of sameness remains comparatively untouched. I notice that the Earth plates indicate a very different location of the various countries from our present time."

Yes. As you have seen, on a greater time scale this scene has oft been repeated.

"Is this related to our floods in Oz and the New Zealand earthquake, and all the other natural disasters that are happening with increasing frequency?"

You compare the human energy-field with bricks being thrown into a giant crusher.

"Yes, the people's energy-fields appear to be as inflexible as bricks."

Keep watching.

Was my question irrelevant? I guess it will be answered in right timing, so I let it drop.

By now, I know this 'look and learn' is about humanity rather than the planet, so I focus again on the human energies below me. I become aware of linear time on Earth, and that the maelstrom of Change is quietening. My bubble of calm is still with me, but I venture outside of it once more. Apart from a brisk buffeting, it is considerably more stable and calm. But the bubble remains? Hmm, seems likely that more Change will come visiting.

Moving away from the bubble's protection, I venture even closer to the surface of the Earth. It is a time of great electrical storms, of powerful, scouring winds and flooding rain. I am unable to recognise any geographical location, none are familiar, and the period seems totally irrelevant. As I relocate here and there, I come across scatterings of people. These are not hairy, primitive humans: they look much like people of today, and despite my brick analogy, they have a very tough, enduring field-of-energy. More so than present-day people. As far as I can see, they mostly seem to have a dark honey-coloured skin tone, or variations of this. It is obvious that this is a time of early nomadic hunter/gatherers. I am rather surprised to see that they have well-made, mostly leather clothing, obviously made by hand, but well stitched, strong and supple.

Nature is not hugely abundant, although it is more plentiful nearer the Poles than at the equator. The equator is very, very hot. At times flooded, often baked, it is a very difficult place for wildlife. Not unnaturally, vegetation is sparse. Toward the Poles, there are forests, great plains of grass, and plenty of wildlife.

From their energy-fields, I glean a few stories from different groups. I am generalising in this overview, but it gives you some idea of what I see. The groups are nomadic and rather male dominated. However, the females are not submissive—on the contrary. The males are similar to us, maybe a bit shorter overall, but with a substantially stronger build. I guess these are survival bodies! They are competent and capable, but the slender, smaller females are mostly much smarter. In each group where the alpha male recognises and accepts this, they are thriving. The alpha female is very capable of organising the females to their mutual benefit. They coexist in harmony and goodwill. They even have small families, if somewhat loose-knit by our standards.

Some of the groups I scan have a dominant male who, although good at hunting, proves to be a poor leader. And dominant males mostly lead. Such groups struggle, they quarrel, they have poor adhesion as a unit, members often leaving the group to struggle and perish alone. Such groups have few families. Everyone is involved in a personal struggle for survival. It is the old story of teamwork. Intelligent males unite the whole group into a cohesive unit, and they thrive, while the less intelligent males create friction and discord. This leads to the group's eventual demise, or, as sometimes happens, their integration into another group.

None of this really matters in the great scheme of human life. What is important is how these people cling to the subconscious content of their lives—from prior incarnations! I am able to read in their energy-fields that, although they have been involved in minor Earth changes, they are still energetically attached to their old patterns of behaviour. Their energy-fields are still carrying the subconscious imprint of their lives *before* this minor Earth Change. They are still mentally and emotionally approaching life as they did in a past, more ordered, era. Although this is a whole new scene for them, they continue to follow the dictates of their old subconscious programs, their old fears, their long-held deep anxieties. These are old programs and inner conditioning that are no longer *appropriate*.

Are we not doing exactly the same today? I sigh. It is as it is. How do you bring about Change that is not changeless? Whatever period this is in this different Earth time, has nothing changed in our human consciousness? One factor is apparent—essentially, these people are us! They are our ancestors, the progenitors of our current attachment to dangerous-safety and new-sameness. (Go

Michael! Two oxymorons in one sentence.) I am saying that there comes a time in the evolution of your soul-self when *safe* becomes dangerously *unsafe*, and what we call *new* is *sameness* in disguise. Too much safe-sameness and we sink into the mire of stagnation. We think we are changing, but under the banner of change more-of-the-same continues, undeterred. We like to modify, and think of it as change.

"It would seem that our fear of real Change goes back a long way."

It certainly does!

"But why? What is it that is so abhorrent about Change?"

This is part of your look and learn. I suggest you observe their signature-energy.

Hmm. This makes sense. I only metaphysically see that which I focus on. Perhaps I have been too involved in the overall fields-of-energy of the groups.

"Okay, I will."

I deliberately relocate a few times, searching for a group that seems to be cohesive and capable. These clans of people are very widely scattered for the very reason of hunting and gathering. I suspect that most clans are aware of others, but meet only for trade and, possibly, finding a mate. Finding exactly what I am looking for, I close in on quite a large clan of about a hundred people. In all honesty, if I was suddenly cast back in time to a hunter/gatherer era, I could find no better than this group of people. I would seek to join such a clan.

The dominant man is definitely intelligent. He is the equivalent of a benign dictator, which in this situation works well. He is the authority, but he shares it with a woman, and he is sensible enough to heed her advice. It is the energy-signatures of these two people that I choose to read, seeking to learn about the way they function.

As I attune with the energy-signature of the man, I become aware that his approach to survival is very sensible and logical.

Taking my cue, I focus on the activity of his head/brain area, and it becomes apparent that he is left-brain dominant. I already know that a left-brain approach to life is generally competitive, habit-forming, dogmatic and inflexible, and quite quickly defensive and aggressive. Yet, this leader is clearly much more than this. Still focusing on his brain activity, I see that although he is left-brain dominant, he is operating more from his whole brain; left-brain and right-brain hemispheres in sync. Glancing around at some of the males in the group, I see one whose energy-field suggests that he is unpopular, people keeping well away from him. He is very left-brain dominant and aggressive, operating totally from that area.

Interestingly, the man who is the leader is within a family group, but his mate is not the woman who shares his authority. His co-leader is considerably older than he is. This seems very sensible. And she, too, is more of a whole-brain person. Hmm, interesting. It is obvious that this group is really thriving, with both leaders operating from a whole-brain perspective. I try to read further into their energy-signatures. The leader has a clear and open energy-signature, nothing at all devious in him. I am attempting to see how he relates to the unknown. Does he fear the unknown? The answer becomes clear—a surprising *no*. He is not afraid of facing and dealing with new situations, or the unknown. He is rather unusual in this aspect! The older woman who shares his authority *does* fear the unknown, but she has a great respect for the male leader, trusting him.

Something does not quite add up. I scan a number of the other men, and I find what I expect. Mostly they are left-brain dominant and afraid of the unknown. I relocate to a number of the other groups, and left-brain dominance is the predominant energy—always accompanied by this fear of the unknown. Okay, now it makes sense. My first alpha man is an unusual person. And probably the most capable man that I thus far have encountered in his time.

"Okay, Pan. I've figured out why we humans are so afraid of change. It is almost as though it is part of our genetic code . . . even though it isn't. Perhaps we have made it so!"

This should be interesting.

"Actually, it's rather simple. Like our present humanity, these people are mostly left-brain dominant. The most outstanding among them are the whole-brain people. They use the feeling, heart-connected, intelligent/wise aspect of self, while the left-brain dominance has a far more fear oriented, isolated, clever/intellectual approach to life. Whole-brain actually knows it can choose change, and will do so, freely, while left-brain clings to more-of-the-same. So there we have it. The unknown is not known, therefore it is a threat to the safe and known. Change *is* the unknown. Change is the herald of the unknown and the unfamiliar. So with a left-brain addiction to more-of-the-same, people of this time—my time—have an inherent fear of big Change. The left-brain intellectual cannot understand the unknown quality of Change, so it fears it. Is it a coincidence that fear is a product of left-brain people's inability to understand the unknown? I think not."

This is a very succinct summary.

"Fundamentally, whatever may threaten our lives that we do not fully understand . . . we fear. Fear allows no room for trust. We have to choose trust, but by the very nature of trust, this is impossible for a left-brain dominant person. A whole-brain person has no problem with trust. Whole-brain, heart-connected people . . . trust easily. For a left-brain dominant person, such trust is incomprehensible . . . and cannot be a choice. I notice that during this time, as in my own, left-brain dominance is by far the dominant brain pattern in humanity. I think this is to our overall disadvantage. Left-brain has spawned the rapid growth of our technological age, but at the cost of conscious intelligence and wisdom."

Is there a solution?

"You . . . are asking . . . me?"
Purely to invoke a response.
"Response invoked! As a right-brain/whole-brain person, the answer is obvious. We need a method, beginning before the birth of a child, to encourage right-brain/whole-brain activity and development. This would also involve a completely different educational system: one that focuses on nurturing our natural intelligence rather than force-feeding our intellect. The human intellect holds a vital and necessary position in the outworking of our lives, but it should not be at the cost of our natural intelligence. In my present time, the media show us daily that the intellect holds hands with stupid. Many people today do not even know that there is a difference between intelligence and intellect. That's scary. Common sense is the companion of intelligence, but in our society today, common sense is a *very* uncommon companion."

I inner-feel laughter. *A good response! Let us continue our journey.*

Involuntary and intuitively, I step . . . Between.

Quite a number of times I step into, and out of . . . Between . . . always into situations similar to where I began. The bubble of calm stays with me, and I need it as I observe more, smaller Earth Changes and their aftermath. I continue to notice that the human addiction to more-of-the-same continues. This, even though humanity seems to handle imposed changes rather well. One prime factor has already become obvious: prior to an agricultural system, when people are nomadic as a means of survival, they handle the unexpected very capably and well. The unexpected is not always Change, but I notice that it often invokes changes in the way a clan operates. And the unexpected happens far more to a nomadic society than it does in a more static agricultural one. From my observation, the greatest growth in human consciousness takes place when they are nomadic hunter/gatherers. Once they move into agriculture and pasturage, thus denoting ownership, the 'greed and want' syndrome seems to kick in. Then, over a cyclic period of around twenty-five thousand years, a decline in consciousness becomes evident.

When, in more recent and calmer times, I overview earthquakes and volcanic activity in an agricultural period, the need to cling to the same piece of ground, the same area, the same village, determines very much the way that people behave. They do not simply move on, they cling and stay. Watching their energy-fields, I see that their piece of land, their homes, their villages, their *possessions* all represent security. People become very attached to the security that possessions offer. The only strong aspect of this security I have seen among the nomadic people is the security that is to be found within the clan as a whole.

"I can see now why you brought me so far back in time."

Then you see wrong. I but accompany you. When you step Between, it is you who determines where it is that you will step out. As it was above New York City, so it is here.

I chuckle in surprise. "I'm glad I didn't know this when I found the bubble of calm. Surely that was your creation?" I ask.

What do you think?

"I think it was yours. I was surprised by it . . . so how could I have created it?"

Nevertheless, it was your creation.

Hmm, this needs a bit of pondering. "Okay, correct me if I get this wrong. It seems to me that the 'I' of metaphysical journeying, and the 'I' who is learning from the journeying, are both aspects of the One immortal Self. The 'I' who knows my connection with Self is overseeing the aspect of Self who is still learning. In other words, the Being I am is offering protection and guidance to the 'I' with learner plates. Does this make sense?"

Does it make sense to you?

"Actually, yes, it does. It makes a lot of sense. It even answers a few unasked, even unthought-of, questions."

Is this not the way it should be?

I smile. "Pan . . . as you so elegantly lead me to the water . . .
I drink!"

And your drinking is as refreshing for me . . . as for you.

I am honoured by his words. "Thank you."

Once again, I step . . . Between . . . and out over the Queensland
floods!

"Gosh, this is where I intended to come in the first place! I
made a very long journey out of it . . . about five hundred million
years . . . but I've arrived with a much more open and expanded
viewpoint than if I had come here directly."

Which is why you made the detour!

I chuckle. I do enjoy humour with Panache!

I am now back in time a mere month or so. This is so very
much easier metaphysically than five hundred million years! The
floodwaters are widely spread over the Queensland landscape,
bringing turmoil and mayhem to almost everyone involved. I see
town after town in the countryside inundated in floodwater, and
I watch as they help and care for each other, frequently risking
their lives. But I am not here to watch the floods or the many heroic
actions; I am here to see if the abruptly changed circumstances are
actually promoting Change in the fields-of-energy of the people
involved.

I scan many energy-signatures. Every so often I scan a
person who, devastated by loss and emotional pain, is making
an inner-shift of major proportions. Only a few of these people
are consciously aware of this inner-shift, and for them the old
program will be overturned. I inner-cheer! Some people have
made a reluctant inner-shift and are not yet aware of it, but a new
direction will emerge over the months, even years ahead, and
they will take it. Sadly, for so very many people, a strong desire
to have their old lives back is very dominant in their energy-field.
I hasten to say that this is not wrong, or bad, or even negative,
but it is a clear symptom of the stagnation of soul-growth. They

115

have a more-of-the-same attachment that dictates their lives. Paradoxically, they will be magnets for Chaos and Change.

I do a quick scan from my overview. As I expected, it is the same situation now as it was aeons ago. Those who are prompted to make major Change in their lives are more whole-brain functioning. The very large majority who continue to resist Nature's inflicted Change are left-brain dominant. No surprise here! I repeat, these people are the magnets of more disaster, whether in this lifetime or another. When I say major Change, I mean a real Change/Shift in their state of consciousness. They can change jobs, change their homes, change countries, even change their spouse or partner, and all these certainly do have some effect, but generally they just modify their lives to fit the new circumstances. It is only the events that smash powerfully into their personal consciousness that brings about major Change. Unfortunately and increasingly, these events are the **major** disaster events.

With my focus on this Change-resistant factor, I move rapidly around the vast area of floodwaters. Everywhere I go, the energy-signature of attachment is repeated. Let me be clear, everyone has a different energy-field, but the majority of people have this habit of in-built resistance to real Change. How ironic, when this is what the human soul seeks!

"Pan, aeons ago, it would seem that humanity subconsciously decided or accepted that the left-brain, with its more competitive and aggressive aspect, was the needed path for the survival of our species. If my supposition is correct, then we made the wrong choice."

There is a flaw in your supposition.

"Oh!" I thought back over what I had said. "Ah, yes, I see it. If the decision was made subconsciously, then we did not make a conscious choice. Our pattern of left-brain survival is so deeply imprinted, so dominant, it simply continues to this day. Was a lack of conscious choice the flaw in my supposition?"

Yes. Subconscious living belies any choices that could invoke real Change.

I hover over flooded Brisbane, scanning the energy-signatures of many people. Here, the turmoil is greater, the fear more acute, because there are far more people and much more damage involved. Many more people will work hard to reinstate their old lives, but, equally, there are more people who are already embracing Change. These were people already hovering on the cusp, people who were ready to take a step into newness.

"Is this how we have to live, having our lives devastated simply to smash the mould of sameness to which we cling? It seems a poor choice! Whoops . . . it's not a choice! It is a lack of choice. What a sad, crazy way to live."

When you abdicate from freely choosing, then you increase the Chaos factor.

"Yes! I've learned that. We attract it."

Mention of the Chaos factor sends me high into the sky so that I can overview more of the disaster area. When I look down onto a country from this metaphysical aspect, it is not at all the same as viewing it from an aircraft at the same altitude. Metaphysical vision is not like looking through physical eyes, it is very different. It is more of an energetic, metaphysical *connection* with whatever it is that I am scanning. Language fails me as I attempt to fully describe this. I am now looking at the vivid reds of Chaos. How can I describe hundreds of different shades of red when each is without a descriptive name, having only an emotional connection to me? Each shade/tint of Chaos and/or Order touches/tweaks/induces in me an emotional recognition. How can I describe watching the tumbling, ever-changing reds of Chaos, laced with human fear and turmoil?

When I overviewed the Earth Changes of the distant past, the reds of Chaos basically involved the Earth's crust, and the black of Order involved Nature. Here, in the Queensland floods, it is very different. The floods are a creative, almost benign red of

Chaos, liberating the drought-sluggish engines of Nature to re-engage powerful action once more. The many years of drought that I once overviewed indicated the stagnation of black Order, as structure became ever drier, ever more stable; a denial of growth. All this is ended. How fascinating! This red of Chaos is about growth and change, exactly what humanity needs. Looking from this perspective, I see that, inadvertently, many of those people who would normally modify their lives to retain their more-of-the-sameness will make many different choices, leading to changes. Little changes, maybe, but conscious changes. Little conscious steps lead to bigger conscious steps! So too with Change.

I see how the torsion of Chaos and Order ignites human lives as every person involved in the floods, whether a victim, one of the many helpers, or simply one of those who makes a willing financial donation to help the victims and their families, are all energetically connected to the dynamic of Change. Of course, how this will outwork for each person will be shown in as many ongoing personal life-stories.

I step . . . Between . . . and out into my study.

"Gosh, Pan, what a fascinating paradox has been revealed. Chaos and Order are in total, complete, and absolutely unyielding opposition to each other . . . yet they do not oppose! From their opposition flows the dynamic of torsion, creating the growth of Change. In this way, unyielding opposition is transformed into transcendent synchronicity. By opposing, the metaphysical energies of Chaos and Order create Balance; a transmogrification of energy that translates its metaphysical expression into physical manifestation."

Put simply . . . every moment of life is an unseen miracle creating miracles.

"I think, perhaps, this is God . . . breathing!"

An inner chuckle. *I like that.*

"Okay, New Zealand tomorrow. Goodnight . . . my beloved teacher."

SIX

CHAOS RISING

A few days pass by. Tomorrow is a few days late!

I have delayed because I have a niggling feeling that I am missing something. Pan had mentioned looking at the bigger picture—but how big can it get?

Earlier this year, after a period of mild resistance, my study was stripped out and has been completely redecorated. The underlay to the carpet was damp and mouldy, so I ripped out all the floor covering, replacing it with an earthy clay-tiled pattern on glued-down vinyl. No more smell of damp mould. Carolyn and I painted the walls a strange, but pleasing colour; a cross between olive and mushroom, I think! Anyway, that's my interpretation. The ceiling is conventional white, and I bought a new desk. Basically, a slightly smaller version of the previous corner desk, it is of better quality, stronger, more elegant. Under Carolyn's more enlightened concept of interior decorating, most of the wall hangings have been replaced, but this time in a way that, apparently, is more tasteful and colour-coordinated. Actually, it is!

My previous approach to hanging anything on the walls had always been, "Ah, there's a space" — whack! Carolyn shudders at the mere thought! My resistance to redecorating was not about change! It was based in a concern that we might disturb the undoubtedly good energy. Indeed, we did disturb it. We reignited it, and the end result is wonderful. When I am in my study I feel deeply connected with much that is creative in my life. It is a place that embodies Nature, both physical—a houseplant, and my view of the garden and pond through the large window—and metaphysical, via exquisite rainforest sculptures by Lindsay Muir, and a dozen or so little sculptured spirits of Nature. Colourful light shines from a matching pair of Tiffany lamps that Carolyn bought me last Christmas, and a greater universal reality is represented by 'Pages of the Universe', a unique painting by John A. Syrmis. Plus, on what Carolyn smilingly calls my 'wife wall' I have a couple of pictures of my late wife, Treenie, and some of my lovely Carolyn. With her blessing, we have two large studio portraits of Treenie in the house, taken about four years before her passing. I know that Treenie and Carolyn were good friends, nevertheless, for me, this is a living testament to Carolyn's self-confidence and open-hearted qualities.

Anyway—tomorrow has finally transformed into today!

Relaxing in my study, focusing into my Light-body, I step . . . Between . . . and out over Christchurch, New Zealand. A week or so after the earthquake, the city looks as though it has been bombed. Even though the immediate terror has dissipated, the energy-fields of the people who were most involved look as though they, too, have been bombed. The energetic effect here is different, and far greater than in Brisbane. The Queensland floods and resulting damage and deaths were very traumatic, but compared with the energetic effect of this earthquake, all similarity comes to an end. Sure, the structural damage is similar—smashed and broken is smashed and broken—but energetically, the overall difference in the whole field-of-energy is huge.

As I overview the area, I learn that an earthquake is the result of the distortion in torsion between the metaphysical expressions of Chaos and Order within the planet itself. Order— the stability of structure—holds together the structural integrity of the physical planet, while Chaos—the engine that drives— continually seeks to break it loose, thus promoting Change and newness. The plates of Earth are continually on the move, often grinding against each other and, over many millennia, moving and relocating our continents on Earth's upper crust. Deeper however, the huge plates float on molten magma, moving through stable and unstable periods according to the torsion between Chaos and Order. There is always an ever-varying place of Balance within the torsion of these opposing forces—this is the very dynamic of creation. As that place of Balance loses its equilibrium, the resulting turbulence affects the surface of the Earth. For us, it seems that the Earth's surface crust is mostly stable. We are alarmed by the physical effect of great upheavals of energy, yet deeper in the Earth these disruptions are continuous as the vast metaphysical forces of torsion erupt and subside in the interplay between Chaos and Order. Our lives are disturbed only when the physical manifestation of those disruptions reaches the surface: an earthquake. We know that seismic activity is constant, but we ignore it. And what else can we do? This is the planet on which we are currently living. We are living in a time when we are not yet ready to recognise that seismic activity is the physical manifestation of Chaos and Order. We still think and believe that all cause is physical—rather than metaphysical.

Reading energy is rather like watching a movie, except that I am not the onlooker as in a cinema. By the very nature of the act, I am an energetic participant. As I openly observe, so I learn from the Chaos/Order torsion held in the energy-field of the Earth, and in the people.

We live in a boiling, bubbling, stewpot of creation. We need our long periods of stability. This allows us time to develop and expand on the lessons we have learned from life, enabling us to keep expanding in consciousness. Unfortunately, as a collective species we do not do this. We expand in technological achievement, in warfare, in industry, in corporate and personal greed, and in the everyday fear of the masses, but as One humanity living subconscious lives, we cling to more-of-the-same. Although millions of people make clear individual choices to walk the path leading to an expansion of consciousness, nevertheless, consciousness-raising is very low on the basic human agenda. Conversely, making more money is very high. There is no intelligence in this. At death, all our wealth is relinquished, whereas we keep forever the content of an enriched and expanded consciousness. In consciousness, wealth often equates as poverty. Not that it has to, but it so often does. When the fear of not having enough wealth, or the illusion of wealth-based power, or the accumulation of material assets is the accolade of ego-driven success, no matter how much money or property is accumulated, fear-based poverty consciousness will exponentially grow.

I move much higher above New Zealand. I intend to look for the bigger picture.

Oh, my gosh! What I see almost causes me to reprimand myself for not doing this earlier, but I instantly realise that everything is in perfect timing.

I go higher, wishing to overview the whole planet.

Now, from my elevated position above the planet, I metaphysically connect with the vast fields-of-energy that I am seeing/perceiving/experiencing.

As I bring my focus to the period that embraces our present Earth time, one factor is immediately apparent. We are in a time when Chaos is rising—sharply. Throughout all this, I become aware that the sun also goes through cycles that affect our cycles. We are told today that the sun has a tremendous influence on the cycles of our planet, but I see also that our Earth cycles have some influence on the sun. Holistically, each 'heavenly body' has an effect on the whole galaxy and, in turn, is affected by it. Imagine all the sixty trillion cells in the body of a human; what affects one cell, affects the whole body. This is equally true of humanity. What affects one person in consciousness, affects all people. Using the same scenario, Earth is a cell in the body of our galaxy. Then take the galaxies as cells in the body of our universe—and so on! Call it a holistic ripple effect. And so it continues, right throughout the multiverse. Yes, I do mean multiverse! Most people are metaphysically unaware of a greater reality, so for them the multiverse is not a reality. People reduce their reality/experience to fit in with the more common beliefs and perceptions of life.

I notice that each of the Great Cycles of the ebb and flow of life on Earth are hugely influenced by the solar flares and great cosmic winds that stream past the sun. The Chaos-driven changes of Earth upheaval seem to be when those immense and powerful wind-streams are closest to the sun. The Order-driven changes of an ice age occur when the great cosmic winds are much further away from the sun. In all this, the solar flares and their timing also have their influence. I should say here that I am simply attempting to share my metaphysical experience. I am struggling to describe something that is outside my normal terminology and expertise. But then, so much of what I write nowadays falls into that category!

Having mentioned that I see Chaos rising, I notice that the great cosmic wind-streams around the sun are becoming increasingly powerful. I also see a disturbing phenomenon; Chaos is rising *faster now than at any stage of the five human cycles* that I have witnessed. This is what I am seeing, and my unique perspective is all I have. Chaos is rising—fast. Whether it will take a month, a year, or several years to reach the point of mass plant and animal reduction is all part of the probability factor. Or, something quite different may occur.

As I scan all this, I bring my focus back to the probability factor of our current humanity. Let me state clearly that every probability factor is, and will continue to be, a response to the overall mass human consciousness. This means that the way each person thinks, and their subsequent emotions, their reactions or choices, their beliefs, their openness or closed-ness, etcetera, will affect the whole human consciousness. In effect, this means that blame and mass fear will create one of many rather unpleasant probabilities, while mass loving concern for each other will create other, very different and more pleasing probability futures.

One probability that is energetically held with many other probabilities is that Earth Changes will be geographically massive. Another probability is that it will involve Change more in the magnetic-fields of Earth, with less physical geographic upheaval. Yet another probability is that Change will be rather like a great cosmic wind that will scour the Earth, taking away all the people who are unable to resonate with the higher energy-field of the cosmic winds. These will not be like our regular normal winds, but cosmic winds of newness that will leave a permanent, higher vibrational energy in their wake. Winds that herald Great Change.

One probability indicates that billions of people could lose their physical bodies. Let me re-establish here that we are all immortal Beings. We can lose our bodies, and we do so with monotonous regularity, but we *never lose our lives.* Our unhealthy fear of physical death is a blot in the human consciousness. The ability to truly *let go* is only possible when there is an absence of fear. Fear lowers our vibrational energy-fields. Unconditional Love uplifts our vibrational energy-fields. In times of Change we need to make positive choices, and not allow negative reactions to overwhelm us.

One probability I see is that the great cosmic winds of Change will create huge energy-gates. Some people will become aware of these almost invisible energy-gates, and will be able to walk through them—into Change. By 'almost invisible' I mean that they may be seen by people whose lives and practices have opened their heart chakras and brow chakras, re-energising them. In yet another probability it will appear that many millions of people are simply vanishing without trace, disappearing from all countries of the world. This is quite a probable probability. These energy-gates will appear as subtle folds that envelop space in a fifth-dimensional probability. This means that two people could be walking together and unknowingly walk into an energy-gate. Moments later, one person has disappeared into a fifth dimensional reality, while the remaining person is looking for a vanished companion. Two people with two different states of consciousness.

One probability around the Mayan speculation that linear time is predicted to end—is that it will end. And with its ending there will be a period of great darkness. I say 'great' because it will be a total darkness. During the darkness, Change will take place beyond the sight of humanity. Another probability is that nothing will Change at all, and life will continue as it always has. However, within this probability lies another probability. This probability indicates that as each person reaches the end of his/her current life—entering whatever their beliefs create about death—and they eventually reincarnate once again, it will be with people who share a similar state of consciousness. We will not all be in the same 'mixed bag' as we are now. We will be with people of like-consciousness in the reality we have collectively created.

Yet another probability indicates that when there is a great raising of consciousness, such as millions have chosen in this current time period, so there will be a mass ascension. Stop, you might think! Ascension is for Gods, not mortals. Yet during this period, when we are engulfed in the winds of Change, a higher-energy-field means a raised consciousness. During this crux of Change, as our consciousness raises to the point where it transcends our current reality, so we may ascend. To ascend is to raise up. The sun rises. We need to raise up! Although this is a minority of the people—as always—it involves the millions of individuals who have walked the path that uplifted their consciousness as one incarnation followed another. They made wise life choices when it mattered, rather than followed the masses.

I learn that we, the people of today, are the sum of most of the people of the five human cycles. It seems that as many as possible of the souls of the five, fifty thousand year human cycles are here en masse, all incarnating to be at this grand, major Change event. Obviously, we have incarnated many hundreds, even thousands of times over the period of the five human cycles, but never have human souls stood in line to be at a single event as is happening right now. I also notice that just as many souls wait to come in, minor events will take away others who are not yet ready for major Change in their lives.

In the energy-fields-of-probability, one precipitates another. This means that the only certainty is Love. The only firm and stable ground is Love. The only place to be is Love. The only springboard is Love. Love—not emotional love—*unconditional* Love. Absolute Love. Divine Love. Love is an earthquake to every probability that could exist. Love shatters all probabilities, creating the certainty of Love.

I see probability after probability unfolding its possibilities. I also see another certainty. The greater the number of people who are Loving and in-their-hearts, the more optimistic the future scenario will be for *everybody*. The greater the number of people who are fearful and in-their-heads, the more pessimistic the scenario will be for *those of that energy*. I have repeatedly spoken and written of how we each create our own reality. This will continue. You and I will enter the perfect reality of our creation. This is a certainty. What we *know in our brains* will make no difference. *Who we are in our hearts* will be the deciding factor. We can hide our inner deceits from people, even from ourselves, but never from consciousness. It will not be our knowledge or perceived needs that determine our paths; it will be the consciousness of the soul we are. Fundamentally, the probability patterns I am watching apply to the mass consciousness. A conscious, Loving, and aware person is free to make the choices that influence their moment, and thus, their future.

I scan the volatile fields-of-energy below me, paying particular attention to the red colours of Chaos. When you are dealing with hundreds of tints and tones of a single colour, it is no longer a single colour. The reds of Chaos impact me emotionally, creating never before felt emotions. There are, literally, as many emotions involved as there are shades of the colour red. Oddly, in this brilliant, clear, intense, luminous-red of Chaos, I *feel* a deep respect for humanity. I pause; this is at odds with my previous experiences. I take a deep, steadying breath; holding my focus on the rising sun of Chaos, I again *feel* into its energy. Yes, I am right. It is, indeed, a Chaos of rising-sun energy. The rising sun is a universal symbol of a new dawn, a new day, of newness. And this is what I am *feeling*. I am elated.

It is as though we are almost—not quite—standing on the threshold of a new age of enlightenment. For the minority of people, this will be a long-awaited deliverance from a world that has become too aggressive, too suppressive, too corrupt, too energetically heavy. For the great majority, other probabilities await. One factor is very certain; we will gain the outcome that our focus, our emotions, and our thoughts have created for us over the millennia.

Good, Michael. You reached beyond your own awareness.

Did I? I'm not sure when or how, but if Pan says so, who am I to argue? "Thank you. I do think I've seen some more of the bigger picture."

There is more.

I chuckle. "I have no doubt. There's always more!"

Taking my focus back to the rising Chaos of Earth, I see that it has been strongly rising for about fifty years. For about the last

127

twenty-five years, it has been rapidly accelerating. I am aware of many of the Earth predictions for the 22nd of December 2012 period. Without knowing anything about the complexities of the Mayan calendar, it apparently comes to a rather abrupt end at that date. Although even that date and the year is disputed. A few of the great enlightened and respected Indian mystics have for a long time predicted major Change around that time. Also the noble Hopi Indians of America, Nostradamus, and many others have all predicted major Change in our present time period. All these are detailed in various books, so it is well documented. Extremists, along with gloom and doom merchants, talk of the end of the world, but you can dismiss this. Although, to be fair, if you are caught up in a huge tsunami you could be forgiven for believing it! One way or another, the probability is that there will be a major Change event. It may be metaphysical only, or both metaphysical and physical.

A journalistic viewpoint I recently read was refreshingly different. The writer said, "Personally, I think the end of the world already happened on the 2nd of April 1982, which was when Revlon stopped making 'An Evening in Paris' lipstick." It is good that most journalists take a cynical and humorous viewpoint rather than an alarmist one. To be honest, all the mishmash of so many predictions combined to put me off the subject. I know that death is an imposter, so I am fairly comfortable with all or any scenarios of Earth Changes. Now, as I gaze over Chaos, I realise that I had an inner reluctance to making my own statements about this. I had closed my eyes to what I am now seeing. I did not want to add to the large miscellaneous collection of predictions. So I avoided and delayed this particular journey with Pan, yet a greater insight suggests that this, also, is perfect. Everything has its own timing—and this is mine. I had felt previous inner promptings, but I had no wish to add confusion to an already confused humanity. I chose to ignore them. This is no longer appropriate. Just as I now own being Mixael as a soul, so I am entering my time and purpose.

I look to see if there are any hot spots on the Earth, but even these are strongly affected by the probability factor. I get the feeling that they are here, but I am unable to clearly see where they are, or to get an idea of their timing. I suspect that some of the hot spots are strong probabilities, but the where or when eludes me. All in all, I prefer it this way. As a person who travels via physical transport into many countries, I really do not want to know. I would rather live with *it is as it is* than try to avoid certain places at certain times! A spiritual teacher attempting to create a schedule like that would surely be a contradiction in terms. As I have mentioned, the Chaos factor of a hot spot suggests that soul-growth in these areas is becoming increasingly stagnant. This, along with resistance to Change, ignites the Chaos factor. In certain key areas Chaos is attempting to break the stranglehold that Order holds over a stagnating humanity. There are many large clusters of people who are so stuck in the more-of-the-same disease that only a major Change crisis will break it. Of course, the logical rationale of the intellect is that a hot spot is all about movement in the tectonic plates—and this *is* involved—but this is a physical effect rather than the cause. Cause is always metaphysical. Metaphysical cause places physical people where they need to be!

Energetically, Nature has learned that the destruction of a physical human body is not enough to promote the Change that is part of Nature's design. Our powerful, tough, yet also frighteningly brittle emotional bodies are becoming the target for an intelligent, constantly readjusting Nature. We are the only species needing this emotional shattering—and the probability factor suggests that this requirement will probably be met.

Feeling rather overloaded by this vast, all-encompassing metaphysical vision that transcends time and space, I step . . . Between . . . and into my study.

I need time to digest the input of my journey.

I spent a few days in the garden. Quite often when I go to work/play in our garden, it turns hot, and this time was no exception. I will be going away on our annual tour of public speaking and 5-day Intensives in a few weeks, so I want the garden to be in good order. Because of our wet, wet, wet, wet summer, everything has grown far beyond normal measures of growth. A lot of pruning and trimming has been needed.

I then became involved with about fifty people in the 5-day Intensive that we hold in our own area. It was at the beginning of this that we heard the shocking news of the earthquake and tsunami in Japan. I have hundreds of friends in Japan, so I watched the news with great attention. Although I have not been to Sendai, I know a few people from that area. I decided that when the Intensive was finished I would go back in linear time and see it from a metaphysical viewpoint. Yasumi, our Japanese organiser, emailed us to say that she had been in contact with most of our friends in the area, and they were safe. Good!

A couple of lovely ladies from Botswana stayed with us for a few days after the Intensive, so I was quite occupied. I allow life to present the timing of something to me, rather than me trying to push or manipulate it to fit in with my schedule. Eggs hatch in perfect timing, and buds turn into flowers. So also, in perfect timing, the earthquakes!

A couple of weeks slid quickly past. A multiple of blinks, a few sleeps, and almost without notice the weeks have passed.

One morning, relaxing in my study, I focus into my Light-body, and step . . . Between . . . and out, far above Japan. I have deliberately arrived a few hours after their disasterous tsunami. I have no wish to gaze on the first onslaught of human suffering.

Do you have clarity on what it is you are looking for, or wish to learn?

"I'm clear . . . but I have no direct focus. I plan to be open to
. . . whatever!"

So be it.

I rise up higher above the Sendai area. The first big impression
is total confusion. More confusion than fear. Confusion based
on the scrambled energy of mass shock—unbelievable shock!
The energy of the emotional turmoil is a match for the physical
turmoil caused by the tsunami. My heart goes out to these souls
so suddenly snatched from their physical bodies. This is nothing
like the energy following the earthquake in Christchurch.
This is anguish and shock magnified by thousands of times.
Energetically, it is very different, although apart from the huge
scale of this disaster, I am not quite sure why.

At this stage tens of thousands of Japanese are dead, so I
focus toward this. Oh, my gosh! I see many thousands of souls in
dim Light-bodies, lost, confused, and in utter turmoil. The area is
flooded in swirling water, yet so many are attempting to cling to
homes that no longer exist.

I descend rapidly. No more look and learn. It is time to roll
up my metaphorical sleeves and help in any way possible. As I
join the people who have lost their physical bodies—not dead—
so I notice many other workers-of-Light assisting the helpless.
Several angelic helpers smile at me in recognition, knowing my
field-of-energy. We are all attempting to restore some sort of
order to the lost souls, but at this time and place, Chaos rules.
Realising the hopelessness of this, I try a different approach.
Pointing to some nearby higher ground, I ask a few angel helpers
to go there and wait for the lost-souls that I will bring to them.
I then expand my Love/Light of Self just enough to enclose one
small area where a cluster of houses have all vanished. It is here
that fifteen or so dim Light-bodies are trying to find their homes,
despite being beneath ten metres of swirling, manic, pounding,
debris-loaded seawater. As I embrace them in my energy-field, so
I hold them, transporting them to the higher ground. Most do not

go willingly. They struggle, attempting to cling to the known, the familiar, the more-of-the-same.

I give them no choice. As soon as we touch ground, the angelic helpers move in, calming and soothing the newly transitioned. And so it begins, as I and others bring group after group of dimly lit Light-bodies to the angelic helpers on the hill. I work fast, urgently, and, in a way, ruthlessly. I almost rip non-physical people away from their dead bodies or vanished homes. It is very strange to find non-physical people deep underwater, acting as though the water is not there. Yet, at the same time, their roiling, pounding waves of fear, confusion and terror as their old life is torn and ripped from them, emulates the waves of the tsunami in which they are engulfed.

Now, many other Light-Beings are helping with this work. The crowd of rescued souls on the high ground is growing, even though angelic helpers are already transporting as many as possible of them to another metaphysical reality, most likely a half-way hospital. No matter how many I transport from the scene of death and destruction, it seems there are endless numbers of them as I go back time and again for more. Some of the sights I see affect me emotionally, and I am aware of tears trickling from the eyes of my physical body.

As I glance at a few of those helping to transport the lost people to the higher ground, I notice that most of them are non-physical Beings of a high consciousness. Like me, they toil tirelessly. Actually, I am getting tired for I am anchored to a physical body while they are in their metaphysical element. Although feeling a growing fatigue, I am a long way from finished. Sometimes I find clusters of souls still awash in the ocean, clinging to their bodies drifting in the surge behind the massive waves. They so often call out to me, begging me to save them, not yet accepting their transition from physical to metaphysical. I reflect on how my earlier experience when following the process of dying and death is now of great benefit to myself and these poor people.

I wonder occasionally what it is that drives me so strongly, and it registers that the lost souls in London have touched me more deeply than I realised. I see quite large groups of astral-body people who have come to help, but most of them are unable to stay for very long. Nevertheless, every soul lifted to a higher reality is a triumph, and the astral-body helpers are invaluable. By now there is quite a crowd of angelic helpers on the high ground. It has become a type of sorting place where those who are ready to depart are taken away, while those too shocked, confused, and upset by death are being comforted and stabilised.

With some of the people I am now collecting, I have to almost forcibly remove them from their dead physical bodies. Some clutch them frantically, while others lie within their physical bodies, as though defying the truth of their plight. In more normal circumstances, I would be very gentle with them, but with so many thousands of disoriented souls, I do not have much choice. Even though they and I occupy a timeless realm, there is a need to get these people into a reality of comfort and acceptance before their trauma becomes too deeply embedded.

And so it continues. I am thrilled by the numbers of Light-Beings who are now involved. Without doubt, this is a mass migration of souls away from their physical bodies. Energetically, I can see they all have a few things in common besides nationality. They are all attached to a home, to a family, to a tiny piece of land, to a way of life, and so deeply attached to more-of-the-same. To be fair, there are many who, having developed a higher consciousness, have the ability to let go. Seeing the constantly growing number of non-physical people on the higher ground, they *consciously will* themselves there, and they are there. Having included soul-growth in their busy lives, they are now reaping the benefit.

Fatigue is growing stronger in me, so I continue at a slower pace. A few of the Light-Beings give me a wave, almost a salutation to my staying-power. I notice that in addition to being a mass migration of souls, the large majority are souls who have chosen to leave early. By this, I mean that they have no wish to be part of the major Change probability. It occurs to me that there could be more mass migrations of souls who are prepared to repeat this cycle one more time. When I say prepared, I do not mean this as a preferred choice, but more as a result of the way they have lived many of their incarnations. Nobody is lost, nobody is saved. It is a probable time of major Change. Life, as always, continues. I repeat, *bodies* are lost, constantly; *life* cannot be lost. Every time the media reports the number of lives lost in a disaster, they inadvertently feed the lie of the mass illusion of death.

I feel a touch of despair, for I am now deeply fatigued. There are so many more souls that need retrieval, but I know I cannot continue much longer. I have no idea how many people I have ferried to higher ground and the angelic help, but it is not enough. I continue on in a slight daze—when my Light-body shoulder is firmly grasped.

Enough, Mixael. You will do yourself harm.

I glance wearily at a Being-of-Light. He—it is a masculine energy—has a strong energy of authority with him. *Do you not remember me?*

More alert now, I stare at him, recognising his energy-field.

"Oh my gosh! Ben . . . what are you doing here? Sorry, stupid question. It's obvious why you're here. I'm a bit tired."

Ben laughs. *I will let that pass. You have done magnificently, Mixael. I am truly amazed.*

But . . . enough. A bit tired is a joke; you are exhausted. We are here in sufficient numbers to deal with this.

I sigh. "I have a feeling this is just the beginning."

Ben nods. *At a later time, we will talk. Consider it a date.*

I laugh wearily. "Okay, Ben. I like that. A date it is."

With a sigh, I step . . . Between . . . back to my study.

Sitting for a while, I reflect on my experience. I have never been involved in anything like that before. I feel weary, but it is a weariness that is difficult to define. Getting to my feet I wander out into the garden, touching the soil, connecting with Nature, and watching my goldfish in their pond. Very quickly, the weariness is gone, blown away by the inner freshness of Nature.

"That was something that I didn't expect," I said to Pan.

You continue to surprise me. Needless to say, you did very well. I need to add that you were not in any danger regarding exhaustion, but you certainly pushed yourself beyond the limits that I expected of you.

"You expected! I didn't know Pan had expectations."

An inner-chuckle. I adopt your own self-expectations . . . which you far exceeded.

"No explanation needed. I know what you meant. Gosh, what an experience. It was both heart breaking and pure exhilaration, simultaneously. I inner-wept for the shattered lives and lost souls, while feeling joy that this is part of a process of eventual soul-liberation."

As you so aptly describe it, the de-structuring before the re-structuring.

"Yes. So easy for me to say, but not so easy to experience."

Michael, any price, no matter how high, is far more acceptable than the frightening cost of a stagnating human consciousness.

"I agree. But I have never seen so many people simultaneously pay that price. So much despair, such shock, confusion . . . it lingers, it hurts."

Be aware that the Earth also needs its cycles of renewal. This is a holistic process. Earth is not paying a price for the lessons of humanity. The life on Earth, and Earth itself, are already in the process that humanity avoids. Whole species are leaving this physical time-frame, and while people are to be commended in trying to save them—for this is a demonstration of their innate compassion—their reasons are all bound up in the illusion of extinction and endings.

"When all life is really about Change and transformation."

135

Exactly. Humanity has no choice in this Change factor. The only choice is in how each person deals with it. Physical death is a heavy blow to people who believe that death is final, but it is these people who have created this belief. Such a belief needs shattering, for it anchors its believers with the heavy chains of fear, loss, and despair.

"It's ironic that our Christian religions teach about 'life everlasting', yet clearly have no understanding of what this actually means. It's even more ironic that it was the so-called pagans, heathens, and the early primitive people who had a far better understanding about death. For them, death was a transition, not The End. Even their beliefs in ghosts and the dead continuing to be in their lives were far more accurate than the pap we are fed today." I chuckle. "After London, I can attest to ghosts!"

I feel his inner-smile. *You are the ghost who haunts the ghosts.*

I laugh. "Well . . . something like that. Maybe for them in their negative attachments, I am more of a . . . a . . . holy ghost! Gosh, I've just given a vague, nebulous term a whole new meaning. Mixael, the holy ghost. I like it. This will probably rattle the cage of a few Christians. Ah well, a shake-up is good. Not that Christians are ever likely to follow my journeys with you, Pan. You, apparently, are a pagan God. You did lots of naughty things with nubile maidens."

Your humour is definitely restored. Clearly you are well recovered!

I laugh. "Yes, actually I am. I'm feeling good. I'm going to return to Japan."

Pan said something that I did not quite catch—but I dismiss it.

Returning to my study, I relax, again focussing into my Light-body. I step . . . Between

. . . and out, once again over the devastation of the Sendai region.

I rapidly descend, meaning to once again be involved in transporting lost souls into the care of Light-workers. But it all goes wrong. I am falling—overwhelmed with loss, despair, and crushing fatigue. I am—falling—with a jolt—into the study I only just left.

Another lesson for you, Michael. The heart may be willing, but the price you paid to last as long as you did in your rescue mission is a deep, metaphysical fatigue. You need to soundly sleep, and find the lightness of heart-laughter. This should be easy for you.

"Gosh, talk about an aborted attempt! I had no idea that would happen. Yet, when I think about it, on my return I felt an odd weariness that was somehow . . . different. Metaphysical fatigue, hmm. I've had that before, but never like this. Now I know why Ben so firmly stopped me from continuing."

A wise and capable soul.

"And in hindsight, you obviously tried to warn me, but I dismissed it."

Tut, tut . . . you dismissed your wise and capable teacher.

"Dismiss my beloved teacher . . . never!"

Time for relaxed rest and restful relaxation.

Although I woke up the next morning fully refreshed, a couple of days passed while I was busy in the garden, and Carolyn was busy with travel preparations. Packing my suitcase is a breeze! On my twentieth year of travel, it takes me about thirty minutes. No exaggeration! Along with the new lightweight T-shirts that wick away moisture, I use the ultra-light materials of our modern sport and hiking technology wherever possible. They are super efficient, with clothing to keep you snug and warm, or well ventilated and cool. Also, all the clothes I use for my travels are already packed in clear plastic zip bags, only used for the five months I am away.

One afternoon, nicely relaxed, I focus into my Light-body. I step . . . Between . . . and out once more above Japan in the tsunami zone. This is a *now* time visit. About three weeks have passed, with the world focus now firmly fixed on the leaking nuclear reactors at Fukushima Daiichi. Despite being built to withstand an earthquake, they were primarily damaged by the inundation of the tsunami, or the combination of both.

First however, I bring my immediate focus to the area around Sendai where I helped in the retrieval of so many lost souls. When I say lost souls, I am referring to the first, immediate impact and confusion as the tsunami struck the coastal towns and villages. Most of the souls recovered their equilibrium quite quickly, moving on into the metaphysical zone that most suited their field-of-energy. If no Light-workers had been involved, the soul impact would have been far, far greater, and the after-effects much more stressful and damaging. Death of the body does not mean the end of stress! A mass exodus such as this needed all the help it could get.

I have learned from the media that over twelve thousand people/bodies are now accounted for, with over fifteen thousand people/bodies missing. What interests me with this visit has to do with the reports of the calm and controlled way that the Japanese survivors are dealing with their loss. This includes and involves the over two hundred thousand people who have been made homeless by the tsunami and the radiation leakage at the nuclear plant.

After about ten years of visiting Japan, conducting our 5-Day Intensives and doing a fair bit of public speaking, (my books are in Japanese), I have learned that they are a people who keep their emotions very controlled. This is not a criticism or a judgement, it is simply an observation. When they feel safe and comfortable with the people they are more familiar with, their emotions are not quite so tightly reined in. With newcomers or strangers, anger, affection, and other strong emotions are suppressed. This is their way. I have made some very good friends in Japan, and they are comfortable with me. Despite this, as a spiritual teacher, most of them present themselves to me in the way they would like me to know them, rather than the way they usually are. This may also happen in other countries, but to a lesser degree. My observation now is to see if the emotional calmness, the kindness, the sharing and caring that is being so widely documented on the Internet is genuine for them, or if it is an aspect of their emotional control.

One glance shows it all, for energy-fields cannot lie. All the kindness, the sharing and caring, the loving concern for others is absolutely genuine. But, at the same time, their emotions are being held under tight control. I see energy-fields of people weeping in privacy, and with overflowing emotions, but as much as possible their emotions are controlled, even within and from themselves. It is the way of most of the Japanese people.

This concerns me. By far the strongest body of a human is the emotional body. It is, of course, a metaphysical body. This is the body that has the greatest influence on building a person's life, of regulating their personality, and of determining their overall well-being during each lifetime. A major Change that destroys the physical body, while leaving the emotional body untouched, is failing to bring about Change. Physical bodies are not so important in this; the emotional body is. The mental body is generally overrated. The thoughts of the mental body are very much linked to the emotions, whether balanced, introvert or extrovert.

I am touched by the energy-fields of genuine kindness and consideration for others. It is exemplary. But I feel sorrow that for the majority the strong emotional discipline continues as before. For many people, however, there are public tears where none have been shed before, and grief and despair are given more freedom. When grief, loss, sorrow, despair, and fear are held as prisoners in the emotional body, they damage the physical body with their negative energies. Not bad or wrong energies, but negative.

When you see television footage of cultures where the people scream and wail, tearing their hair at a funeral, or over a dead body, it is easy to judge them as emotionally over-reactive. But even if it is disconcerting to watch, these people are releasing their negative emotions. They will recover quicker, and be emotionally cleaner, so long as they do not go on to embrace self-pity. Our Western culture seems to be a mixture of both emotional extremes, with most people somewhere in between them. We also seem to have more emotional confusion.

"Pan, in view of my observations, do you have any comment."

You were expecting a lot for a single event to break the emotional control of a nation.

"But it was a major event."

No, Michael. This was not a major Change event. This was a preliminary event, to allow those who, on a soul level in this time-frame, wish to take the opportunity to join an exodus from Earth. As seemingly unpleasant as it may be, it is also merciful.

"Oh. I thought this was a major Change event!"

You have seen the energy-imprints of major Change events. Being within the physical reality is something else again.

"Yes. I think I got emotionally involved. Are these major Change events a certainty?"

Michael, you know perfectly well that all such events are an ever-changing probability.

Oh well—I tried!

I bring my focus now to the nuclear plant at Fukushima.

With all that I have read and heard about the radiation leaks— and knowing absolutely nothing about radiation—I expected this to look something like Chernobyl. I was wrong. It does not. Energetically, it is nothing like Chernobyl. I cannot explain the difference in terms of radiation, but there has not been a nuclear explosion. This is radiation leakage. At Chernobyl, the explosion caused an inside-out, outside-in energy, as I explained in *Book Two*.

Energetically, this is an energy contamination. The water that is being used to cool the heating reactors is being energetically damaged. Water is not just a substance. We give it a chemical code and tend to treat it with indifference—to our loss. Water could be described as a unique form of liquid consciousness. Water energetically knows our energy-fields. Yet we, so clever, have little idea or concept of the living energy-field of water. If you water a plant while consciously aware, feeling a sincere reverence and gratitude to the water, it becomes a form of liquid fertiliser. Water consciousness, combined with aware human consciousness, raises the performance of both. So also, if we drink it with this awareness.

In an expanding area around the nuclear plant, I see a distortion in the energetic quality of the water. Metaphysically, I feel 'water pain'. Not emotional pain, but a Chaos pain such as I have never seen or felt before. Chaos is red, angry, distorted. Very nasty. The torsion is twisting and tormenting the water on a metaphysical molecular level, all to our eventual detriment.

Naturally, the greatest impact is in the water closest to the nuclear plant, but water knows nothing of separation and division. As water experiences this, so, to some degree, all water on the planet feels a resonance of discord with this radiation-polluted water. This includes the over seventy percent of water that makes up a human body. To counter-balance this it is important to maintain a focus of Love on your physical body. Love and bless the water you drink. Love and bless your body.

High above the nuclear reactors, I expand my Love/Light of Self to embrace the whole plant and all the water involved. Strangely, nothing at all seems to happen. I continue holding the Love/Light in position for what seems like a long time in timelessness. I still get no indication that I am doing anything constructive at all. I continue for as long as I can. I continue until I feel myself wobbling! Then I withdraw my Love/Light.

Almost instantly I feel a vast multitude of tiny, infinitesimally tiny shafts of Light connecting with my Light-body. I feel physical goose-bumps as a shiver of Light runs through me. It seems as though the water is responding. I feel this from the molecular level of the water, combined with the spirit of water. A well-known (or certainly should be well-known) Japanese man, Masuru Emoto, who has a remarkable insight and empathy with the spirit of water, has called for a world simultaneous prayer for the water that is being used to cool the leaking reactor. He calls for people to Love the water, and ask forgiveness for the way it is being used with the nuclear reactors. He is right. This would make a difference—if it happens! In fact, it would not only powerfully assist the water, but it would beneficially affect the physical bodies of all the people involved.

As I look at the field-of-energy of the radiation where it penetrates the homes, the water, the land, in fact every substance in its energy-field, I get the impression that when it is finally held, or contained, no longer leaking into the environment, the area will clean up and recover reasonably quickly. Unlike the three-kilometre exclusion zone of Chernobyl, which I doubt will be clean in centuries—although who knows what major Change could achieve?—this will be quite quickly cleansed. And that cleansing could be accelerated by human awareness, by Loving and blessing the nuclear plant, rather than despising and fearing it. By Loving the water, and by imagining and visualising Light over all the area involved.

As unlikely as it may seem, negative human reactions have an energy not so hugely dissimilar to negative nuclear reactions. Negative nuclear reactions tend to create negative human reactions. As I watch, I see that in the fields-of-unbalanced human energy, repetitive negative human reactions also have the potential to precipitate negative nuclear reactions. We create nuclear power plants. They are one of our most unwise creations. They are an incredible source of energy. We are linked to their energy, for we gave them birth. As crazy as it may sound, energetically, they are our children. Not the children of a few scientists or physicists, but of all humanity. In our intellectual world of isolation, we think that time and space and individuality separate us from each other, and from events in other times and places. This is not the reality of life. In reality, all is connected. All is One. We are the parents of nuclear plants, and, like it or not, we are always energetically linked with our own creations. In Europe, old, outdated nuclear power plants are to be found dotted around all over the place, and horrifyingly close to town and city populations.

Our human negativity is the prime factor in the probability outcome for the current major Change events. The more negative we are, the more ways Nature will find to trigger negative reactions from our own negative creations. This could also involve our stores of negative, mass destruction weapons that so many countries hold onto in the name of peace. What incredible hypocrisy. Weapons of peace would have to be the ultimate in left-brain human insanity.

I sigh. Why was humanity not given the ability to see life as energy, the way I am now doing? I smile. Silly me. If I can do this, it means humanity does have the ability. It is just that so very few people explore their metaphysical potential. We explore our physical and mental potentials, applaud them, and make as much money out of them as possible. And there it ends. Oh well, new opportunities will abound when this cycle is repeated *once again* by the big percentage of humanity.

It will probably be back to the future—hunter/gatherer style.

Time for me to return home, I'm getting morbid!

I step . . . Between . . . and into my study.

Carolyn and I are off on our annual tour in a few days. Bye!

SEVEN

Reappraisal With Ben

Home again!

Although you may read this from one uninterrupted chapter to the next, Carolyn and I have recently returned from four months of travelling. This was my twentieth year of our annual tour giving our 5-Day Intensives, seminars, and talks in many countries. Four months is plenty long enough for me. I get the 'suitcase blues' after being away for too long. But it seems I may need to get over it; apparently, next year I will be speaking in fourteen different countries. Yikes! Sometimes during a tour, Carolyn or I come out from an early morning shower, and just stand, wet and uncertain, not sure which way to go while slowly drying with a towel. Uncertain because we have just arisen from maybe our fifth different bed in as many nights. As we adjust to the new bedroom/bathroom layout, we are trying to remember where our suitcases and clothes might be located this morning. We spend so much time out of our comfort zone that we are now comfortable outside it. Despite this, the first couple of weeks are definitely the most stressful, then we settle in and accept living in the zone of divine discomfort!

When we return home, Carolyn tackles all the accumulated office work—despite keeping up with it on her excellent MacBook Air—and takes care of the many various items that cannot be dealt with while travelling. I go into the garden and begin the work of generally overhauling and cleaning up, along with all the pruning and preparing for the annual deep mulching. I really enjoy mulching the soil. I feel a deeper connection with it by taking care of it in this way. All this work often takes me a month or more, depending on the weather. It is my time of happy, down-to-earth reconnection with Nature. This is when I get out of my head—as in all the public speaking—and back to the basics of love in action on the land and among the plants that I enjoy growing. For many thousands of years my impoverished mountain-ridge soil had most of its nutrients washed down into the valley. Now, after twenty or so years of heavy mulching, it is rich with organic matter and humus. This does not change the fundamental nature of the soil, but it has certainly made it far more garden friendly.

For Carolyn, office work never comes to an end; it is an ongoing commitment. For me, there comes the time when—for a little while—the garden is up to date. As I sit now, relaxed in my study, this is one of those times. Although my metaphysical journeying and writing takes priority over gardening, I like to find a balance between both.

During my travels I get several ideas of things that I would like to metaphysically investigate, plus quite a few people give me various suggestions. Invariably, I misplace them all. Although I do a little metaphysical journeying while on my travels, I never write about it or record it in any way. On my return I have several loose ends to follow up from my earlier metaphysical travels. I have a date with Ben, and I have many people in their astral-bodies, both in New York City and London, who will be expecting me. It is odd to think that I can go back in linear time to keep those dates even though six months have passed by.

※　　　※　　　※

Relaxed in my study, I turn my focus to Pan. How wonderful! I feel an inner glow igniting deep within. It is something that affects me emotionally, mentally, and even physically, rather like the sun gently shining brighter within me. I Love my beloved teacher.

Your beloved teacher Loves you.

"You *are* Love, Pan, but . . . thank you."

Love is an ever deepening connection.

"Yes, it is with Carolyn. I'm grateful that it is with you."

Do I understand that you plan to meet with Ben?

"Yes. This is what I have in mind."

Are you making ready?

"Yes, dear enigma, I am making ready."

Consider this another solo journey. You will learn more this way.

"But . . . you are my teacher!"

There are times when my absence is a better teacher than my presence.

"Okay, if you say so." I focus into my Light-body, and then on Ben, visualising him as I remember him near the fabulous garden. Easily, so easily, I step . . . Between . . . and out into an area of great Light and beauty.

Hello Mixael. I felt your focus of energy as you decided to keep our date.

"Hello Ben. It's wonderful to see you again."

He looks much as I remember him from our first meeting, even if a bit more radiant and spiritually mature. Of course, the last time we spoke was at the time of the tsunami in Japan, when I was fatigued and preoccupied.

"I assume that you were able to retrieve the remaining souls in the flood zone after I departed in a bit of a wobble."

Ben chuckled. *Yes. What an interesting and early mass migration of souls. It is not easy to comprehend that on a soul level they all made a*

146

conscious choice to depart.

"Prior to more upheaval, maybe?"

The probability is high that this will be so. Anyway, if we are going to spend some time together, even if timeless, why don't we relax and make ourselves comfortable.

This needs explaining: you cannot actually be uncomfortable in any Light-body situation, but human habits of relaxing, of sitting or reclining with something to drink are very much part of our psyche. Can you imagine throwing a party with no food or anything to drink? It is the way we are. Beyond habit, it runs surprisingly deep in our psyche as a pattern of relaxation.

Ben waves his hand gently, and suddenly the Light is less powerful and we are in a beautiful garden. Close by is a star-dusted table with comfortable recliners around it, along with cool drinks in star-dusted glasses. With a smile, he indicates a recliner.

The recliner is, as usual, ridiculously comfortable. Why can't we make them as good as this physically? But then, this is not a physical body! I pick up a glass of liquid sparkles, having already learned that it is possible for me to drink in some of these situations.

Well, Mixael, how is life for you?

"Hmm. The older I get physically, the busier I become," I replied. "Not that I have any grumbles. Personally, I don't really relate to getting older. I'm relating ever more easily to my immortality. Mind you, there are the odd twinge moments of age when I lift a large, heavy potted plant that I should not be lifting."

Ben laughs. *Why not teleport it?*

"Ah, yes. That's a trick I have yet to learn. I would like to be able to teleport Carolyn and me around instead of traveling by air, but I hesitate from sheer 'how to' ignorance."

Ignorance is a good reason to hesitate. Would it be a fear of teleporting into an object and getting stuck in it, like in the middle of a brick wall, or tree?

"You said it perfectly."

Has Pan never suggested how you could do this?

"The subject has never come up."

It would seem to me that you have the required state of consciousness, but you do not have the required mentality.

"Seriously! I need a different mentality? That's the last thing I expected to hear."

You have a very simple and direct way of approaching life, even though intense. Be honest, would you, or could you, adhere to a quite lengthy mental process prior to teleporting?

"You'll need to elaborate on that question."

I'm asking you a question about attitude.

"I have the attitude that I would like to teleport without . . ."

. . . too much rigmarole involved. You do not like processes. Right?

I nod. "Okay, I don't like long drawn-out processes."

And yet you travel with the most awesome companion/energy possible.

"Maybe . . . but Pan does not need or require drawn-out processes."

Ben throws his head back with laughter. *So you are suggesting that Pan waltzed up to you one day and said, 'G'day, Michael . . . wanna go travelling?'*

It is my turn to laugh. "No, it wasn't like that at all . . . as you well know."

No, it was not. It took you about twenty years to overcome your fear and resistance, and to fully process and integrate the energy of Pan into your daily life.

"Well, I suppose you could put it like that."

Is there any other way?

"No . . . but I think I'm being outmanoeuvred in this discussion."

We laugh together. *Mixael, you are a wonderful character,* Ben says solemnly.

"As Mixael, I have no problem with teleporting, but my current psyche is deeply imprinted with an emotional resistance.

It was that sub-emotional resistance to Pan that took so long to overcome. As you well know, we are as much sub-emotional as we are subconscious, although this is seldom recognised. My sub-emotional body avoids the emotional confrontation of teleportation. Nevertheless, I am gradually moving my way toward a basic acceptance of teleporting. Intellectually it is a big step; emotionally, it is a H-U-G-E one. This is where I hesitate. I am hopeful that in the appropriate timing I will break through the emotional blocks of our everyday normality."

Ben smiles. *Well said. I can relate to all that. But you must be aware that metaphysically you are constantly teleporting.*

"Gosh, that's a thought! I have never once considered it like that. Any-where or any-when is easy metaphysically. All time occupies the same moment. But in a physical reality, linear time rules, okay?"

Only if you let it. The same Truth prevails; all time occupies the same moment.

"Yes . . . of course. This opens up a whole new way of looking at it. Thank you, Ben." Taking a sip of liquid sparkles, I consider a way to describe the taste. The closest I can get is lemon, with a dash of starlight.

"Do you have any insight on Earth Changes that you could share with me?" I ask.

It would not surprise me if you have more insight than I do. Not being in a physical reality does not make me all-knowing.

I chuckle. "I thought you might have the low-down from high-up!"

Ben laughs. *Actually, I do have something to share with you. When I became aware that you were keeping our date, I was filled with an inner-knowing that you have missed something in your overview of Earth changes. I suspect that Pan is behind this knowing.*

I nod. "He so often says, *'There is more.'* In truth, there is *so much more* I get overloaded. As you may have noticed, he did not accompany me this time."

Perhaps, together, we can have another look.

"Oh . . . can you travel that far back?"

Yes, with you.

"You really need me?"

Whether I do or not is irrelevant. You have a remarkable any-when ability that together we can utilise. All I need is to be within your field-of-energy.

"Ben, one thing puzzles me. Why did you go through your transition while so physically young? Surely you would have been a tower of strength during our times of change."

I have learned that my transition from physical life was made so that I can be of far greater assistance when Earth Changes get underway. There are many others like me. On a soul level we made a deliberate and conscious choice. This obviously suggests that the probability is strong that major Change will take place.

"I agree. One way or another, Change will take place. We are an immortal species—as are all life-forms—and the negative expressions of the many power-mongers will not be allowed to block the growth of consciousness that we all humanly represent."

Ben gives me a shrewd look. *Does humanity annoy you?*

I sigh. "A good question. No, I'm not annoyed . . . not now. I used to be. I used to be annoyed by *me!* For a species that has such a magnificent potential, we have not done too well. But . . . whether we are recycled or continue onward, we have each made our choices by the way we have lived, and it is time to reap those choices, however inadvertent they may have been."

So be it, says Ben, getting to his feet. *Whenever you are ready for us to explore the frontiers of space and time, I am willing and able.*

Taking another sip of sparkles, I smile. "That's dramatic: frontiers of space and time. I thought they only existed on a three-dimensional basis."

This is true . . . but three-dimensional is still your physical reality. So, let us travel, my friend. I am keen to experience how you do this.

150

Standing close to Ben, I expand my Love/Light-body just enough to embrace him. Not sure of what will happen, I focus on the one hundred million year Earth cycles, stepping . . . Between . . . and out, far above an earlier planetary time.

Wow! That was neat. Good stuff. I could not do that.

I smile to myself. Having a human companion is *very* different.

"Well . . . it worked. Here we are. So now I have to look for what I previously missed. I don't suppose Pan gave you any idea of what that is?"

Not really. But I did get a distinct feeling that you have been too restrained. A bit too reined-in . . . as it were. Any idea what this means, or why?

Pan is very astute. I know exactly what he means.

With a sigh, I decide to explain. "Yes, I do know. You must realise that what I see and experience on my metaphysical journeys is all written down, eventually becoming a book. You, Ben, will be featured in *Book Three*. So, also, will all my Earth Change observations. I am aware of a deep inner reservation of not wanting to stick-my-neck-out too far regarding them."

I think I understand. A fear of ridicule, perhaps?

I shake my head. "No . . . I don't think it's that. I've had my share of ridicule, and it no longer bothers me. No . . . to be utterly honest, I have a tiny fear of being completely wrong about Earth Changes."

*But they are inevitable. You could only be wrong if you state **this** or **that** will happen, allowing no room for the ever-changing probabilities.*

"Yes, I know. It's completely irrational . . . but it's there. And the only way I can move beyond this old block is to acknowledge it, accept it . . . and move on."

I agree with that. Any idea of why the block is there?

"I think so. You know that as Mixael, I am a walk-in. In quite a number of his earlier incarnations Michael was tortured to death for being different. He was a heretic, radically opposed to the church and the way it misrepresented the teachings of Christ. He was a spiritual teacher, going against all normally accepted thinking . . . and he paid for this with the high price of pain. The residue of the inner-block this created is still in his/my psyche. Right now I can look at it and dismiss it. Those identities of Michael's earlier incarnations were tortured because the common belief said he was wrong, despite his knowing otherwise. This is now the residue of the block. Even though the soul I am is Mixael, I cannot ignore the deeply imprinted emotional program of Michael. I am in his physical body, with his sub-emotional and cellular memories. This is another of his remaining memory-pain-associations that I need to overturn. Does this make sense to you?"

Yes, it certainly does. I, too, have paid the high price of Truth in earlier incarnations. I understand only too well.

We smile at each other, and hug: Love/Light embracing Love/Light.

"I can overturn the pain-induced program by letting go of all reservations and fully seeing and experiencing whatever is awaiting me."

Sounds good to me. Let's go for it.

Together, we assume my position of hovering in a lotus position high above the Earth of this early period. As much as possible, I relax into a full acceptance of *what is.*

Almost immediately Ben asks, *Mixael, when you were here earlier, did you notice the cycles within the great cycles?*

I am puzzled. "I saw the five, one hundred million year Great Cycles, yes."

No. I mean the cycles within each one hundred million year cycle.

"I saw them in the last Great Cycle, when humans appeared. But I did not see them in the previous cycles. I wonder why? But I can see/perceive them now that you have drawn my attention to them. It's almost as though you have drawn a veil aside. Oh my gosh, I did not expect this. I can now see that the magnetic Poles of Earth reversed their polarity many times. Gosh, this happened far more than I allowed myself to see. I thought maybe once in a million years, but it seems as though the Poles flip a dozen times or so in each of the twenty-five million year cycles. Do you see what I mean?"

Yes. I am also rather surprised by their frequency. There seems to be a bit of a pattern to the reversals, but I am not sure that it matters right now. I also notice that some reversals are fast, a few days, some a year or so, while others seem to take considerably longer.

"I'm glad you are with me. This is more than I expected."

Ben laughs. *Can I say that two pairs of eyes are better than one?*

"You could if it made sense. Tell me, how do you see what is below? Do you see through your non-physical eyes, or through the eyes of perception?"

Both. How about you?

"Ah ha! There *is* a difference between us. You are non-physical, while I still have my physical body. I do not see through my physical or non-physical eyes. I see/experience/connect with this reality very much on an energetic and perceptual level. Tell me, can you see the energy of Chaos and Order beneath us?"

I can see earthquakes and volcanic eruptions . . . if that is what you mean.

"No. Can you see the many different red colours of Chaos, or the fewer black colours of Order? Colours of pure energy. Literally, the energy of creation."

Now Ben is puzzled. *No. I cannot see anything vaguely like that.*

"Okay. This means that you can see more than I, while I perceive beyond you."

And so betwixt the pair of us, we lick the platter clean!

I laugh. "Good one! Yes. Between the pair of us we should be able to have a far greater experience by each sharing our observations. Tell me about the cycles within the earlier Great Cycles that you can see."

Ben is quiet for a while. *I can see the five great cycles. I agree, each is about a hundred million years . . . as if it matters. I . . . !*

"Sorry to interrupt, but do you get the feeling that linear time is not very meaningful on this scale?"

Very strongly so. But then, I live out of linear time! Okay, this is how I see it. If a single hundred million year cycle is one hour on a clock—there are four cycles—each is of fifteen minutes. In other words, there are four, twenty-five million year cycles in each of the hundred million year cycles.

"That's what I can see . . . now! Yet when I was here before, I only saw extra cycles in the last of the Great Cycles. Most odd. I wonder why?"

Maybe if we continue with this all will be revealed.

I laugh. "Yes . . . hopefully!"

Fundamentally, the four, twenty-five million year cycles in each Great Cycle are showing us more cycles of Earth Change. Nothing Earth shattering, but very much about big changes in Nature. In many ways it is a similar scenario; minor Earth movements instead of major, but with extensive changes in the many expressions of Nature. Deserts become flooded, while flood plains become deserts. Land sinks beneath the ocean, while land rises from beneath the ocean. And always Nature adjusts to these changes, re-clothing in verdant green the new land that emerges, while re-mineralising the oceans from the land that sinks.

"Basically, it seems to be minor Earth changes within the cycles of major Earth Changes. Certainly I missed that, though I honestly don't understand why. I think what I missed has more to do with the last of the Great Cycles than with the first four."

Yes, I think you could be right.

Focusing now on the last of the one hundred million year Great Cycles, I am aware of the need to be free and open in my appraisal of what I see. No more reservations, no sub-emotional editing. No longer need I fear the stark terror of torture. I can see/experience what unfolds before me, and simply share it in the written and spoken word. If I am wrong, so be it. *It is as it is.*

Fear closes doors, clouds vision, limits experience, erodes self-confidence, and makes life more static. None of this is my reality anymore, so I will release my sub-emotional censoring.

As these thoughts cross the mind in my metaphysical reality, tears are freely flowing in my physical body reality as I feel *very* old cellular memories of deep physical and emotional trauma being released. I have been increasingly aware lately of my body changing in ways that I cannot easily interpret, or understand. I am comfortable with the changes, even when they are indefinably uncomfortable. It is apparent that aspects of Mixael are appearing more strongly in me, yet they are still intertwined with the old programs of Michael. The old is being released while the new continues to fortify itself. Undoubtedly, this is part of my physical and psychological discomfort. However, body changes are also affecting Carolyn. I am fairly certain that Earth changes are subtly harnessed to physical body changes if we are open and receptive to the new. At the most simple level, it might be a sudden chilling of the body for no apparent reason, or an abrupt need to sleep when we do not feel tired. We have found that keeping warm and getting plenty of sleep are good antidotes for both of us.

With Ben alongside, I zero in on the last of the one hundred million year Great cycles. Yes—this also has four, twenty-five million year cycles. And yes, within the most recent of the twenty-five million year cycles, there are the five, fifty thousand year cycles, with each of those containing two, twenty-five thousand year cycles. Cycles within cycles within cycles!

I have no idea what I am looking for. I can only be open to—whatever.

Ah, openness reveals that this is not so much about what I am seeing/experiencing, but what this triggers within my inner-self. Previously, the subconscious censoring and the sub-emotional editing have taken place within my psyche, unknown and unrealised—until now.

I am aware that a lot is happening within you, my friend.

155

"Yes, Ben. A whole lot of inner realisations about my inner blocks . . . and all the little negative aspects that hold hands together." I smile. "In this moment I'm learning more about myself than about Earth changes."

Well . . . that has to be good.

"Yes, it is. But it suggests to me that even though I chose to come and review these Earth cycles, seeing more in these cycles is not why I am here. I deceived myself. I am fairly certain that my inner-limitations placed me here, with the cycles, rather than where I truly need to be."

And where is that?

"I need to be back in the frame of probable Earth Changes that I visited earlier."

So saying, I expand my energy-field to embrace Ben. Stepping . . . Between . . . and out, we are at the scenario of Earth changes.

Wow . . . that was a quick transition. You do it so easily.

"Yes, I guess I do. This is where I am meant to be. I can *feel* it."

Everything is pretty much the same as when I was previously here. The solar winds are blowing close to the sun, and the solar flares from the sun reach out a tremendous distance. The full scale of the red energies of Chaos is obvious, along with considerably less of the full scope of the black energies of Order. There is not much evidence of the white spectrum of Balance in the many probabilities that I see, yet Balance will undoubtedly be the final outcome. We humans have eroded the great creative Balance of the Earth, thus destabilising all Nature—of which we are a part. As has been said many times, what we do to the Earth/Nature, we do to ourselves. I am seeing this Truth in action.

I am now seeing patterns in the energy of Change that I previously missed. This time I see other Beings involved in the probability factors. Although human consciousness is very much the determining factor in the probabilities facing us, there are many Beings of Light involved in the process. These Light Beings

156

are gently—this is very difficult to describe—winnowing the warp and weft of the patterns of probability. In other words, we, the human factor, are being given the greatest possible opportunities to move with the energy of Love, rather than succumb to the overpowering, destructive, negative energies of fear. It is as though higher Beings of Light will spiritually encourage us to choose Love, to choose Light, to choose God, to choose the Buddha, or Mohammed, or Krishna, or to choose whatever is a positive and uplifting focus for our own higher spiritual good. The focus needs to be spiritual, not survival.

I realise now that I did not see the Light Beings previously simply because I was too restrained. Writing about them is definitely sticking my neck out—for me. With a new, more open approach, I now see probabilities when we are visited by spacecraft, with our brothers and sisters from other parts of the galaxy assisting us in our major Change. I do not see them taking us en-masse off the planet since we are here for a purpose. I see space people who remind me of home, golden skinned people who look like a slimmer, fitter, healthier version of us.

With them, and other space Beings, I see the foundations of a new Earth being laid. In fact, this is happening now. The old ways and those who promote them are already faltering in their last desperate struggles for survival, but for them, their time is finished. Those who fight for the old, who seek only the harvest of money with its associated power and material wealth, will find themselves repeating more-of-the-same as they reap their reward in a new/old society of hunter/gatherers.

I also see the probability of a mass exodus of souls from Earth. I see the probability that for great numbers of people this whole Change in consciousness is just too confronting. They hold onto the rigid structures of their old beliefs even to the death of their physical bodies. I suddenly have the insight that people who *believe* in death and endings attract death and endings to themselves, even when confronted by eternal life. Death is their

157

reality. They hold to the belief that you cannot get out of physical life alive. They have rejected eternal life for so long that they have denied themselves the choice to choose. If your consciousness is closed to a certain doorway, even if you stand before that open door, you cannot walk through it. This is how it is with so many of the people to whom the Beings of Light offer opportunities of conscious Change.

I see the probability of the greatest gathering of angelic Beings that has ever congregated on Earth. It appears as though they throng the Earth in their millions, particularly in the areas of mass exodus. Fear is the greatest attractant to the disruptive reds of Chaos. Fear, turmoil, anger, blame, and mass desperation—these attract the destructive power of red Chaos like nothing else. And yet, with even greater clarity, I again see the paradox: just as Chaos raises fear to ever greater levels of destruction, so Chaos raises Love to its greatest levels of creation. It is so easy to link Chaos only to destruction, yet this is a huge error. Chaos is the engine that drives. Chaos drives Love to its greatest levels—*if Love is our choice.* Chaos will not give us Love, or teach us Love. Chaos will bring forth from within us that to which we have long adhered, whether it be for better or worse. In the midst of mass turmoil and confusion, Chaos will show us the content of our individual psyches, of our own hearts, of our lifetimes of conditioning. And we will know the Truth of ourselves. By its very nature, Order allows us to hide our anger and blame and all our negative energy within our psyches; a structure of self-defeat. The nature of Chaos is to smash this, thus exposing our self-deceit.

I see the probability of new technologies that are in harmony with Nature and with life. I see where water is honoured for the life force it contains, and all systems of water transportation are replaced, away from the restrictive pipes and into energy channels where water can spiral, forever renewing and re-growing its energy as it travels to where it is needed. I see where water that

158

is honoured will become the fertiliser of the land and the plants, along with the natural ecological cycles of growth and return. I see the probable potential of zero-point energy, where the human consciousness has the maturity and wisdom to use this vast free energy for the benefit and the welfare of all humanity. I see the collapse of the monetary system and the ending of poverty as humanity finds ways of trading based on meeting needs, not on profiteering.

I see a probability where all meat animals leave the planet, their spirits lifted to a place of rest and restoration, before returning as part of the natural fauna and flora of Earth. I see the probable return of many so-called extinct species, as Nature provides the appropriate timing. The new humans will no longer exploit animals or eat meat, nor will they exploit the land to grow crops that are forced into unnatural growth by chemical stimulants. All the ways that humanity has found to produce our food involving the exploitation of Nature or humanity will end.

I see a probable future where there are no armed forces, no police, no law enforcement of any kind; in fact, no laws at all in the way we know them, for these are people of a higher consciousness. These are people who see all as equal, who seek only the welfare of all. These are people who live holistically. I see people walking the Earth with other Beings, mingling as though this has always been the way of life. And I see the arrival of souls from other, different frames-of-reality, bringing gifts of new technologies, revealing new, previously unknown methods of creating and guiding new energies, energies which have no name within our languages. And I see the end of the language barrier, as humanity learns to telepathically communicate with the language of the heart. I see the end of sickness, for with a humanity of pure consciousness, sickness is no longer a reality.

I also see the probability where keeping pets comes to an end. No animal or bird is penned, caged, or held in restriction. I see animal companions, but not in the current way of cats and dogs.

These are meat eaters, and live by our slaughter of other animals to feed them. This will not continue. Many of these species will return to their natural order for a period of time, rebalancing their energies as they assimilate and integrate their experiences with humans. For all those who were beloved pets and treated honourably, there have been countless numbers of so-called pets starved, beaten and exploited. As new fruit, vegetables and fungi of a very high protein level are developed, so the companionship of the predator animal pets will begin again in a very different way.

Let me be very clear; although I have released all my former restrictions, and I am sharing what I energetically see/experience, all this depends on the probabilities of about seven billion people. *We will not all share and experience a common reality.* The masses of people today adhere to an overall consensus reality. As people adhere to this, so they will share a consensual experience. Those who have left a consensus reality will experience the reality of their own making. Nobody will pay for the so-called mistakes of another person. We are all accountable to, and for, ourselves, only.

I can see energy literally whirling through you, Mixael.

I smile. "Yes, I'm feeling almost overwhelmed with input and insight. I feel as though I have been unleashed for the first time in a long while."

Mixael unleashed. Sounds interesting.

"Even more interesting will be Michael unleashed."

How do you reconcile Mixael and Michael?

I hesitate. "I'm not sure how to answer that. In everyday physical life I am Michael, but Mixael is also present. When I travel metaphysically, I am Mixael, but Michael is also present. I suspect the inner relationship is constantly and slowly changing. I think that if I am part of a probable Golden Age on Earth, then I will be much more Mixael than I am now. If the probabilities place me with an old order, then Michael will prevail."

*That all makes perfect sense except for your last statement. You **are** part of the Golden Age of humanity. You are living it here and now. 'If' is irrelevant.*

I look at Ben and smile. "Thank you. Even if, or when, Mixael becomes more apparent, or a bit more dominant within me, I love Michael's sense of humour too much to let it slip away. Quite honestly, I truly enjoy and love my Michael-ness."

Even though I never met Michael, I know him in you. He is very apparent.

"I'm flattered . . . thank you."

I become aware that polarity is becoming a major player in Earth Changes, but I am not sure how or why. I can speculate, thinking of a huge shift in magnetic polarity where North and South no longer polarise each other, but I have no idea of the outcome of such a shift. Oh gosh, even as I speculate, I see unfolding probabilities of my speculation.

Okay—in this probability, all the polarisation on Earth is disrupted. Physically, this is spectacular because it affects the stability of our planet, oceans, and wind, but energetically, it affects all Nature; i.e. all plant growth, along with animal and birds' directional ability. It affects us, however, in other ways. Quite apart from having to deal with an unstable planet—as though that is not enough!—we find that our inner systems of belief are no longer stable. Just think for a moment about everything you believe in, then abruptly having the stability of those beliefs erased. In other words, all that is based in illusion and polarised by belief is shattered. Equally, all that is based in Truth, and polarised by the heart/soul-knowing is empowered.

The effects become powerfully obvious to me. For those whose beliefs are based in illusion, and their illusions are shattered when faced with Earth Changes, a form of insanity prevails. Not so much insane, but no longer sane—unsane! For the people who have just felt the empowerment of their heart/soul-knowing, they are spiritually fortified, knowing that they will endure. They will know that, no matter what happens—Love will prevail.

As this probability unfolds, I see what I can only describe as the basic principles of growth. Chaos, the engine that drives, Order, the stability of structure, and Balance, the state of greatest potential, are all revealed in every cell of every life-form there is, from the great trees to the tiny microbes. It is all too easy to assume that scientific thinking, with its logical laws of physical life has got it right—especially when they fly under the banner of *scientifically proven*, along with their derision and scorn of anything *not scientifically proven*—but they see so little of the overall expressions of life. If physical law determined the cause and effect of life, scientific reasoning and thinking would be valid, but this is not the way of life: all cause is metaphysical, even though the effects are seen and experienced physically. The energies of Chaos, Order and Balance are not even visible to normal psychic or metaphysical vision, never mind the electron microscopes which are obviously correlated by physical vision to physical reality.

As I gaze at the universal principles that govern physical life, I am almost overwhelmed by the metaphysical input. The most obvious of these principles expresses within the polarity that ripples through and within all life. Polarity could be viewed as the balance of opposites, yet, metaphysically, I see that there are no opposites in natural life other than Chaos and Order. And these, while appearing to be opposites, are more of a dynamic; opposing and thus strengthening each other simultaneously as they seek Balance. This *is* creation. I sigh. I am at a loss to find suitable words to physically explain something that is metaphysically impossible for physical words and concepts to explain.

You really do have a deep insight into this.

I look at Ben, puzzled. "How do you know I do? Or even *if* I do?"

Are you able to . . . shall we say . . . read my energy?

"Yes . . . to some degree, anyway."

Well . . . !

"Oh . . . of course. You can also do this?"

Ben smiles. *To a degree. Enough that I can see an orderly riot of energy-information as it escalates within your energy-field.*

I chuckle. "Physically, we cannot have orderly riots! It's an oxymoron."

Maybe . . . but oxymorons are often useful for metaphysical explanations.

My chuckle becomes a laugh. "You're right. I often find myself using them simply because they are often so very appropriate."

So what is it that you are attempting to understand?

"What we are now talking about. I am struggling to find a clear mental path for my metaphysical insights of the universal principles as they apply to life. I need to be able to clarify my thoughts. This is a struggle. In other words, Ben, if I can formulate clear thoughts about what I am seeing and experiencing on an energetic level, I will be able to write about it."

Are you always able to do this?

"By no means . . . no. I have metaphysical knowing within me that I cannot put a thought to, never mind an explanation. Not even for myself!"

Are you able to accept this inner knowing?

"Oh yes. I know that I know, just as I know that I don't know."

Meaning?

"Meaning that I know the picture in the frame, and I know that a bigger picture exists in a bigger frame that I do not yet know. And I know this will continue."

Well said. So is there conflict in all this?

I laugh. "There is no actual conflict, merely a mild frustration when it comes time to write all this down in words".

And mild frustration is not mild conflict?

I shake my head at Ben. "You're rather provocative. Mild frustration is only mild conflict if I am unable to accept that it is as it is. And that, I accept. I'm naturally right-brain dominant. I live my life on those terms . . . *it is as it is."*

You see . . . I have provoked you to clarity.

Chuckling, I agree. "You have indeed. So tell me, how much have **you** learned about the universal laws of life since you left your body?"

He glances at me obliquely. *Do you remember the Garden?*

"Do you mean your physical garden, or the garden we arrived in when we went to your metaphysical home?"

He smiles slyly. *Come on, Michael of Mixael . . . you know perfectly well which garden I refer to.*

I sigh. "Yes. I do. And the universal laws, according to the way that I have learned them, collapse in the face of that Garden!"

Which you would rather not happen! Amazing how we try to avoid the unavoidable.

In the Garden where Ben and I arrived at his departure from his physical life, all the physical laws of Nature came to an end. I saw hot and cold climate plants growing side-by-side. I saw waterfalls which fell upwards, and plants that grew toward and into semi-dark caves. I saw plants that are extinct on our physical Earth. In fact, I saw plants that defied all the physical laws of Nature.

So, Mixael, how do you reconcile the Garden with natural law?

"I'm glad you brought this up . . . because it has triggered more insight. While here, in this place of Earth Change probabilities, I am seeing life through the lens of physical and natural law as I know it. The Garden to which you refer is a wonderful reminder that life is multidimensional, not just three-dimensional. I am currently learning about three-dimensional natural law, which I have called universal. Clearly this was an overstatement. Universal law is a term used by scientists, and I have inadvertently fallen into the trap of believing that our physical three-dimensional law is universal. It may be universal on a physical three-dimensional level, but we live in a multi-verse, and this far transcends our physical reality as humanity knows and experiences it."

Very good. Pan would be proud of you.

"It's a good reminder not to make hasty conclusions. Come to that, any conclusions are inclined to close the door on further inquiry. Hmm . . . did Pan ask you to tutor me?"

No . . . not in so many words.

"Okay, now you are being a bit evasive."

Fair enough. Pan very mildly suggested that you cannot be led, but you can be prompted.

"Well . . . of all the cheek! Prompted or provoked?"

A bit of both. So tell me, how accurate is his assessment?

"He . . . I . . . well . . . maybe just a little tiny bit accurate."

I sigh, deeply. "Okay, so I will apply what I have just learned to the probability of Earth Changes . . . which is why we are here."

In Truth, nothing really changes—except my way of approaching this. I had been trying to be clear, fair enough, but without realising it, I had been rather attached to explaining 'things' on a physical, three-dimensional basis. Now, as I open myself to as unlimited a reality as is currently possible for me, I see that the probabilities and possibilities are not only attached to the human consciousness—which they very firmly are—but also to many other races of Beings, both physical and non-physical, that coexist with us. I say—coexist! We do coexist, but most of humanity is completely unaware of it. It's rather like in London and other older cities; people of physical and non-physical reality coexist in the same cities, but for the most part, unknowingly.

What I am saying here is that everything connects with everything—and this is both universal and omni-dimensional law. Think about it for a moment; nothing is separate. Not even a thought. Thought is energy. Thought connects with the energy of similar thoughts. Right now, if a significant percentage of humanity took the thought, 'Freedom and Liberation through Love and Care for All Life', then this is what would become manifest on Earth. This is natural law on every level. The natural

165

law of thought is multidimensional in its application. We are immortal, metaphysical Beings pretending that we are mortal, physical Beings. This pretend game has gone on long enough. We are no longer playing this game to learn anything; we have *become* the pain and suffering that we have created in the game. It is time to wake up. It is time to choose Love. And not just thoughts of Love, but the actions and intent of Absolute Love—the Love that creates newness.

I share these insights with Ben.

Without being judgemental, the current Earth time is rather like a harvesting of humanity. The chaff shall be with the chaff, and the grain shall be with the grain . . . this sort of thing.

"Probably, yes. And I have no doubt that the grains will be graded. The grains filled with the nutrients of Love and wisdom will go one way, while the grains that have starved themselves of such nourishment will fall in a different direction."

Ben smiles. *Good lines for a preacher.*

I laugh. "It's meant to be more poetic than preachy. Anyway, you started it."

He gives me a speculative look. *I wonder how humanity will handle it when the world as they know it falls apart.*

"That's rather dramatic. Do you think it will fall apart?"

Not literally, no. But I think that life as people know it will definitely fall apart. Imagine the financial system collapsing. What will people do? How much panic will it invoke? How much violence will it invoke? How many people will blame the government? How much rioting will there be? How many people will just wait for someone to fix it? How much looting will take place? And what happens when the shops are stripped of food?

"Gosh . . . what a terrible scenario."

No, that is a mild one. Imagine what would happen if the magnetic polarity is lost, or North and South Poles reverse, or something like that. And we both know that this has happened many times during the history of Earth. We have seen it. Suddenly, there is no electrical power

166

or communication. Vast numbers of people will go crazy, literally. Once the magnetic field of Earth is disrupted, then the electrical energy that is generated between the inner core and the mantle of Earth will become destabilised. This may result in massive volcanic upheavals, and the human population will implode rather than explode the way it is now. Just the destabilising of the Earth's magnetic field will be enough to cause mass hysteria . . . and insanity.

I stare at him in amazement. "Finished?"

He looks at me levelly. *No. It is known that the Earth reverses polarity around every four hundred thousand years. It is now something like seven hundred and thirty thousand years since this last happened. Would you say it is well overdue? A shift of the magnetic Poles is no longer an 'if' . . . it is a 'when'. And sooner is just as likely a time as later.*

I attempt a joke. "Okay, so now I know why you left your body."

Mixael . . . you know what I am saying is true. You do not want to frighten people in your writings, and I understand this . . . but humanity is running out of time. CHANGE is knocking on the door. BIG CHANGE. You cannot, nor should you, sugar coat this truth. I think that you should present this in the manner that I have outlined.

I have to admit that the force of Ben's words shiver up my spine, metaphysically and physically.

I am aware that my words disturb you, they are meant to. And you, in turn, need to disturb the people in your life. You have been pussy footing around. Clarion says that you should give people hope and not frighten them, and this is true, but you need to speak with courage and conviction about the coming Change, not speak in a way that implies this is only a probability. Be very clear that the probability of Change is almost certain; what is not certain is just how this will take place . . . but one way or another take place it will.

"I guess, in all truth, Ben, that the way you are so powerfully expressing your knowing of Earth Changes makes me feel vulnerable. We live among trees, and I am unable to grow all my food and vegetables in the way that I would like. Too much shade and not enough water. The Michael-me says, sell this home and shift to a place where self-sufficiency is possible. Then the Mixael-me says, these thoughts are fear-based as well as practical. Mixael says if I have total Trust and focus in Love, all will be well. Mixael tells me that I am not here to shelter from the storm, but to trust that it will carry me into the countries and among the people who need my inner strength, my vision and clarity. I am not here to be safe, but to inspire. Brave words and true . . . I only pray that I can live up to them. Any comment?"

Ben places a hand on the shoulder of my Light-body and gently squeezes. *You came here by choice. There are things I may say, and things I should not. Let me state simply that you are one of those who will see the Changes through on a physical and metaphysical level. You need give no thought to survival . . . nor will you and Clarion ever be alone. And you will know that you are not alone. You are both Bearers of Love and Light, and your role will unfold in your ability to lovingly respond to every moment of Change. LOVINGLY, not fearfully. And this, my dear friend, I know you will both do. This is a certainty!*

"Thank you. Your words are very encouraging."

For the time being, I have had enough.

Embracing Ben in the Love/Light of Self, I step . . . Between . . . and out into the Garden of botanical wonders that I am still waiting to explore.

After thanking him for the strength of his advice and all the insights that he triggered in me, we share a farewell hug. We also plan to meet again.

Once again, with a focus on my study, I step . . . Between . . . and I am home.

EIGHT

KEEPING MY APPOINTMENTS

While we were on our annual tour of Intensives in 2011, I spoke about the trickle trace of humanity I had metaphysically witnessed. I mentioned how those early primitive/humans and advanced/human visitors from space had conjoined, and how later down the time track the surviving reptilian/humans from their vast battlefield above Earth added their diversity to the growing human gene pool: maybe they gave us our violence and aggression. I emphasised that what I metaphysically witnessed was my own personal experience. I spoke of the incredible air battle I had seen over Earth which involved the reptilian/humans fighting each other in a battle of such magnitude that it made Star Wars a pale comparison. I mentioned heat-ray weapons of an intensity far beyond anything in our modern comprehension, scorching huge areas on the planet, turning forests into churned-up pieces of a glass-like mix of wood, soil, animals and minerals. Multiple other enormous areas were scorched and melted into massive fields of a glass-like substance. As I spoke of this, it sounded crazy and unlikely to be believed. And I was okay with this. I mean, there is no shred of evidence.

On my return, I received an email asking me if I knew of tektite. Through the power of the Internet I learned that an estimated ten percent of the Earth's surface is covered in tektite. Its colour varies; in Libya it is a greenish to yellowish colour, while in many other countries it is darker, more black. It is estimated to be about three-quarters of a million years old, and mostly it is believed to be caused by asteroids and/or meteors— even though they cannot always find accompanying evidence of craters or the like. Another theory considers it volcanic in origin and natural—and some of it may be. Nevertheless, it remains a scientific mystery. Despite all the scientific speculation, for me, the glass-like element described as tektite fits in perfectly with the timing and the heat rays I metaphysically witnessed. I found this strangely satisfying. On reflection, I realised that although this proves absolutely nothing to anybody as evidence of my experiences—nor do I need it to—for me it held a very gratifying affirmation and emotional validation.

A few months later, Carolyn and I set off for Japan.

In 2010, after a long, tedious and unnecessary delay, the immigration officers at the passport control denied us entry. We were detained from five o'clock in the evening until almost midnight, by which time the whole of Narita Airport had closed down. They claimed that I did not have the correct visa, even though I had been advised by the Japanese Embassy that it was correct. Finally, to add insult to injury, they then expected us to pay 92,000 yen ($920 AUD) for two guards to stay with us for twenty-four hours until we could be put on the first return flight home. This, on a small island and with them holding our passports. They told us we were not criminals—then proceeded to treat us as though we were! We were not allowed to make any phone calls, or talk with Yasumi, our Japanese organiser for the past nine years who was waiting at the terminal. We were treated very unpleasantly. We refused to pay the guard money—and that resulted in a long standoff. Finally, around midnight, and against Carolyn's wishes, I agreed to pay one quarter of the amount, to which they hurriedly agreed.

We were then escorted to the prison wing of an airport hotel; it was cheap, dirty and nasty. Although the guards could not speak English, they were quiet and courteous. Needless to say, the remainder of the night was uncomfortable and sleepless. The next day we were under constant and discreet surveillance by the guards until we were escorted to the return flight around nine o'clock that evening.

In 2011, having got a special visa from the Japanese Consulate in Brisbane (which was issued from Japan) and having made sure that we had the appropriate cover letters from Yasumi detailing our every move, and having the phone number of the Australian Embassy in Japan, we were well prepared. Yasumi had done everything that the immigration office specified. Of course, on the entry form I had to put 'yes' to the question: 'Have you ever been denied entry to Japan?' Once again we were detained. Last year we both handled the whole affair good humouredly; this year when we were led away, my humour deserted me! I told them in no uncertain terms that we had complied with everything required to enter the country. As expected, they came out with the usual stupid forms asking all the same questions that had already been predetermined and well documented in the forms from the Consulate in Oz which they had just been given. When it came to another interview, I went first. One of my most regular quotes to people in difficult times is to 'choose Love'. As I departed, I could hear Carolyn saying to me, "Choose Love! Choose Love!" I did choose Love—but with a stern expression. I told them exactly what I thought of their process—tough Love! The interview lasted five minutes. Finally, after an hour and twenty minutes, we were told that we could enter the country. They made a point of stipulating exactly the same conditions that we already had and knew about. It matters not which country you are in, bureaucracy means crazy-bureau in any language! However, while last year the immigration people involved with us were arrogant, impolite and unpleasant, this year, they were quietly insistent and very polite.

Yasumi was hugely relieved and very happy to see us finally emerge. Her joy was shared by people from all over Japan when we eventually met them at our Intensive. A couple even came from Singapore. All went wonderfully well, with very positive feedback, so this journey had a happier ending!

With regards to travelling, it occurred to me recently that I had a couple of appointments to keep in very distant places. I remembered telling Angela in New York City and Anne in London that I would return to them. No date was set. I told them that they would energetically know when I returned, and if they did not—that would be okay. About five months had passed, so for them I am probably overdue. I decide that I would go back about three months to reduce the wait—if waiting they were! I confess, I really do enjoy the timelessness of a greater reality. So convenient.

Naturally, I share my travel plans with Pan.

You do not need my energy to accompany you for these rendezvous.

"True, but I would still enjoy your illustrious company."

I feel his delightful inner-smile. *Look and learn, or teach with Love, but do not meddle or interfere. You have a fondness for getting too involved.*

"Well . . . thank you, Mister Panhandle!"

The inner-smile becomes an inner-chuckle.

Relaxing in my study, I move my focus into my Light-body and step . . . Between . . . emerging over New York City during the early evening rush hour. I say, rush hour! Maybe I should say when rush becomes frantic! I came early to give Angela and her fellow astral travellers plenty of time to become aware of my energy-field. As always, time does not exist for me, but I choose to be with the people of New York as they hurry and scurry their various ways through the ending of another day.

I sigh in sympathy. Okay, when Carolyn and I physically travel the world each year, time and physicality make their demands on us, but it is only a few months of the year. These people live with this—hectic-mania—daily. (New word. Good, huh?) I have no wish to judge, but the crowds I see are slaves to a lesser god—money. With some exceptions, it is clearly revealed in their energy-signatures. They are some of the 99% of unaware people who are being manipulated by the corrupt 1%. This unsavoury 1% is aware that those who control the money control the people. And to the degree that we unwittingly allow it, they are correct. They also believe that by controlling the money they control the world, but this is not so. Controlling the people of the world is one thing, but controlling the world itself is something else again. With Chaos rising, Earth, the planet, the world, has its own agenda to meet, and the corrupt 1% is not going to like it. What goes around comes around. There is a huge bill to be paid for the high cost in human suffering through their global networks of unscrupulous manipulation and murder. And be paid it will. Knowing this unfailing reality will come to pass is definitely satisfying. This surprises me. I am not an advocate for revenge and retribution. But of course, this is neither of those. It is as simple as cause and effect; *that which we sow, we reap.* I always did like harvest time!

As I observe the hurrying crowds, I notice again a thin scattering of Balanced people among them. Some of these people are also hurrying, but whereas the energy-imprint of the crowd is basically harassed and negative, with the Balanced people it is no more than speeded-up movement. The haste and hurry does not reach their inner place of peace and calm. For the majority of the crowd, there is no inner place of calm or peace. The great mass of humanity lives in a way that does not work. To accommodate this we have created a society to support this intellectual and emotional insanity, and it still does not work. Today, one in every seven of the seven billion people on this planet is constantly hungry; that is a billion people living with hunger. This, along with the tens of thousands who die of starvation every day. Very clearly, the system does not work—except for the criminal few. In all this mass insanity, the small minority of aware and Balanced people who live in a way that does work, are the outsiders of society. They take what they need from society, and contribute what they can. Nevertheless, society judges the healthy, happy minority to be wrong in their approach to life, while the sick and suffering majority have it right. Why is this? Because the majority think that the majority must be right; the 'safety in numbers' theory! Interestingly, history proves the opposite; it was always the minority who were right—and so it continues today.

These are my thoughts as I watch the people eager to finish their day of work. I also acknowledge that each and every one of these people is a Being of Love and Light. This is not something they have to achieve, this is who they *are*. This includes the depraved few. These two different types of people have one thing in common—Self-denial. The denial of the Being of Love/Light whom we each truly are. The corrupt-few walk unknowingly in the darkness of fear engendered greed, power and control; far too great a percentage of the victimised-many walk just as unknowingly in the shadows of ignorance and fear. The happier, healthier remaining small percentage walk in the Light, and generally this is a path deliberately chosen. Today, there are ever-increasing numbers of people moving toward the Light, along with those who are already dedicated workers-of-
˙   ˙. And we need them! These are the people who *know* that
Change is approaching, and they welcome it. These are the
˙f Balance. I smile. These are the people most likely to
vords in this book!

Enough of my musings. I bring my focus toward midnight, the streets less jammed by the day people, while the night people pursue either their entertainment or their skulduggery.

Like phantoms emerging from the mists of the night, astral-bodies are weaving in my direction. Many of them. I stare. Many, many of them. Angela appears by my side as if by magic. She certainly has the art of astral travel down pat.

Welcome, Mixael. I began to wonder if you had abandoned us.

I smile at her. "Hello, Angela. I could hardly abandon you when I made it clear that these will only be occasional visits."

True enough, but I began to think you might never come back. Three months is quite a wait. But I'm glad you are here.

"The very last thing I want is for you to depend on me. I encourage independence."

Yes, you make that very clear, and fair enough. However, I and many others who are here have been reading and learning about the approaching Earth Changes. Much of what we learn is very alarming. Do you have any words that can clarify things? Maybe alleviate our fears?

"Can everyone hear me?"

The nod from Angela and the energy from the many astral-people are affirming.

Settling in for a long explanation, I remain just a tad provocative. "Why create fear and then try to alleviate it? That makes no sense. Surely it is better to not create fear."

But fear is automatic.

"Yes, for the many. But it should not be for you, the few. You especially, Angela, as a spiritually enlightened person should no longer maintain a relationship with fear."

Yes . . . I know what you mean. For me, fear is not really an issue, but for the majority of the people here it is a big issue.

"Okay. In every moment of life there are choices. All the truly meaningful choices have been eroded over our lifetimes of incarnations until choice is now no more than mundanities. We have . . ."

What do you mean by 'no more than mundane choices'?

"Let me finish. We have slipped into making subconscious choices over a period of many incarnations. We live on automatic. We are able to choose our houses, our cars, our clothes, our friends, where we work, etcetera, but even this is mostly based in a subconscious reflex of the people we are, based on our program of conditioning. The conscious choices that create and maintain our physical, mental and emotional well-being are seldom made. Thus . . . overall, we lack it."

I pause, inviting comment.

Angela is in telepathic communication with the others. She nods several times.

We agree. The big question is, how do we address this?

"Let me fully clarify my meaning and maybe this will answer your question. If, living in New York City, you decide to fly to Sydney, Australia, you are not going to just wander into an airport and get on the first plane going anywhere. You are going to determine your destination and buy tickets accordingly, making sure you get on the correct aircraft. On that basis, if, when you wake up in the morning, you get out of bed and mindlessly go about your day . . . as you have every other day . . . it is going to be a day, a year, a life of endless repeats of all your yesterdays. Literally, lifetimes of repetition.

"If, however, you wake up in the morning, and placing your hands over your heart, you murmur, 'Today, I choose Love. Today, I am going to focus on loving myself, on loving other people, and loving my life.' This, Angela, is a prime, life-changing ice. With this beginning to your day, you consciously revisit *hoice, living it, feeling it, and reaffirming it* as often as you can hout the day."

God! It's so obvious when you state it like that.

"Yes, but no matter how obvious, it has to be a choice. Conscious choices are rare. Most choices are subconsciou., following an already predetermined pattern of which most people are unaware. So, another morning, hands over heart, 'Today I choose appreciation. Today I will appreciate myself, other people, and my life.' Choices like this are life-changing. Another day, 'Today I choose respect. Today I am going to respect myself, other people, and my life.' And so on. Day-after-day you make the choices that remodel and renovate your life. But, it all has to be *conscious* choices, and those choices *must be consciously lived.*"

Why are you so strong on conscious choices?

"Because the majority of people live subconsciously for practically the whole of each day. This means that almost their whole lives are lived less than fully conscious. The subconscious dominates and controls us by habit, by conditioning, and by endlessly repeating the same old, same old, same old . . . ! Interestingly, the subconscious will resist conscious choices. If the astral people listening to this decide to do as I have suggested, they will find it very easy to forget when they wake up each morning. As unlikely as it may seem, the subconscious will avoid the conscious memories that could disturb the subconscious program of repetition. This could be termed the power of habit. It is very strong and very clinging."

It all sounds a bit scary!

"Angela . . . you have no idea. This is one of the main purposes of Chaos rising in our approaching time of Earth Changes. Chaos . . . the engine that drives, is attracted to the human clusters of habitual fear and attachment. And these are *big* clusters. When we consider the negatives of humanity, we find that negative energies cling to a fixed-and-stuck position. By its very nature, Chaos is attracted to these fixed-and-stuck negative energy clusters. The effect is to destroy them, for they are the very antithesis of human growth and expansion.

"By stark contrast, Chaos will also be attracted to the fewer clusters of human Love. Chaos . . . the engine that drives, will uplift Love to a new and higher energy expression. In other words, with negative energy it will be a de-structuring power, while with positive energy it will be a restructuring power."

Angela smiles. *The choice is obvious . . . Love!*

I nod. "And *live* it. For the last few years, this is what I have been telling all those people around the world who listen to me. Choose Love. In every situation, choose Love. Instead of anger, choose Love. Instead of suing for legal retribution, choose Love. I mean in every, *every* situation . . . choose Love. This is the manifesto that will carry a person through the period of Earth Changes in the best possible way."

You were right. By clarifying you have answered the question.

I watch Angela as she listens to other telepathic questions. *Another big concern . . . and I buy into this one . . . is about how we can help family and friends during all this change?*

I study her thoughtfully. As Mixael, I am beginning to realise just how much extra I brought in with me, particularly regarding inner-knowing. When I have a superficial question, I have to look for answers like everyone else—Google!—but if it is an appropriate and meaningful question about life that is in perfect timing, then the inner-knowing seems to emerge into my awareness. I used to think that this came with spiritual enlightenment, but I have long realised that this is not always so. It can happen, but this depends on the consciousness of the soul.

"Angela . . . every person is a soul on their spiritual journey. Life does not begin at birth or end at death. Life is the continuity of the immortal soul whom we are. We are Beings of eternity. This means that our children, parents and grandparents are no more than souls in either the early stage of a physical incarnation, or in a middle stage, or in a considerably later stage. Regardless, they are immortal souls in mortal bodies. Let go of your concern. Your family and friends will continue their journeys throughout Earth

Changes. What will happen to them physically has everything to do with their state of consciousness and their choices, and nothing to do with any attempts to save them. Nobody will be lost, so how can there be anyone to save? What is wrong with us? We are either doing everything we can to keep people alive, or doing our diabolical worst to kill them."

Not everyone is as sure and certain as you are.

Her words are sobering. "Yes, you're right. My many metaphysical experiences are creating a depth of knowing in me that is so clear and certain that I am inclined to overlook the fact that not everyone has this inner-knowing to such a degree. We all have it, but most people do not focus on consciously developing it. Understandably, making enough money with which to live is their main priority."

I take it that this development has been your conscious focus for a long time?

"Yes, for about the past fifty years. But it is in the more recent years that so much more has developed. Clarity and certainty sound like very ordinary words, but energetically what they describe is quite a rare state of consciousness awareness . . . or inner-knowing."

Can you teach clarity and certainty to other people?

"I think not. They are the medals of experience. Clarity and certainty hold hands with wisdom. Wisdom is the distillation of experience and intelligence. These are not things you can teach; they are an honorary degree you earn as you teach spiritual Truth. To me, it has always been very important that I am constantly growing in consciousness. If a spiritual teacher is not growing in this way, they cannot convey the consciousness of inner-growth. They can speak the words, but the words will be empty of the required energy."

When I am faced with a person . . . soul, like you, it makes me feel very humble.

I smile. "When I am faced by the Love that so many of the people I teach hold for me, I too am humbled. We tend to expect Love from family . . . even if we don't always get it. But when people I have known for a few years, or a short time, look me in the eyes to express their Love and gratitude, and I know it is real . . . this is *very* humbling."

I know that some of us are losing focus. Do you have any last words for us?

"Trust. Trust Self. Be aware that you can only trust consciously. There is no such thing as subconscious trust. Subconscious doubt is plentiful, but trust is a conscious choice. Where you have full trust, there is no anxiety. Where you have anxiety, there is no trust. Choose trust. Choose Love. Choose miracles. Choose to consciously live in the moment. As hard as it is to hear and accept this, physical survival is not important to the immortal soul. Love is of paramount importance to the soul. Choose Love."

Thank you, Mixael. As you said, difficult words to receive. Will we see you again?

I sigh softly, but I am rescued by my humour. "The Lone Ranger will return."

So saying, I embrace Angela within my Love/Light. She watches me as I casually step . . . Between . . . but when I emerge into my study, no one is watching.

❋   ❋   ❋

A couple of days pass, but having kept my assignment with New York City, I am feeling a slight pressure to keep my appointment with London. I accept that it is me who is applying the pressure, and I wonder if it has anything to do with emotional obligation. But no, on reflection it is more to do with keeping my word. Emotional obligation is an insidious little energy/attachment that seems to emerge with the birth of our children. As they develop and grow, unrealised, our emotional obligation grows with them.

Generally it stays for a lifetime, making emotional decisions regarding the family based in obligation, rather than in free choice. It is a subtle, yet binding obligation hiding in the guise of love. It was only when one of my sons, in his long-term anger toward me, told me that I was dead to him that I actually found the substance of my own emotional obligations. Once revealed, I was able to release it. Emotional obligation is a sneaky, subconscious emotional behaviour, so we are seldom aware of it. The malice of my son's words caused me to realise and accept that, son or not, I did not like the person—nor was I emotionally obliged to— although I Love the beautiful soul he continually denies.

Sometimes it also works in reverse, when grown children feel an emotional obligation toward an ageing parent. Emotional obligation is not a bad or wrong thing, but it is seldom based in emotional honesty. Cultivating emotional honesty is much healthier for all concerned. This requires emotional clarity which is uncommon, unlike emotional confusion which is prevalent. Then, of course, emotional insecurity is involved. Gosh, humans— we are so emotionally complex! This is why I teach people how to achieve emotional balance.

Sitting relaxed in my study, I make ready for a London departure.

With this as my focus, I step . . . Between . . . stepping out into the airspace over London. Only now do I check whether Pan is with me.

He is not. I am aware of my ever-increasing independence, and although I am never truly alone, I am unaccompanied by him. This is mutual choice. He said he would not be needed for my two rendezvous, and he is right. Time to earn my wings!

For a while I sit in the lotus position about a hundred metres over the city, just watching the energies of Chaos and Order as they writhe and coil through the traffic and among the people. Chaos is rising. It is so clear and obvious. With increasingly less prompting, anger is quicker to emerge and slower to subside.

The hurry, hurry, hurry is becoming more frantic, the pace of life increasing in a way that is not to our benefit. I see that people are becoming more chaotic in the way they speak, in their driving, and in the way they generally deport themselves throughout their day.

I have the flickering thought of once again visiting the ancient markets for the physically deceased, but I decide that Pan would not approve! After a while of musing, I decide that the Balanced astral people will be aware of my energy-field by now, so I focus into midnight.

Like a swift-changing slide in a projector, midnight emerges. I become aware of very many astral people around me, and I am unsure of how to begin. My decision is made as Anne comes toward me.

Hello Mixael . . . greetings. We have been waiting for a while.

"Hello, Anne. I sat through a period of afternoon so that you would be aware of me. Then I focused into now . . . and here I am."

I smile at her, then abruptly realise that all is not well. Energetically, she looks frail and depleted. Her previous astral vitality is missing.

"What's the matter, Anne? You feel very depleted."

She smiles weakly. *Do you remember me telling you about the two very negative entities in my part of the city?*

"Yes, of course. I suggested you meet them with Love."

I tried to do that. I don't know what went wrong, but they are now feeding off my energy. They are very savage and horrible. I'm out of my depth. I can't handle it.

"Oh, they are, are they! Okay, time for action. I can't have my astral spokeswoman for London sucked dry by a couple of delinquent bullies. Can you take me to them?"

Are you sure? They are stronger than ever.

"I'm absolutely certain. Lead on, dear lady."

I am rather looking forward to this encounter. Not for a moment do I doubt my ability to confront and confound any non-physical London nasties.

Anne leads me swiftly down toward the city. We enter an old, very dilapidated area in the slums that is filthy and smelly. This is not an area I have ever visited. Many of the buildings are obviously unsafe, with doors nailed shut; correction, doors that *had* been nailed shut! They have been forced open and are housing the very dregs of London's drop-outs. The area stinks of urine and vomit, and the smell of old, sour human staleness. Energetically, it is dreadful. Chaos is the red of degeneration and abuse, a foul colour that stinks of erosion. This surprises me. Erosion has a smell? Apparently yes, an emotional smell. When it is the energetic erosion of human emotions and values, it has the stink of a slow and odious decay.

Anne hangs well back, as far from energetic reach as possible. I wonder why she comes to such an area, but that can wait.

This is a whole new experience for me, and I am glad Pan is not here. I will handle this my way. I decide that I will attempt to metaphysically disguise myself. I have never, ever tried this before, so I am not sure of the procedure. However, I focus on myself as a very unsure person who is lost in this area. I cannot be physical, but I can pretend to be a lost astral person.

"Wait here, Anne, and don't come anywhere in their range. How do I look to you?"

Well . . . amazingly, you look a bit like an astral-beginner, although you have not quite managed to hide all your power. It is leaking a little from the illusion. But . . . you know, I think it will fool them. They don't know you, so they will not be on their guard.

With an encouraging smile at her, I stumble-walk, half-fly, half-hover and wobble my way among the buildings. A couple of them have physical people in them, but another has the energy of avoidance. Ah ha, this is my target, the building the derelicts avoid. Moving toward it in my stumbling manner, I pretend to fall through the door after fumbling at it. I am inside. It is pitch dark, but as a Light-Being darkness is not in my reality.

I energetically feel them well before I see them.

It feels like the approach of a sickness, of moving vomit, of suppurating disease. I admit, even I am surprised by this. I have never explored human degradation when the mortal body has been discarded—and I am not sure that I want to. An energetic stench is approaching me with feelings of disease and discord growing stronger. If I was physical, I would be running rapidly away from here, but I am metaphysical, and I truly feel myself to be the master of the situation.

Now I can see them. It is quite a struggle to maintain my disguise, for the Light of Self clearly wishes to be released. Not yet. There are actually three of these lower astral people. This means that at physical death, these people who were/are drug addicts or alcoholics moved deeper into the lower astral realms. In their lifestyle they had been gradually moving into a lower astral reality through drugs or alcohol, as well as through their negative thoughts and emotions. When physical death eventually claimed their drug-sick bodies, they were already within the lower astral realms. They look rather like three very sick people who are encased in dark and angry energy. If you drew a wide, thick, heavy black felt pen outline around a thin pencil sketch of a human, it would give you some idea of how they appear energetically. As ghosts, they are very nasty to look at. Something you would avoid, or run away from, but when push comes to shove, they are not really dangerous if you are without fear. And most people have fear aplenty. Fear is the lure and the food of these entities.

I continue with the feeble, befuddled astral person guise as they swoop toward me. As I said, they really do have a frightening field-of-energy. No wonder Anne was overwhelmed, becoming their victim. Ah well, what goes around, comes around—now it is their turn!

I honestly have no idea what I am going to do. I have not thought this through. This is my typical Aries jump-in-and-see-what-happens approach! Instinctively, I wait until they are nearly on top of me, then I suddenly release my disguise.

They stop abruptly, almost skidding to a halt. Without a thought, I instantly expand and open my Love/Light energy-field full on, enveloping them within it. For one l-o-n-g moment nothing happens. They stand as if frozen, shock and horror on their faces—then there is a huge, somehow loud/silent *implosion* that echoes through the hallways of the building—and they vanish. I am so shocked and startled that I fall forward toward a space of nothingness before me—then it abruptly fills in with another stupendous silent/loud *explosion.*

Oh my gosh! What have I done?

Very good, Michael. In your inimitable way you have managed to reach new and hitherto uncharted heights of meddling and interfering!

"Pan! What are you doing here?"

Considering the astral storm you just unleashed, where else could I be but observing the exploits of my wayward student. And this time you have excelled yourself.

He does not sound annoyed. I think—I hope!—he sounds amused.

"Er . . . what happened, exactly?"

It is very simple. You moved them from such a low astral reality into such a . . . high one so abruptly that their reality creation literally imploded. The explosion was the automatic balancing of astral realities.

I nodded. "Good. That makes sense. I have no doubt the problem is dealt with."

Yes, I have no doubt. After about a century, the unfortunates should be well recovered.

One of Carolyn's expressions surges into my memory. "They created me in their reality, so they got what they deserved. Anyway, they terrified Anne. A century of timelessness should

185

sort them out." I laugh. "I've just given 'Ghostbusters' a whole new meaning!"

Pan is unable to suppress an inner-chuckle. *Do you have any more plans of retribution for tonight? Or have you about finished?*

"No more retribution . . . and my night has just begun. I'll be good . . . I promise!"

And just like that—Pan is no longer with me.

A few moments later I am joined by Anne. *They've gone, haven't they?*

"Yes, I banished them."

Where to? What happened? Oh, golly, the energy is so much better. The place is still a slum, but it no longer contains that . . . that awful malevolence.

I chuckle. "Actually, I'm not sure where they are . . . but they are going to be there for a very long time. Ultimately, those three lost souls will be very grateful for what I did. Anyway, you will not be having any more problems with them."

Thank you, Mixael, so very much. They were making my life hell.

"Yes . . . they found your subconscious fears and amplified them. In this way you became their victim. Along with plenty of others, I have no doubt. They were *very* nasty. So . . . maybe it's time to go back to the meeting place and continue where we left off."

I think that maybe the others will have lost their focus by now and be drifting away.

"No. This is a timeless realm, so we will re-enter when we exited."

Embracing Anne in my energy-field, we return to the moment of leaving. I explain that I have conferred with the New York City astral folk, and now it is the city of London's turn. I also tell Anne that she is already looking far stronger.

I'm just realising that they were feeding energy off me continually, day and night.

I look back to when I first met her on this visit, and note that her solar plexus chakra was looking drained and shrunken. As I look at her now, the chakra is strong and vital once again.

"Yes, they were. They were draining energy from you via your solar plexus. They must have established it during your last encounter. Why were you in their territory?"

I go physically to help the derelicts. There are so many of them living in such appalling conditions. Then I thought I would also help the lost astral souls, and move them toward astral retrieval. I went into their area in my astral body, inviting them to be friends. I was able to help some, but the ones you dealt with rejected me, and were very threatening. After speaking with you, I tried again, opening myself to them in the way you suggested . . . and they attacked me. I barely escaped.

"Oh, Anne. Rescuers invariably need rescuing. Allow those people who have decided on a lower path to stay on it until they *ask you* to help them find a higher path. There are enough people asking and begging for help without looking for trouble. Those three entities have been locked in the lower astral realms for so long that the outcome could only be as it was."

But if I was loving them, how could they so easily overpower me?

"Because, like me, like all of us, we are still learning about the fullness of Love. Love is not about salvation, because nothing is ever lost or dammed. Love is the empowerment of Truth, of Life, of Light. Your Love had little uncertainties, little weaknesses which they exposed and exploited. Your intent was far stronger than your ability. And that's not a fault."

It's been a very good lesson for me. Change what you can, and leave well alone what you can't. I thought I had learned that one. Obviously I hadn't.

I smile. "Okay . . . now forget it. It's all over. Do you or any of the astral people here have any questions that have come up over the past few months?"

Well . . . we have read some and watched many of the contradicting YouTubes on the upcoming Changes. It's all a bit confusing, but we seem to be okay with it . . . if it even happens. It is a bit frightening. But if we survive, what happens afterwards? How do we continue? What happens if our cities become uninhabitable?

I sigh. "This is anybody's guess. The trouble is that you are taking a pragmatic approach to this time of Earth Change. You need to take a more metaphysical approach. Nobody really knows what will happen. It is all about probabilities. The probability future for the more open and loving people will be very different from the probability of the people who will fight and kill to survive. And how do you know there is an afterwards? This is an assumption. Time . . ."

But of course there is an afterwards . . . you are not making sense.

"Anne, hear me out. Stop listening through your mortal identity-self, and start listening through your immortal soul-self. Let us suppose that the Mayans are correct—supposing linear time does come to an end on a specified date. If this happens there is no time; no before, no afterwards. Then we have only an ongoing 'now' experience. This is the basis of living in a fifth dimensional reality. The past and future—which truly are illusions—give way to the continuity of the moment. Why discuss what happens afterwards if there may not be an afterwards? You are demonstrating an inability to stop linear thinking: the 'before and after' syndrome."

Oh my . . . you live in an entirely different reality. I feel like a . . . a child.

"Anne, don't be ridiculous. All I am saying is to stop with the left-brain reasoning and logic. They have their place in everyday life, but Earth Changes are not everyday life. So you have to use new skills. First . . ."

She cut in again. *What sort of skills?*

This must be the revenge of Pan! I bet he is chuckling in the breeze.

"First of all let go of the 'working-it-out' syndrome. Forget it. Put it aside. Develop your ability to trust. Trust your self. Trust you, the person you are, the way you are, warts and all. Trust life. Honour life. Embrace life. You can only do this if you are trusting yourself. Trust is something we have to learn. Let us suppose that I trust you . . . and you let me down."

Oh, I would never . . .

"Ah, ah, no interruptions. You let me down. I continue trusting you . . . you let me down. I continue trusting you . . . you let me down. I continue trusting you . . . you let me down. Now . . . I am beginning to build and grow the energy of trust. I continue trusting you . . . you let me down. I continue to trust you . . . you let me down. Now my trust is growing far stronger. I am building trust-energy into my energy-field. I continue to trust you . . . you let me down. I continue to trust you . . . and my trust is validated. You have learned to be trusted because I continued to trust you. I have learned that trust is not based in you doing what I expected, or hoped for. Trust is an energy that grows from continuing to trust . . . regardless of results. This is how you learn to trust yourself, regardless of letting yourself down."

Anne is looking at me as though I am an alien.

How . . . however do you learn such a thing. I have never heard the likes of it.

"It is Truth. These are the new skills to be learned. Skills that people think they have. Just because we intellectually know the meaning of the word 'trust' we think this *is* trust. It is not. Trust is an energy we have to grow, in the same way we grow a plant . . . except we need far more patience and tolerance. Loving self is exactly the same. We grow Love by unconditionally Loving. For aeons we have judged ourselves and each other; we have criticised ourselves and each other; and by doing so, we have reduced ourselves. And so we continued, regardless. Now, Life/God/Nature is saying, **'Enough.'** After ages of humanity, finally . . . finally, we have reached the place of enough."

189

I really did think that I knew roughly what to expect and how I would deal with it. Stored food and water . . . and all that sort of thing. Now you have turned it all upside down.

"Good. This is what I do. In my Intensives I strip away the nonsense concepts people have about life, while offering a view of Truth. It is up to people whether they embrace the view, or ignore it. This is their responsibility, not mine. The same applies now for you . . . and all these astral people. Cultivate the skill of being conscious, of being aware, of experiencing trust, of an inner-clarity and certainty about Self and life. In other words, *consciously grow.* I tell people everywhere I go . . . choose Love. Instead of confusion, focus on Love. Instead of anger . . . choose Love. Instead of following the masses . . . follow Love. Love will not be running or attempting to survive. Nor will Love be filled with fear. Love will have no confusion. Love will have no doubts. Love is the power of creation. When creation is in doubt . . . choose Love and confirm your creation. Choose Love. Over and over, choose Love. Choose Love and you recreate your reality."

Whew! I feel as though I have been turned inside-out. What can I say? To thank you sounds so trite compared with the wisdom you have shared . . . but, thank you. Thank you for giving me back my physical and astral city life, and thank you for giving me back my blessed spiritual life. I had no idea that it was slipping away. When will you return to us?

I smile at her. "I honestly don't know when I will be back. However, when you feel my energy one afternoon, I'll be here at midnight."

Anne gives me a half-hearted smile. *I would have liked something more definite . . . but I'll settle for what I can get. We need you. People like you are rare.*

"Anne, people like me don't just happen. I am the result of dedicated conscious growth. I made every mistake possible along my path, but I have continued on to the place where I *know* there are no mistakes. Focus on your own inner-growth . . . you do not need me. And please . . . no more attempts to rescue dangerous lower astral entities."

So saying, I step . . . Between . . . and out into my study.

I remain relaxed. I have one last appointment to keep. When Carolyn and I are on our annual tour, we often stay with Bruno Streit, an old friend who lives in Bern, Switzerland. His lovely home is one of our places for a few wonderful days of rest and relaxation. Bruno is a qualified medical doctor, but for many years his work and passion is with homeopathy. I find homeopathy rather fascinating; it uses the energy of a substance to effect a cure, rather than the substance itself. For example, the energy of bee venom—*apis*—is the antidote for a bee sting, when we are literally injected with the substance, hence the pain and swelling. Bruno has a medical partner, and between them they also use applied kinesiology. This is a practice that provides feedback on the functional status of the physical body. Yet again, it is using energy to reveal the energetic status of the body. Good health has its own energetic resonance, while disease or localised discord speak a very different language! When the health issue is rather complicated, both Bruno and his partner work together on a case. If it is reasonably straight forward, as most are, Bruno is more than capable.

I had suggested to Bruno that one day when he is working, I would metaphysically visit him, watching to see what happens on an energetic level when he is involved in his homeopathy practice. Now seems as good a time as any. Of course, Bruno has no idea when I will visit, nor will he know I am there while I am visiting!

Having no intention of arriving out of timing, I focus on Bruno with a patient while he is considering which homeopathic remedy to use for them. To be clear, this could be a time Bruno has not yet reached, or in his past with the patient, or happening in this 'linear moment'. With this as my clear focus, I step . . . Between . . . and into Bruno's medical room.

Bruno is treating a fair-haired boy of about ten, while the boy's mother is sitting in a chair watching the procedure. Bruno is alone, applying kinesiology to test the boy's body for its energetic feedback. I stand as far back as possible, deliberately holding my energy-field well away. Knowing Bruno's sensitivity, I have no wish to influence the feedback—and this is very possible. While the physical components of the body are all contained within the skin, the story is very different on an energetic level. We leak! The more confused and scattered a person is, the more their energy is leaking away from them. Depression and anxiety cause physical exhaustion in a person simply because the more negative they are, the more rapidly they leak energy.

My focus now is to observe the energy-field of the boy and Bruno, and of the eventual homeopathic treatment. From my metaphysical viewpoint, no testing is necessary. The boy has way too much red Chaos in his stomach and upper intestine. The red Chaos colour has a strong emotional content; an energy of emotional rejection! This is a surprise. I wonder if Bruno will be able to identify the cause. The boy's mother has told Bruno that the boy has stomach pains. That is not in question. The question is why? For me, the answer is simple. The red of Chaos metaphysically connects with the boy's father. He and his mother are recently separated, and the boy is feeling emotionally torn and rejected. Of course, in our very human way he pretends that everything is okay—but it is not. Hence, the solar plexus area is seriously over stimulated, causing a negative reaction. It would appear that the extreme acidity in his small intestine is no longer being sufficiently buffered by the bicarbonate that should be continually produced. Acute stress is limiting supply. Energetically, acute stress creates acute pain!

Bruno moves smoothly through his kinetic diagnosis and seems to be confident that he knows what is happening. He and the boy's mother chat for a while in German, so metaphysical or not, I have no idea what they are talking about—physically! Energetically, while I do not understand the words, I can tell from her distressed energy that she is talking about the recent separation. Bruno nods, and energetically I can see the knowledge from their conversation and the knowledge he has already gleaned from his kinesiology coming together. For him, they create a clear picture of the health problem.

Okay, this is no great drama, but I am impressed with how Bruno has picked up and followed an energetic trail that he cannot physically see. What terminology he actually uses to label the problem, I do not know, but the homeopathic remedy he picks out is high in Order, the stability of structure. How perfect. Chaos, the engine that drives, is driving the emotional rejection, increasing it—along with the physical repercussions. With this remedy, Order will stabilise the structure of his emotional energy, thus alleviating the over-stimulating cause of acute pain. In other words, Order will restore Balance, the place of greatest potential. And we all know that stomachs and small intestines need to be at their greatest potential, considering the junk food and drinks that ten-year-old boys frequently subject them to—to say nothing of adults!

So, basically Bruno is finished with this patient, apart from words of advice to the mother and the boy. It is interesting to notice that Bruno has at no time allowed his own field-of-energy to intrude in the process. This must take practice. It means that a practitioner like Bruno needs to keep his or her state of consciousness as calm and collected as possible. By comparison, a regular medical doctor makes a diagnosis based purely on physical feedback—rather than energetic—so they can be as confused and scattered as their patient without it affecting their eventual results. In other words, being a homeopath is, in itself, a path of conscious growth. This applies equally to kinesiology. I have often told Bruno that his homeopathy and kinesiology are the very essence of his spiritual path, but I have never actually seen how it works until now.

I could stay and see more, but I have observed the principle of both practices in action, and this was my intent. Goodbye, Bruno—and thank you.

I step . . . Between . . . and home.

Bruno has often demonstrated kinesiology to me on my own body. He finds my energetic balance through my outstretched arm, then suggests I think the word 'sugar'. Even as I do this, my arm is instantly losing energy. It is impressive, but very basic compared to the potential that kinesiology has to offer. I am convinced that there is nothing that a good practitioner could not learn about the human body. And not only a person's lifetime in their current body, but in past lives in other bodies; all are energetically connected. Time and space are of no account. The memory of a dramatic life issue from a previous lifetime is held within our consciousness. In each lifetime consciousness re-imprints that memory into the cellular structure of the current body—until the issue is resolved. Simply stated; anything unresolved in the past is unresolved now. So many of our current health issues have had their genesis in a previous lifetime, in a different body, and yet—the issue is carried in consciousness and remains with us until we deal with it—or until we fall into unconditional Love with Self. This is the ultimate resolution.

NINE

FINDING MIXAEL

I have often wondered about my origin as a walk-in. There is much I do not know about the walk-in process, or about Mixael, and until recently I have not been particularly curious. Nevertheless, the timing seems to have arrived because recently I have felt a growing need to investigate this aspect of my soul-self. I admit, ever since I walked-in, questions have always been there, lurking disregarded somewhere in the back of my consciousness—but now they are coming forward. I sense a faint reluctance to look into this; it feels a bit like opening Pandora's Box. If I open it heaven only knows what I might find, or even if I will like what is in it. Some things are best not known. I function well on that basis, but, truth be told, I do not *grow* in this way.

Most people function without knowing their own truth as spiritual Beings, but they do not *grow* either. Yet this is why we are here; to grow in consciousness, each and every one of us. We need constant inner-stimulation to grow in consciousness, yet we are addicted to stability and maintaining the status quo. Obviously, stability and stimulation do not sleep in the same bed! It would seem it is my time to once again choose stimulation.

I am in my study, relaxing, when I decide to invite Pan along.

Where are you planning to go?

"Well . . . I'm not exactly sure, but I have a question. Do I need to go through the Gate if I want to meet with Cardifer and Carienne, or am I able to step directly into their reality?"

What do you think?

"I think that I can step there directly. But on my previous visit, *(Book Two)* I had to go through the silver Gate. Maybe I've grown a bit since then!"

If you believe you can step directly into that higher reality, you can. If you believe that you need the Gate, you do. If thought and belief are out of alignment, you will quickly know.

"You mean that if I think I can step there, but deep down I doubt it, then I can't?"

Exactly.

I took a long and serious look within myself. Were my expectations actually my thoughts? Although I expect to be able to step into this higher reality, do I actually think I can? And do I really believe that I can? Yes, yes, and yes. I can see and feel no inner conflict.

"Yes . . . I think and believe that I can step directly into that reality."

Michael, if you can I need not accompany you. Be sure.

Hmm. Am I sure? "Yes, Pan. All my clarity and certainty says I can . . . and I will. But anyway, you are always with me . . . even when you are not with me!"

Meaning?

"Well, on my last journey, when I decided to reprimand the 'bad' guys . . . it caused a big silent bang . . . and you were instantly there."

That 'big silent bang', as you eloquently describe it, was the colossal impact within two realities caused by the instant dislocation and relocation of three shocked Beings completely out of all natural timing. Yes, Michael, you had my instant attention.

"Oh . . . so is your attention normally spread over all Nature on Earth simultaneously?"

Clever! You ask me to put into words something that is beyond any human concept. I am the Spirit of Nature. I am in the All and the One simultaneously. I am the multiple and the single. I am the movement in the moment. If a leaf falls, I am within the leaf and the falling. If the Earth quakes, I am within the Earth and the movement. If you, Michael, transgress all laws of astral cohesion, I am naturally involved! Or in your case . . . unnaturally!

Humour and reprimanded! "Okay. I get it. I also get a strong impression that you trust me, nevertheless."

How could I Love you and not trust you?

"But . . . you **are** Love. You Love humanity . . . but do you trust it?"

A deep sigh. Not mine! *Humanity is as humanity is. Divine Love and Trust are One. Where judgement does not exist, all is divinely Loved. As you have learned, trust is a human concept that is seldom based in a reality of Truth. Love IS. I AM.*

I smile. "Beyond all words and concepts, the soul I am *knows* your meaning. So, I am off on another solo adventure. Thank you for trusting me."

You trust you, I trust you. And make sure it is not a misadventure!

"Ah ah . . . trust!"

Relaxing, I am very careful to focus on Cardifer, the person. I am not sure that I am ready to inadvertently step into the dragon realm. But then again, I have to eventually find out. But not now! Cardifer and Carienne—this is my present focus.

Relaxed, I move into my Light-body focus, and step . . . Between . . . stepping out into a clearing on the edge of many trees. With huge smiles, Cardifer and Carienne are waiting. They both look vital and striking, literally vibrant with health and energy. Cardifer is wearing a belted, one-piece garment of an ochre-coloured material. Carienne wears a similar one-piece garment of forest green, without the belt. I guess we would consider their clothing as unisex, yet nobody could look more masculine than Cardifer, or more femininely beautiful than Carienne.

I gaze at them in astonishment. "My gosh! How did you know I was coming?"

You are still broadcasting, Mixael. How are you? It is so wonderful to see you again. And metaphysically, you are looking stronger than ever.

"Thank you. Gosh! I'm so surprised. Even though I focused on you, I didn't expect it to be this easy. And here you are . . . waiting."

Your intentions were signalled so loud and clear, we could not fail to know. Even though we are separated by a reality-frame of time and space, on a deeper level this is transcended by consciousness. It was within our consciousness that the 'feeling and knowing' of your intended visit was conveyed.

"I'm impressed. We get intuitive feelings, and these can be strong, but they are seldom so definite, even when they prove to be true and accurate."

How is my beloved sister, Clarion?

By now we are walking within the clearing in the trees. "She is very well, and sends you all her Love. She wishes she could deliver it to you herself."

Carienne smiles ruefully. *I wish she could, but what you do is rare. Few are the humans who can move through reality-frames in the way you do.*

"Why do I find it so easy?"

You have had many lifetimes of mystical practice and metaphysical travel. As you are aware, the price paid in pain and torment was high, but the rewards were even greater. Michael developed the ability which you, as Mixael, had perfected on another level. Hence your synchronicity in mutual skill and prowess. When you walked-in, you were inheriting the body and skills of a person who matched you in so many ways. Naturally enough, synchronicity between the people involved is a requirement of walking-in.

"That makes sense. Walking-in was tough; far more difficult than I expected. The actual walking-in part was easy enough, but the acceptance and integration was slow, complex, and sadly, very much resisted by myself. It was baffling. One problem was that it is so far out of context with normality."

Mixael, be aware that neither Cardifer nor I can simply step from one reality-frame to another in the way that you do. I could not visit Clarion in the way you visit us.

"Are you not able to step Between?"

No, we cannot.

"Gosh! For some reason that comes like a bolt from the blue."

Why? Because you have metaphysical abilities that transcend ours? Why should that surprise you? You came from here, my dear.

"Can other people in this reality-frame travel as I do?"

Yes, of course, but it is the few, rather than the many.

We have stopped walking and Cardifer is enclosing us in a bubble. He has a belt device that, when a stud is pressed, emits a transport bubble. As the bubble fully envelops us, we are transported in moments to their home. My questions proliferate.

"Why did you meet me in the woods, rather than your home?"

Cardifer laughs. *Because your energy had no destination other than us, we chose to be in a place that would feel safe and familiar. Hence, trees and Nature. Mixael, let's relax. I am not sure if you are able to take liquid refreshment in our reality. We can but try.*

"I think I need to be in a metaphysical reality for such, and this is not."

He smiles. *No. This is a real and solid fifth-dimensional reality.*

I am astonished. "Fifth-dimensional!"

Carienne looks surprised. *Well, what did you think it is? You know it is more than three- dimensional. That is your world of reality,* but we live in a higher energy reality that comes from a higher state of consciousness.

"Yes, of course you do . . . I just never put it together. Your reality is three-dimensional in the way that I experience it, but it is also much more. That *more* must be a fifth-dimensional reality. So, beloved friends, what can you tell me about fifth-dimensional reality? I am very interested because as we approach Earth Changes in our current reality, one of the strong probability factors is that our reality-frame could lift from our three-dimensional reality into a fifth-dimensional reality. If this happens to us, what happens to you?"

You mean . . . is there a 'kick-up-the-ladder' effect?

I smile. "Yes, something like that."

Realistically, Mixael, what percentage of the people in your current reality are ready for a fifth-dimensional reality?

"Ah . . . now that is something else altogether."

By this stage of the conversation we have walked through the obliging self-opening walls of their home. Close by are their chairs of incredible design; their appearance so extremely uncomfortable you would hesitate to put a cat in them. Yet—I know their comfort is as extreme as their design appearance. Carefully relaxing into one such chair, I feel it change as it gracefully accommodates my metaphysical body. Ah well, if a chair can be so generous, hopefully the liquid refreshment might also prove possible.

Carienne comes in with chime-thin glasses that I can hold, but when I try drinking from it—nothing. I can feel the glass with my lips, beyond that, nothing. I am not surprised. This is a more solid reality than when I visit the various metaphysical realms.

Carienne smiles at me. *I expected that. You are much more etheric than you appear to be.* She raises her glass. *To our beloved Clarion!*

They both drink solemnly and enjoyably.

"So . . . about that kick-up-the-ladder effect. Does such a thing happen?"

Cardifer relaxes with a contented sigh. *Not really, no. Each reality progresses by its own efforts, retaining its own integrity. As you move up-the-ladder, so to speak, it is your ladder you climb. We each have our own ladder within the ladder of realities. And then again, just to make it more complicated . . . all ladders are One ladder.*

I chuckle. "I know what you mean; apart, but not separate. Okay . . . it would seem that you live a reality that *appears* to me as three-dimensional, yet there is so much more. Are the miraculous means of transport, the amazing chairs and suchlike, actually impossible for us in our reality, or is it the result of a far more sophisticated technology?"

Both. Fundamentally, fifth-dimensional reality is a state of consciousness. When you grow into a fifth-dimensional state of consciousness, you find that energies are available to you that are not available to a lower state of consciousness. In your reality you have split the atom as a means of weaponry for warfare. We have no weapons, no warfare. Love does not kill and maim, nor does it need to defend itself. You manipulate the genetic materials of Nature for profit and control. We use far superior genetic engineering with the full cooperation of Nature for mutual benefit. And so the story continues. None of this makes you bad or wrong; it is a statement of the overall state of consciousness.

"When you say *we* split the atom for warfare, and *we* use genetic manipulation for profit and control . . . that *we* is the very few. About one percent of our population has a degree of control over the other ninety-nine percent. They determine the *we*."

I understand, but, nevertheless, the one percent simply takes to an extreme what most of the other ninety-nine percent also contain within their consciousness. We do not have that lower state of consciousness in this frame-of-reality.

"Yes . . . I am compelled to agree with you. In some ways that one percent shows or demonstrates to the rest of humanity the greed and depravity that lies either dormant, or active, within most of us. And then again, many others have gone beyond all that. However, overall, the few express the worst of the many."

Unpalatable . . . but in Oneness it is a truth to contend with.
"What is the main effect of a fifth-dimensional reality?"
Living fully conscious in the moment.

"Okay . . . now I know what you mean by a state of consciousness. The people in my reality-frame are pretty much fully subconscious, along with sub-emotional. It's a major journey from subconscious to fully conscious."

Mixael, I asked you before. Roughly what percentage of your reality-frame people are ready for a higher-dimensional reality?

"To take a worst case scenario, maybe three to five percent now. On the other hand, as, or if, we enter major Earth Changes, I suspect that maybe another ten percent could and probably would respond with various degrees of Love . . . rather than react from fear".

Carienne smiles sympathetically. *That is either a very large number of people, or a very small one. It depends on your perspective.*

I nod. "True. I like to think of it as a huge number of people. Ten percent of seven billion people is seven hundred million. This is an enormous, even unprecedented number of people with the potential to ascend from subconscious domination to a far more conscious expression. It is also possible that figure could be increased to fifteen percent as new and uplifting energies sweep across our planet. That would take us to over a billion people living more consciously. I see it as an incredible opportunity for a mass ascension . . . or a major leap in consciousness . . . to a fifth-dimensional reality on our beloved Earth. If Earth Changes take place in the way that many expect, with turmoil and terror, then nothing is more likely to find the truth of a person's state of consciousness. It's rather like a harvesting of soul-growth. The probability is that the many will be recycled back through a similar human experience as they have lived, to hopefully do it better. The comparative fewer will move on to new expressions of their consciousness. But that few can also be looked upon as so many!"

Are you okay with this?

"Why would I not be okay?"

You may have friends and family who will follow the recycling route of souls.

I sigh. "Yes, very likely. But nobody is lost, nobody saved. We are immortal souls in mortal bodies learning the basic human lessons of spirituality. With a single exception, my own family ignores what I have to say or teach. They are each leading their own lives, with differing interests and different spiritual values from me, all of which they can justify. And that's okay; there is no right or wrong in any of this. It all boils down to the journey of the soul. Some of us recognise this and willingly follow our spiritual soul path, while others . . . the majority . . . seem to think of nothing beyond a single lifetime of procreation, profit and pleasure. So be it!"

Carienne refills their glasses, smiling an apology to me. *I wish I could refill yours.*

"It's okay. As a metaphysical Being I don't experience hunger or thirst. Although I've learned that I can get utterly exhausted. I reached a place of overwhelming fatigue when I was assisting after the tsunami in Japan."

We heard about that. I must say we love to have you visit like this. It is an honour, Cardifer said, *but is there a reason for your visit? A reason we should explore or consider before you need to return.*

I laugh. "Thank you for reminding me. Yes, there is a reason . . . beyond your beautiful selves and the pleasure of your company. I want to know more about . . . me . . . as Mixael. I fully accept that I walked-in when Michael walked-out. I understand that Michael is with Treenie in the higher realms between physical births, and I truly Love and honour their togetherness. As I understand it, I walked-in to the body that Michael's soul vacated. My **big** question is what happened to my body? If I was in this reality prior to walking-in . . . where is my body? Did it die? If so, how did this happen? How could I just leave my body and depart . . . to walk-in to another body/reality?"

We wondered when these questions would come to pass.

"Well, for a long time I was caught up and fully engaged in untangling the emotional knots that I had inadvertently tied. Then, after twenty years of avoidance and not doing too well with this, Treenie went through her transition and I was compelled to face my emotional insecurity. Her passing was the massive kick-in-the-pants that I needed. Consequently, during the next year or so I dealt with my emotional insecurities, and I now experience the blessing of emotional completeness. Even so, my curiosity about Mixael was quite low-key, but the timing to know has risen to the surface. I am now looking for answers."

Cardifer and Carienne both stand up, smiling and beckoning to me. *Rather than words to answer your questions we need to go on a small journey. There is something you are now ready to see and accept. Come . . . stand close to us.*

So saying, Cardifer presses a stud in his belt, and the now familiar bubble rapidly expands, easily enclosing us. I stare out as everything around us seems to blur, yet I feel no sense of motion. In moments, the bubble retracts, and we step apart. We are now standing outside a large and beautiful building, surrounded by gardens of pure delight.

"Okay . . . this brings up another question. Does that bubble actually transport us, or do we simply emerge in some other part of your reality world?"

Cardifer laughs. *I'm sorry, but this defies your physics. Both are true. We, and our destination, are drawn together without either actually going anywhere!*

"You mean . . . we, they, move together without actually moving?"

Let me briefly explain. Time and space are not quite what they seem. Whereas they make sense in our daily living, if we need to take a journey then it is sensible to temporarily remove the time/space equation. This is what the transporter does. In that bubble we create a suspension of time/ space so we 'are' where we need to be without actually travelling.

"So could we do this in our reality? Or does it need a higher consciousness?"

Mixael . . . you already know the answer to this.

I nod. "Of course I do. A higher consciousness opens doors that we can hardly imagine."

The sheer beauty of the large garden catches my attention. There are trees that I recognise, and trees that have never known our frame-of-reality; impossible trees that need different light and cultural conditions to be growing here. This is a gardener's delight!

"Carienne, I have seen these silver-leafed trees in a very different reality. They cannot possibly grow here . . . yet they are. How?"

Cardifer answers. *These trees are a perfect example of genetic cooperation.*

With their permission, I wander quickly around a small area of the garden. I know I cannot linger long; the answers to my questions are close by, but this is just too good to ignore. It is not easy to describe plants that have never been seen on our Earth, although I am aware of plants here from our Earth-frame reality long before humanity arrived. "It would appear that most of this garden is the result of genetic cooperation. There is no other explanation for so many differing plant needs growing in a single area."

Very observant . . . but then, you have the advantage of having seen some of these plants in their natural environment, so you are aware of the problems of bringing such biological diversity together. However, despite this pleasant distraction, we need to enter the building.

I sigh. This is it. This is where I open Pandora's Box.

This building is known as The Sanctuary of Repose, Carienne said. *You will understand why very soon.*

The building is another of the sweeping, graceful, impossible acrylic-types; crystal clear, yet with faint blushes of colour. However, I am unable to see through the thin, sheer walls.

"Can either of you see through this?"

They both smile. *No. It is transparent, nothing to stop the eyes at all. We cannot see through it simply because it is designed with the intent to resist the eyes' ability to see through it.*

"I'm not too sure I understand that, but I see that I cannot see!"

Chuckling, we walk to the door. This is high enough to accommodate a person four metres tall, but I figure it is just an architectural flair. The door opens untouched, as though the building is aware of our entry. With that thought, I realise that there is a form of intelligence within the very building itself. We are now in a fairly large circular room, which has a number of doors leading from it. The room is brightly lit, and I assume that sunlight enters through the sheer walls. Unlike my vision, sunlight is allowed entry.

Cardifer opens a door of natural oak appearance, and gestures me in.

Gently, he asks, *Do you want us to come with you? Or would you rather be alone?*

I gaze at him blankly. "I don't understand. Why would I need to be alone? What are we going to see? I mean, why are we in this building? I feel a tinge of apprehension. "Why might I need your help in there?"

Carienne takes immediate control. Holding up her hand for Cardifer to remain in the circular room, she takes my hand and leads me through the oak door. *This is the Forest Room.*

Even with her words, the room is a complete surprise. I am in a room, yet I feel as though I am walking into a lightly wooded forest. Bird song rings out, and it all seems completely authentic. Then I see birds flitting around on some of the lower branches,

with a breeze tickling the leaves! It is definitely a living forest—
yet it is more.

There are a number of what appear to be huge coffins
hovering about half a metre above the forest floor. They are dome
shaped, and as I approach one of them, I see they have a clear lid
covering the contents. I look into a coffin-like container, but as I
look through the transparent lid, I am actually looking through a
window into a small, room-sized reality. In this I see a large block
of . . . something?

It is a soft, clear, resilient, yet firm gel of a very special substance.
Carienne's words are spoken very softly and gently.

"Oh!" There is a body lying on the gel, sunken halfway into it,
and deeply asleep. It is a man, completely naked, and he looks as
though he is settled in for a long sleep. He is tall, strong-looking,
but slender. As I look at him, I am shaken by tremors running
through my Body-of-Light, and I struggle to contain a deep inner
shock. Abruptly, I am emotionally overwhelmed. I know this
person. It—it is the body of Mixael. He is alive. This is—me!

I feel Carienne holding me gently as I sob. I cannot help it. To
see myself, alive, and sleeping, or in a coma, is emotionally too
much. I metaphysically cry, and I feel tears trickling down the
cheeks of my physical body. I have no idea how long this lasts,
but it is no quick sob and all finished. I am too deeply shaken. I
stare at—myself. This—person—is me! It is obvious to me that
my body is in suspension awaiting my return. God! I had no idea.
Needing an explanation, I am choked with words, but I do not
know what to say.

Hurriedly, we leave the room.

Cardifer is looking rather anxious. *Are you all right? We knew
it would be a shock for you, but we also knew that you had to face it.
There is no way to prepare for this, except to be sure of the timing. And
you were ready.*

I hurry outside the building to the gardens, where we sit on
a bench of miracle comfort. Even as I struggle to regain my calm,

another shock wave of emotion hits and overwhelms me to the point that everything blanks out.

I am automatically back in my physical body reality, copiously weeping in my study. All I want is to be held by Carolyn, my Clarion. I call out to her and she is quickly with me, holding and comforting me while I sob out my emotional shock.

Next morning, fully recovered, I return to my study. Moving into my Light-body, I focus on the moment I left Cardifer and Carienne sitting on the bench in the gardens of The Sanctuary of Repose. I step . . . Between . . . emerging close by the bench.

They smile at me. *We knew that you would be back, so we waited.*

"I figured this was the same moment that I fell away from here, or very close."

Carienne laughs. *About five of your minutes. I wish I could have been of more help, but nothing can really prepare you for a shock like that. Are you fully recovered?*

I nod. "Oh, yes. In fact, I would like to have another look at . . . myself, without all the emotional turmoil. I admit, seeing my own body was about the last thing I expected. Why didn't you tell me, or warn me?"

Because, Mixael, we know you well enough to know that you would not have wanted that. Despite your shock, this is the way you would have preferred it, Cardifer replies. *Also, really, how do you prepare a person to face such an experience?*

I sigh. "Yes, I agree. I always prefer to jump in with both feet. All or nothing, that's me! Come on. I'd like another look at my original body before you explain the details of how!"

We enter the building and walk to the door of the Forest Room. Cardifer opens it and steps back, but I beckon them both in. "It's okay. I'm over the shock."

We gaze at the real body of Mixael. Now, with the shock well past, I look more closely. He is tall and obviously strong, with his skin the same golden-honey colour of the people here. He is fair, appearing to be in his mid-thirties. He is completely relaxed, yet his energy is very alive. Not for a moment does he appear dead, or in a coma. Even in this state of suspension, he looks very vital and dynamic. I like what I see.

"When I came in here previously, I thought of these cubicles as coffins. I now realise this misconception increased the shock. I can see there are other cubicles among the trees in this forest. How big is this forest reality/room?"

Carienne replied, *It is big . . . but not huge. It holds maybe a few hundred cubicles. What you see through the transparent lid is called a suspension cell. It is actually a tiny reality-frame of its own, and each is unique to the occupant.*

"Is suspension dangerous? Could the occupant die?"

It is no more dangerous to the life of the occupant than my life is in danger between one heartbeat and another. Your body is suspended in the moment between heartbeats. Time does not exist. Countless years or lifetimes could pass. It makes no difference.

"Gosh! Impressive. We often play with this theme in movies and books, but here it is a reality. Are the people in these cubicles now in my time-frame reality, or in different ones?"

Quite a few are in your reality-frame, but some are in others. Mostly they are where the need arises. This applies to either their own particular needs, or the needs of a reality-frame. The block of gel that each person relaxes on is a high-tech marvel. It supplies everything the body needs in the moment. When time is suspended, bodily needs are suspended, but, paradoxically, we found that a certain dynamic interchange of magnetic and biological energy was required. The properties of the gel maintain and enhance that vital alchemy.

"That explains why I could see, even feel, the obvious vitality of my body."

I stare for a while, marvelling at my own body. I like it! As we leave the Forest Room, I again notice a breeze stirring the leaves on the trees in our vicinity. Even though the trees are much wider spaced than in the forests I am familiar with, this is clearly a living reality.

"Is this forest self-maintaining or do people tend to this?"

Cardifer chuckles. *Are not all forests self-maintaining? This forest is both, growing perfectly naturally in its enclosed reality, while it is also maintained by the team who cares for the whole Sanctuary of Repose. You will notice there are no fallen branches. These are picked up and removed, yet it supports a certain balance of wildlife. Just as each cubicle is a sanctuary for the body it contains, so this forest room is a sanctuary for some of the more vulnerable species of wildlife that need a higher degree of protection.*

We have left the Forest Room and are again in the circular room with the doors.

"Very thoughtful. I like that. It creates a beautiful and peaceful living environment for my body . . . and the others. I notice that some of the other doors are of differing sizes. The door to the Forest Room is what I call normal, but that one over there is very tall, while over there the door is very small. Why is this? What's in there?"

You are at liberty to look . . . if you choose.

"Why did you hesitate? Why say, 'If I choose?' This is just a tourist visit . . . right?"

They both laugh. *Yes, Mixael, there is nothing alarming, even if a bit different.*

Cardifer opens the very tall door, and I look in before entering. Nothing. So I walk in.

"Oh, my gosh!"

I am in a desert of ochre-red sand. Okay, we have places a bit like this, but not with a thin scattering of the same ochre-coloured tree trunks, with pale orange leaves. I am in another room environment. This is small, or so it appears! I am learning that appearances here can be *very* deceptive. There are what look like car-sized shells lying here and there, as though washed up on some alien beach. Except there is no ocean. These shells look rather like the shell exterior of a paper nautilus, except they are thick, rather than wafer thin. These are also pure white.

We walk in. As we do so, I see what looks like a huge seed pod lying not far from a shell! I walk over to it. Only now do I notice that the seed pod is not quite on the sand, but hovering slightly above it. I quickly realise that the seed pod is not a seed pod! As I lean over it to see the surface area, it is transparent, as expected. By now I am braced for another shock. What I see is a big surprise, but not a shock. Inside the pod, obviously in a similar state of suspension, is a tall—very tall—Being. Naked and relaxed in/on a similar, but much bigger block of gel, is a completely genderless Being. Or at least there are no discernible genitals. This Being has an elongated, cone-shaped head on a long slender neck. He or she is alien and very beautiful. Definitely human-like in appearance, but very exotic. The Being is, at a guess, about four metres tall, and would have to come from a low gravity reality. She/he is extremely slender, without being thin. The body conveys a feeling of great endurance, an impression of some alien, high tensile strength. The skin is as white as the shells.

This is one of the Star People, Carienne explains. *They come to us when they, also, wish to be placed in suspension while their souls enter other experiences. Mind you, this is not a common occurrence. Rarely are there more than two or three of these people here at a time.*

I indicate the shell-like 'things'. "What are these?"

She smiles, wistfully. *Quite honestly, we do not know. Despite appearing to be heavy, they weigh almost nothing. They float and propel themselves around. They are alive, yet appear lifeless. Whether they share a symbiotic relationship with the Star People we are not sure. It has been explained to us, but the connection between the two Beings is too utterly alien for us to comprehend. Enough to say that wherever one is, the other is close by. This Star Person is in suspension, yet the other Being apparently has no relationship with time, therefore they do not require suspension. Very occasionally they move, but we have no idea why.*

211

"Hmm, a bit like a pet rock . . . only more so."

Carienne looks puzzled, but we leave the room, and I indicate the very small door close by. "Are we allowed to enter that room?"

Any room that we can enter, we are allowed to do so, Cardifer replies. *For example, that room over there is impossible for us to enter.* He points to a very ordinary door on our extreme right. *The caretakers here may enter, but they have to wear special sealed suits and breathing equipment. Apparently it is a very harsh, alien environment.*

With one accord, we enter the room with the small door. Cardifer and Carienne have to crouch down a bit, but in my metaphysical body I simply reduce my size to fit.

Once inside, I look around in awe. Many years ago, I climbed to the top of Mt. Scenery on the Isle of Saba. This reminds me of it. The room environment is filled with a thick mist and a single, not tall, but very wide, outspreading tree with fern-like foliage growing among low, lush vegetation. Its branches are dripping with metre-long strands of what appear to be greenish moss. Not exactly as Mt. Scenery, but strongly reminiscent. There are five small cubicles evenly spaced under the branches of the single tree.

Walking to one of the cubicles, I look into the suspension cell.

Oh my gosh! I see what appears as a small girl of about three years of age. She looks so exactly like a human child, I gasp.

"How did she get here? What's a human child doing here?"

Look again, Mixael, without jumping to instant conclusions.

Okay, calm down. Look for the unfamiliar, not the familiar. With these thoughts I gaze more carefully into the suspension cell. At first glance she appears as before—but there is so much more. This is no child. This is an ancient Being who looks young and vulnerable while naked and asleep. I now notice that her ears are extremely pointed, and her eyes, while closed, are obviously slanted far beyond anyone of our humanity. Her fingers are very long and tapering, each with a small retractable claw. I only realise this because each thumbnail is extended, sharp and pointed, yet the fingernails are retracted. She looks supple and fragile, but the overall impression is of alien strength. As a Being, she looks wild and fey. She looks like a spirit of Nature, like an ancient and unfamiliar elfin-person.

She is another of the Star People, Carienne explains, *and so very beautiful.*

I realise that, yes, she is very beautiful. Not a conventional beauty, but very exotic. She looks so young, so childlike at first glance, but as I continue to observe her, an ancientness becomes obvious. I get an energetic impression that she is very, very old.

"Has she been here long?"

Carienne smiles. *Centuries of our time, several millennia of yours.*

"Oh my gosh! That's a long time. Is she is perfectly okay?" I look again at the Star Being who looks as though she just lay down for a nap only moments ago.

Yes. All five of them came here together, and together they went into suspension. Why, we have no idea. We have never encountered any Star People like these either before or since their arrival. Maybe they are the last of their kind. To us, they are a mystery. However, this is a service we offer, and we do not question the history or motives of any who wish to use the suspension cells. We know they have the required consciousness . . . and that is enough.

"Suppose they did not have the required consciousness?"

They could not be here, or if they deceived us, they would quickly die.

"So these Star People were here long before either of you?"

Yes, long before us. But the continuity of care for the Sanctuary of Repose never lapses.

Amazing. I indicate my readiness to leave, so we walk out of the building and into the gardens again. The miracle bench awaits.

"I have a question which harks back to an earlier discussion. You told me that only a comparatively few people in this reality-frame have the ability to travel metaphysically as easily as I do.

I've thought about this and it doesn't make sense. I mean . . . in a higher reality it must surely be easy for everyone."

Cardifer looks at me strangely. *Mixael, you seem to have forgotten some of the basics. A higher reality does not automatically convey greater spiritual or metaphysical knowledge. A higher consciousness results from a higher degree of unconditional Love, from a greater care and compassion for your fellow humans. This is what raises human consciousness. You can, and we often do have both spiritual/ metaphysical knowledge and a greater Love, but this is not so common.*

I stare at him blankly. "Of course . . . you're right. This is so very basic. I'm not sure quite how I overlooked it. Many people in my frame-of-reality are growing in Love without much spiritual understanding. Different cultures, different beliefs . . . but One Love."

We stand, and coming together Cardifer's belt bubble encloses us. Again, that shift without a shift, and we are outside their home.

Looking around, I remark, "It never seems to rain here, or to be inclement weather. Do you control it, or is your weather more stable than ours?"

Both are true, Cardifer replies. *We do have specialists who have learned how to harness the various energies of Nature that we term weather, but mostly our weather patterns are stable.*

"What do you mean by the various energies that make up weather? Do you mean like the atmospheric wind and moisture, and suchlike?"

Well . . . yes, I suppose I do. This is not something I know much about, but apart from sunshine, which I think is beyond our ability or need to control, we have people who are able to attune with cloud moisture, whether very cold or warm, and with the air or wind elementals.

"Very cold . . . do you get snow?"

Oh yes, but we have snow where we want it, rather than wherever it might fall. Our snow is all in the highlands, creating wonderful seasonal snow fields. We enjoy snow sports as much as your people, although we are not really competitive. We explore sport from the aspect of cooperation, rather than competition.

"Gosh, that would be a novel idea for us. I can hardly imagine how it works."

Simple enough. Our sports are not devised to create a winner, but to develop skills. When you remove the 'win' or 'lose' equation, it allows a far greater degree of relaxation. The more you are relaxed, the more you are in-tune and balanced. We extend skills in this way for all to enjoy.

"But our competitions also increase skills."

I'm sure they do, but competition also creates stress, tension and anxiety. This does not allow the very best of skills to emerge; it engenders a 'winning' mentality. This is seldom the full potential of a more balanced dynamic.

"Hmm, I think you're right. So many of our athletes get sick shortly before a competition, or during pre-competition training. Some call it bad luck, but the smarter ones call it pressure . . . which is stress, tension and anxiety. After an ice skating competition is all finished, competitors often give displays of their skating skills. It is so obvious that once the pressure is removed, their displays exhibit far greater skill than when they were competing, hardly daring to take a risk in case they lost a point. Competitors often fall, or make a slip during a certain intricate movement, yet this seldom happens with the same move during practice rehearsal. Although still stressful, practice is without the unrelenting pressure of direct competition. So tell me, do you *have* sports where two teams or two people are in direct opposition?"

No, we do not. I find this difficult to understand. People or teams in direct opposition is not sport, it is a type of warfare . . . even if friendly. Can you explain this? Our sport is sport. Much of your sport seems to be based in either gain or loss. As I said, our sport is based in cooperation, not in opposition.

"Yes, to the winner the glory is certainly piling on the pressure. In our Olympics, the difference between a gold medal and fourth place may be less than half a second. Yet fourth place is the pits in the world of sport. Gold often means fame and fortune. Fourth means you remain an unknown. Obviously, there is a huge amount of money and ego involved. I admit, when I watch part of a rugby league match and witness the terrible injuries that all too often occur, or the anger that flares into a punching match, it definitely relates to warfare. But they also share a huge overall camaraderie . . . and they hone their skills . . . and this is the way it is in our frame-of-reality."

Nor am I implying this is wrong or negative. We were discussing the difference in sport using cooperation, or sport using competition. In our way of sports, excellence is a shared or even collective achievement, rather than bestowed on a single person or team.

"I think that would be wonderful for us . . . but it isn't going to happen. Aggression comes in here somewhere. Our violence and terrorism, along with our general aggression which results in road rage, car park rage, surfing rage and shop sales rage, just to name a few, all indicate that we have way, way too much aggression and anger. And all this is based in self-hate and self-attack. Anyway, enough of this!"

About time, Carienne laughs. *I can see from your field-of-energy that you will not be with us much longer. Is there anything we can do for you before you have to leave?*

"Thank you, but all is well in my life. Perhaps you could drop in on Mixael occasionally and tell him from his soul-self that he is loved and remembered. Let him know that I will return one day. Now there's a question . . . what happens when my physical body dies?"

Carienne smiles at me. *No great drama. You hold an energetic connection with your Mixael body. This is how you almost instantly knew it was yours. What happens when you release your current physical body will depend on your state of consciousness. If your transition is peaceful and loving, you will swiftly come here. If you are deeply traumatised, or afraid, you will enter one of the halfway hospitals with which I believe you are familiar. Either way, this body will be waiting in perfect readiness for your arrival. And time is of no concern. Of course, you could also make a conscious soul decision to incarnate elsewhere, where you would be naturally born.*

"Hmm . . . thank you. I think the trauma or fear will not eventuate, although I don't lightly dismiss it. I would like to think that I can leave my body as gracefully as a certain dolphin once showed me. And I cannot . . . nor do I want to . . . imagine a reason to incarnate again in my present frame-of-reality."

I have the familiar feelings that come when I am in danger of overstaying my ability.

"Gotta go. I Love you both. And thank you . . . so very much.

Goodbye, Mixael. Give our Love to Clarion. We Love you.

I focus into my study, and step . . . Between . . . back to my Carolyn/Clarion.

TEN

STALKING THE TORUS

I have been feeling a touch of excitement lately. Recently we bought the documentary created by Foster Gamble, *THRIVE: What on earth will it take?* I thoroughly enjoyed it. It is very well presented, highly ethical, and positive. I recommend that every adult should see it. For me, it verified much that I already knew about global dominance, while greatly extending that knowledge. But this is only a part of the picture they present. The section that excited me was the talk and description of the torus. Having left school at fourteen, and never having been a scholar, there are several holes in my education. Over the years I have read a reasonable amount of layman's quantum physics, but I did not always understand everything I read. Now, when something catches my attention and I want to know more about it, I often visit my subject on a metaphysical level. Mostly—not always—this fills in the missing spaces. In all my reading, any mention of a torus completely passed me by.

THRIVE changed this. When I saw the three-dimensional images of a torus, goose bumps walked my shoulders, trickling icy cold down my spine. Oh my gosh! I have seen the torus countless times in so many of my metaphysical experiences, I literally gasped. I have seen it in the cells of my body, in the very cells of Nature. I have seen it in mountains and in the grit of mountains, in oceans and in the water molecules of oceans. I have seen it rising through countless trees, returning to the soil to rise again, and I have seen it everywhere I look at life on a metaphysical level. I had no idea that what I was seeing was a torus, and I had no words or way to adequately describe it—so I made no attempt to do so!

The torus is the basis of the energy of Chaos—the engine that drives, and Order—the stability of structure. Each is composed of a different shaped torus, as Balance, the place of greatest potential, is different again. But the torus is within and without all that I have seen in Nature. In the early years of my association with Pan, I often told him that I was a poor choice for his attention because of my lack of education; okay, my ignorance! He always indicated that what needed to be known, in timing, would be known. He considered my lack of complexity, my simpleness, and my passion for life as far more important than knowledge for the sake of knowledge. Well—I feel I have proved my simplicity, but this is the first time I have ever truly regretted not having a greater knowledge of quantum physics. And yet, metaphysics is taking me to the same places, usually on a far deeper level.

The double helix DNA is a physical construct, and no matter how many zillion times it is magnified, it remains physical. Metaphysically, I am able to see/experience the metaphysical construct of DNA. As I have written and spoken many times, the metaphysical world/reality *precedes* the physical world/reality. The physical construct is a physical reflection in the mirror of a greater metaphysical reality. When you see the metaphysical DNA, you are seeing a vortex, or wormhole, that transcends physical reality. And this, I now know, is a perfect torus. Not only that, but this torus connects the metaphysical world with the physical world, taking them through the miracle process of creation, both in time and space—and beyond time and space.

THRIVE gave me the torus! Foster Gamble, you have my gratitude.

It was with all this in mind that I brought up a proposition to Pan.

"Could we take a journey into the eye of creation . . . or something like that?"

In other words, you are not sure.

I sigh. "You're not going to make this difficult, are you? No, I'm not sure exactly what it is that I want to explore, but I do know it has to do with the torus. Why didn't you tell me about a torus, or at least make it known to me?"

Why were the native islanders unable to see the explorer Magellan's ship?

"I think they did see it, but because their brain had no reference to such a ship, their sighting of it could not register in the brain."

That is a different answer! The general human consensus is that the islanders could not see it. Like the islanders, even though you saw the torus, in effect it did not register. To speak to you of a torus, when a torus had no reference in you, would be out of timing. My point . . . timing. Now that you have a reference, you have created the timing.

"Fair enough. I concede your point. Er . . . where do we go?"

An inner chuckle. *Where would you like to go?*

"Okay, you've made your point again. I have no idea where to go . . . and you know that! But I trust you implicitly to take me where I need to be."

Time to make ready.

"Making ready! Er . . . when or where do I step Between to?"

Leave that to me. I will guide the journey.

"Thank you. Making more ready. Er . . . sorry . . . but I've been thinking about this just lately. Pan, why do you do this for me? I mean, with all the vast multitude of happenings in the world of Nature, why do you do this for me?"

I also sometimes wonder. Just joking! Michael, as you know I am not an I. No place, no plant, no animal, no person holds my focus, for I am All. A vast cosmic sigh. Language reduces that which I would say . . . so let me share like this.

Suddenly, I am lifted as though I am snowflake and tossed into the All of Nature. I am air; here a hurricane, here the softest breeze. I am water; here a great ocean, here a tiny bead of moisture. I am the planet breathing; here the whole of Earth, here a particle of mineral dust. I am every plant on Earth; here every towering tree, here all the creeping moss, here a wisp of pollen. I am every insect, every bird. I am *all life* on Earth. From the largest to the minutest, all is connected, all is One. Nothing holds me more than anything else, for I am the All in the All. I see Michael travelling on his metaphysical journeys, and I see that the very essence of Nature accompanies him. I see that the growth of Michael is the growth of all life on Earth. Everything that lives is an expression of One consciousness. Humanity grows in consciousness as Michael grows in consciousness. Equally, Michael grows as humanity grows. The growth in consciousness of every single person is the growth of the All. All is One. I see the planet Earth as just one cell in the cosmic body of a vastness that is perpetual creation.

Sadly, language has also reduced my own description from magnificence to mediocrity. I am in awe of the immensity of my experience, overwhelmed by the sheer wonder of the infinite vastness of the physical universe, the metaphysical multiverse, and the sheer volume of life on Earth. The description of life on Earth as a unified field of energy is very accurate, but it is purely conceptual. It is rather like watching a microbe through the most powerful microscope: even though connected in consciousness, the observer is always physically disconnected from the observed. To experience Self *as* the unified field of energy — words fail.

Words are simply inadequate. But at least I know how trite and ridiculous was my question!

No, Michael, not trite or ridiculous. Your question was based in your consideration and care for me, and of all that I represent. Your need was not intellectual, but emotional.

The metaphysical me is expanding out so far beyond any previous experience that I am struggling to retain my humanness, the 'Michael me'. Even as I hear Pan's words, I realise that this struggle is also emotional.

We are already journeying, Beloved. Let go of the struggle; you need retain nothing. Just allow your pure Being essence to merge into the All. This . . . is life.

Pan called me . . . *Beloved.* When Carolyn calls me 'My Genius Husband', I am inspired. Now, as Pan calls me *Beloved*, I feel a denial. Why should I feel this? I instantly realise it is a distant echo of an old emotional program that no longer runs my life, a program called 'Not good enough'. I let the echo go. I *am* good enough to be beloved of Pan; I know this for certain.

"Thank you, Pan . . . Beloved. I can do this. Another lesson learned."

*In just such a moment, you make every instant I spend with **you** worthwhile. Now, focus into our journey . . . and let us see what unfolds for all life on Earth . . . through you.*

Expanding out further than I have ever experienced, I relax. This is okay. I need to let go of my emotional need to relate to myself as a body. In this moment, I realise how we relate to being in a body, or in a car, or an aeroplane; if we are moving, we need a vehicle for our reference point of stability. Normally I have two stable references: my physical body or my metaphysical body-of-Light. Now I have none. I am stationary—and I am moving! I have no real awareness of my physical body or my Light-body. I am the All experiencing Self as All.

Michael . . . become aware of the movement of energy in life on Earth.

Pulling my focus back to Self as nothing, I experience the flowing forms of energy. Oh my gosh! I see now in detail what I have been only vaguely aware of in earlier travels.

First I learned to see the huge range of reds in Chaos, then the range of blacks in Order, along with the dynamic of torsion and the luminous white of Balance. Then I learned to see and read energy-signatures and energy-trails. Now this becomes apparent. What next?

"Why was I unable to see this at other times?" I regret my words as soon as they are mentally fabricated. I know why. Timing.

I feel an inner smile. *Yes, timing. Out of timing . . . which includes self-acceptance, a greater openness, easier expansion, the releasing of fear and need, among other qualities both acquired and released, all that is before you now as perfect clarity was blurred by the veils of containment.*

"Containment?"

People contain themselves in the boxes of their beliefs. The greater your expansion, the greater are the boxes that continue to create the illusions of safety. In this experience, another box of containment has been released.

"I like that explanation. But does it imply I am in yet another bigger box?"

Oh, yes . . . more boxes remain. Remember your dream/experience!

My dream. Funny how I instantly know *which* dream. I have mentioned it before; it is the dream in which I was over-lighted by Self, while on a beach late one evening. Put simply, in the dream I experienced the Oneness of all Life.

"So are you implying that the Self I experienced was un-contained by any boxes?"

Exactly.

"It is a dream that continues to lead me on to such a goal. Once I thought it impossible, but the dream was so real, I realised that it was showing me a reality that awaits."

Not so much a reality waiting as a state of consciousness to be achieved.

"Yes. I understand."

My attention is drawn back to the vast movement of life in which I am involved. I gaze at a torus so immense it seems to hold the creative streams of energy of the whole planet, when abruptly, an inner realisation blossoms in my awareness. I see clearly that life is only unfolding for each one of us, each person, if we are actually involved in the creativity of life itself. Oh my gosh! If we are living in a continuation of the past, we are uninvolved in the unfolding of the moment. When this happens, we become static—or a non-growing state of consciousness. This is not bad or wrong, but we place ourselves in a different frame of reality. Suddenly, I see why humanity has intellectually grown so much, while hardly growing at all in consciousness. I have known for a long time that these are very different energies, but never had I seen the difference as powerfully, or with as much clarity, as in this moment.

There are two streams of energy in which a problem can be solved; one is the energy of the brain and intellect, the other is the energy of conscious intelligence.

Brain and intellect energetically take a person out of the moment. As I have said many times, "You can think your way out of the moment, but you cannot think your way into it." By using the brain and intellect they develop and grow—obviously! This has been the path of the majority of humanity. This has led to our left-brain dominance. But the growth of the brain and intellect has absolutely nothing to do with growing in consciousness. Hence our continuing violence, warfare, inner-conflict and self-attack. By living *out of the moment*, we are living out of the energy stream of conscious growth. In other words, humanity is stuck and static regarding consciousness. The Balanced people and the 'newly-aware' people who have a regard for the environment, for humanity, for loving and caring for more than themselves, are the forerunners of the state of consciousness that awaits a slowly awakening humanity. They are the people who are already involved in the dimensional shift.

Conscious intelligence, as a way of living, takes a person into the moment. Problem solving through conscious intelligence is a very different energy from the intellectual approach. First and foremost, there is no problem to solve! These people see a situation that is offering growth in this moment, and that timing will see where resolution is to be found. They disregard force, knowing that timing is everything. A flower in bud is not a problem; it is a flower waiting its timing to unfold. For a person living *in the moment*, this is the conscious and intelligent approach to any so-called problem. When a person is in the flow of conscious intelligence they are consciously growing and this, in itself, opens the door to resolution. The so-called problem becomes part of the process of inner-growth. When people live in this manner, they continuously grow in consciousness. Generally, this is the approach of right-brain dominant people or whole-brain people—which is the holistic way to use the brain. I know people who are strongly right-brain in their creativity, and strongly left-brain dominant in their way of living life. If only they could synchronise to whole-brain living for everyday life, they would have it made!

All this flashes through my awareness in micro-moments.

An immense torus is holding my attention. (If you are unclear about a torus, I recommend Wikipedia. Their definition is far more scientific than mine! They describe the basic torus as a surface of revolution generated by revolving a circle in three-dimensional space about an axis coplanar with the circle.) The torus I am watching is composed of the overall energetic flow of Earth. I will describe it this way: imagine the planet as a vast jellyfish, soft and undulating; let go of the fixed and rigid physical construct. Imagine that this huge jellyfish is drawing water/energy in through its rear and moving it up through the interior of the jellyfish to exit at the front. As it exits, the water/ energy flows over the entire jellyfish surface to once again enter at the rear of the jellyfish. Simultaneous with all this, the interior of the jellyfish is revolving round and around with the exterior, all happening in a continuous fluid movement. Moreover, as the jellyfish/earth swims in the ocean of space it undulates, its whole body moving with a soft outer rippling effect. Energetically, our planet undulates in space, but the undulations come from the inside, flowing over the outer surface, only to return via the surface back into the interior. The North Pole on the top of the planet seems to be the entrance for this energy, while the South Pole seems to be the exit. The jellyfish analogy can only take us so far! When we have an earthquake, the ripple effect from the interior is far more powerful than normal, actually affecting the physical construct. This is not a denial of the apparent physical causes of an earthquake: this is about the metaphysical *affect* that is the precursor to the physical *effect*.

As I watch the incredible (impossible to describe) energy-field of Earth, it almost appears to be swimming in space via the torus. I have never seen it in this way before, and I concede that I was not ready to! Metaphysically there is no *real* space between the Earth and the planets that physically are so vastly distant to us. Energetically, the metaphysical undulations of Earth connect and blend with the undulations of our moon, Mars, the sun, and so on throughout the galaxy. On an energetic level, it is difficult to see the Earth torus as a mathematical geometric concept. To me, it is far more a metaphysically living field-of-energy, interfaced with, and within the physical reality of our planet.

After a timeless no-time of gazing in awe at the energetic toroidal wonder of our planet's field-of-energy, I feel as though I am falling into the vast planetary torus, while at the same time following a trajectory into the energy-fields of the forests of the world. I am a mote of cosmic dust slowly settling onto a branch of a large tree in the northern hemisphere, yet in the same moment my awareness is expanding over the whole tree. I am both the micro and the macro.

On a micro level, I feel the discord in the branch on which I rest. Tree energy moves in waves both within the branch and along its exterior. Tree is both physical and metaphysical. Within the physical tree, the energy holds a thread of discord. This affects the tree in the manner of disease—out of harmony—which is evident by a few of the once-healthy branches that are now dying. The tree energy no longer holds the harmony it once did. Fungi invade some of the branches, along with the bacteria of rot. All this will take a long time to cause the death of the physical tree, but it *will* happen. To most people this is part of the natural cycle—and it is—yet the base cause is not actually physical.

Within the metaphysical tree, Chaos is rising. This affects the equilibrium of the torsion between Chaos and Order in the tree. As the energy of Chaos rises in this tree, harmony is lost, along with Balance. This is not a sick, negative red Chaos the tree contains; it is simply an imbalance in the torsion of the Chaos and Order ratio. Overall, just as the physical tree takes in mineral and nutrient energy with its roots to travel throughout the tree and finally transpire back into the atmosphere, so, on an energetic level, the toroidal energy of the tree is taking in a flow of energy from the Earth to flow over the surface of the tree, metaphysically connecting it with the torus of every tree in the forest. This, in turn, connects with every forest and every tree on the planet—and on to connect with the toroidal energy-field of the sun and moon, returning with this extra energy into the Earth via the North Pole. As I share this, I am describing the basic torus in every plant.

How many ways are there to say and describe it? Everything of Nature is energetically connected with everything of Nature, including us: *the unified field of energy*. Okay, having read a bit about the scientific concept of the torus, and taking note of the several different types they describe, I have probably metaphysically seen toroidal shapes that mathematics and geometry have yet to comprehend.

As I metaphysically connect with the moss in this forest, becoming the many types of moss growing here, so I embrace the changing shapes of the torus. Maybe I am attempting to explain the inexplicable, but so many varieties of moss are held within the framework of one great torus that the many different moss expressions cause the energetic framework of that torus to continually change its species shape in the way of a vast amoeba. Yet, never for one micro-moment does the ever-changing torus fail to perfectly fulfil its energetic purpose. To describe this is complex, yet it is simple to witness. Each species of moss has its own type of torus energy-shape, each being the most perfect energetic expression of that species of moss. While the variation is not big, it is there. Within this framework, the toroidal energy of each species flows smoothly into the vast, overall torus of moss, fully integrating the unique torus of each species without any violation of its individual integrity. To me, this is the miracle of energetic creation, and all creation is first and foremost energetic.

As it is with moss, so it is with other plant varieties within a species. While there is an overall toroidal shape for the whole forest of trees, so each individual species has their torus. Not only that, but each cell of each plant energetically follows the creative path of the torus. Even though the words are difficult to grasp, this incredible flow is aptly described in geometry as an energy surface of revolution generated by revolving a circle in three-dimensional space about an axis coplanar with the circle. Coplanar meaning on the same plane. I have done my best to give you a more simple, right-brain description of a torus, but I recommend that you see *THRIVE* and watch a torus in all its beautiful, three-dimensional flowing action. Then take a moment to realise that this toroidal movement is within your own body, both on a multiple cellular level and as a single body.

The torus in Nature does not just follow the shape of a plant or a flower; rather the reverse is more accurate. A flower is as affected by the toroidal energy within, as it is by external energies. By external I mean, for example, the flowers which specialise in their own unique pollination processes, whether by insect, bird, or animal. That external forces play a major part in the way a flower evolves is obvious; while internal forces of a metaphysical influence are anything but obvious.

Guided by Pan, I drift through many forms of Nature within the forest. I realise that this whole forest is but a microcosm of the greater planetary macrocosm of Nature, yet it is certainly a fair representation of the subtle changes in toroidal energy.

"Pan . . . looking at the planetary torus, I noticed that the toroidal energy appears to enter around the North Pole, while exiting the planet around the South Pole. Is there such a thing as a polarity torus? I mean, are the Poles simply an energetic way in and out, or is toroidal energy attracted or expelled by the polarity factor?"

We will continue with your look and learn. It is refreshing that in these circumstances there is no possibility of your meddling and interfering!

I know that Pan has a huge influence on me, but is there a sneaky possibility that my sense of humour is slowly infecting the great God of Nature?

I feel an inner chuckle—but no comment.

Still with no sense of my Light-body, I am 'awareness' wafting like an autumn leaf through no-time no-space, drifting down toward a vast expanse of snow and ice. I get the feeling that this is the Antarctic beneath me, the current location of the slowly drifting South Pole. As a metaphysical field-of-energy, I seep through deep, thick layers of ice, deep down through the crust of the Earth. Drifting downward deep within the planet, I see some huge strange shapes of what seem to be pure energy. I have never before seen anything like these vast blobs that very slowly drift deep in the ocean of the Earth's crust. My impression is that they are pure polarity. I have read quite a bit of the literature about polar shifts and geomagnetic reversal—which apparently are different—and it is obvious there is very little agreement about any of this. As a layman, I read one allegedly informed article, only to find it completely contradicted by another also claiming scientific validation. Most scientific reports seem to scoff at any likelihood of a shift of the Poles, while a few that claim scientific endorsement confirm that it is likely to be sooner, rather than later. How much sooner involved further conjecture! Obviously the sciences of a physical world do not allow for the metaphysical probability factor, while such things as human and/or planetary consciousness are totally dismissed.

Most *New Age* theories on a Pole shift seem to be based on prediction and channeling, with plenty of assumptions thrown in. I know little about the physical structure of our world, apart from the basic layman's knowledge. I have learned that the inner core is assumed to be solid, while the outer core is assumed to be liquid. It is speculated that the interaction between these two states, separated only by a complex mix of solid, semi-solid and semi-liquid states which may be anything from tens to hundreds of kilometres thick, produces masses of unstable, magnetically-charged particles of polarity. Some of these stream upward toward the North, while another stream heads toward the South. Right now, I can see that, while the outlets for all this energy are the magnetic Poles, huge unmentioned quantities of these magnetically-charged particles coagulate into the enormous blobs of polarity that float in the space of Earth around me.

I recently learned that evidence indicates the North Pole is speeding up in its wanderings to around fifty-five kilometres in a year, while the South Pole is apparently much slower, moving between three to five kilometres in a year. I have a good grasp of the evidence suggesting that we have a lot to learn about our planet before we kill all life on it with our ignorance. Apart from this, I have few technological facts cluttering my metaphysical awareness. This means I will share what I see/experience in the way that I see/experience it, without any prejudice toward so-called scientific facts. Although I always share my experiences as they happen, I am pleased when so-called facts are inclined to favour me, as with the torus. Now, having summarised my knowledge of the Earth's core, it seems a good idea while I am here to have a metaphysical peek!

"Can we go to the inner core of Earth, Pan, or am I likely to get . . . cooked!?"

An inner chuckle. *There is nothing of you to get cooked. However, on a serious note, while you are nonphysical you come under the influence of the metaphysical aspect of heat. Although this cannot harm you, it may well frighten you.*

"Let's keep it simple. Am I in danger or not?"

*No . . . this needs to be seriously considered. No danger if you remain calm! However, at some stage you will be totally surrounded by molten rock, liquid lava . . . not so easy then to keep your cool. In effect, **you** are the determining factor of high risk or no danger.*

"Okay . . . I'll keep my cool!"

For the first time ever with Pan, I feel myself being inner-scanned. With a touch lighter than mist, I feel 'something' sweep through me—or did I imagine it? Honestly, I am not sure.

"Are you checking me out?"

My question is ignored. *We will continue.*

As I/awareness drift downward, I see vast caverns of stalactites and stalagmites, taller and bigger than anything I have ever seen photographed. There are caverns with crystals as big as our houses and churches, and enormous underground lakes of clear black water. I see rushing, roaring rivers and tiny trickling streams; it is as though all that lies on the Earth's surface has a beautiful underground counterpart. I drift down through seams of precious stones, of caverns littered with a rubble of semi-precious jewels, glittering to my perception as though they are illuminated. As I continue my downward drift, I come close to a huge blob of polarity. I do not understand what I now see. Back to my jellyfish analogy: I see an immense undulating torus, twisting inside-out in a continuous flow, with energy drawing in one end and out the other to flow over the convoluting surface and endlessly around again. But it is twice split in the middle, so there are three jellyfish involved in the dynamic of creation, all connected yet apart, while connected as one—a treble torus. Okay, you do not understand—all connected yet apart. Neither do I!

"Will you please explain to me what a blob of polarity is?"

Michael, trust your own knowing. It is as you have already summarised. The polarity blobs, as you call them, are pockets of pure energy which have filtered or drifted from the streams of magnetic energy according to the hemisphere. Over time they accumulate, becoming large fields or pockets of polarity energy. Because the pockets are pure energy, they cannot be contained or restrained. They are able to drift . . . as is now happening.

"Thank you, Pan. Validation tastes as good as vanilla ice cream!"

We continue drifting downward. I am acutely aware that time is no factor here, nor is distance; we are travelling metaphysically. I have an impression of the vastness of the planet. To describe this I can only say that when you fly around the world in an aircraft, you have a similar impression of how big is the world. But this is only the skin of the planet; the interior is vastly bigger. If you sail a boat over the ocean, you are on the surface only, and it seems huge. Imagine the immensity of the depths beneath you. So when I tell you I am drifting into a vast open space, probably as big as the whole continent of Australia, in the immensity of this inner-world, you will understand my feelings of total awe.

"Oh . . . my gosh! How is it possible for a . . . a cavern to be as colossal as this?

This is one of the biggest, but there are others.

"It seems to be light! Is there life down here?"

Of course.

A thousand questions are born—only to be somehow terminated! I gaze around as I drift down through a tiny part of this prodigious, cavernous space, but I can see/experience little. I get a vague impression that the cavernous/space is roughly the shape of a vast rugby ball, and that it has its own illumination, but overall I feel as though a smothering veil has been thrown over me.

I am indignant. "Pan . . . you've closed me down!"

Timing . . . Michael . . . timing.

For a moment I struggle against my restraints, then I relax. Timing must not be discarded, nor my total trust in Pan.

"Okay . . . some other time when we both know the timing has arrived."

That is acceptable.

"So what is involved in my timing to explore an inner Earth?"

You have a block . . . and in perfect timing you will let it go.

A block—me! Hmm, I don't think I like that. I wonder what it is.

We continue drifting down, down, down, ever downward. Even though I am nothing more than 'awareness' I am feeling the growing energy of awesome heat. It is a different heat feeling than any I have ever experienced. Very different. Abruptly, I feel sick. Why, I have no idea, but a rapidly growing sense of nausea is sweeping through me.

"Pan . . . I'm feeling very nauseous."

I was waiting for you to acknowledge it. Denial now would be extremely foolish. I did wonder if your pride would allow you to admit it.

We have come to a stop, no longer drifting downward.

"I don't get it. You warned me about the heat of molten lava, but you said nothing about me feeling sick. What would you have done if I just kept going?"

As I said, I need to know how well you have developed your sense of responsibly to yourself. Pushing yourself into fatigue is one thing; pushing yourself into extreme hazard is another. A few more moments and you would have been back in your study.

"Why do I feel like this? Actually, that's a stupid question. Suspended here, I feel as though two titanic forces of intense heat are not only pulling me in two different directions, but also as if they are about to tear me apart. And I'm . . . metaphysical nothingness!"

We are immediately lifting, slowly rising at an angle up through the planet.

Michael, you have absolutely no idea of the enormity of the forces of energy that are continuously generated deep in the interior of a planet. The atmospheric pressure at the bottom of the ocean is crushing, but the forces of energy close to the planet's core make that pressure as nothing. One aspect of this journey is to teach you to respect the environment of combined metaphysical and physical forces. The other aspect is to teach you to know when to withdraw, to know when your limits are reached. You did well. To tell you that you still have metaphysical vulnerabilities does not carry any impact. To demonstrate your vulnerability does. While you retain a physical body, you are not impervious to all and everything.

I feel myself coming back to balance. Balance! Ah . . . the Chaos factor! That's what happened. The energy of Chaos in the vicinity of the Earth's outer and inner core must be utterly awesome. Chaos rules—and by gosh, it's a chaotic Chaos!

Yes, Michael, that says it well. Were the magnitude of Chaos near the planet's core to be unleashed in Nature on the surface, it would be instant death.

"Oh, my gosh! Such a thought never occurred to me. The Chaos on the Earth's surface is just a multitude of mild expressions of Chaos compared with the stupendous energy of Chaos near the Earth's outer molten core. That is something else again."

I have discovered that there is Chaos, and then there is— CHAOS!

We continue our upward drift. I realise that I have learned a very valuable and important lesson. I really *did* think that I was invulnerable while metaphysical, and learning that I am not is a bit of a shock. It leaves me with a greater feeling of respect, both for Nature and, oddly, for myself. Of course, I was in no danger, but had Pan whisked me back to my physical body, it would have been a case of—wisdom failed, foolhardy proven. I acknowledge also that had Pan told me about the danger of such titanic forces, it would have been an easily-dismissed concept. Instead, Pan made it into an actuality that has really impacted me.

In moments we drift out of the Earth, and I actually breathe a sigh of relief. My quest was the pursuit of the torus, but I found more than I had bargained for. I feel queasy at the very thought of those titanic forces near the Earth's outer core, nevertheless, my nausea has ceased.

"Thank you, Pan, for an unpleasant, but enlightening experience. I am the better for it."

More than you yet realise.

"Was this part of a plan?"

No . . . simply an opportunity seized.

"Hmm . . . any further down and I might have had a seizure!"

Thinking of how it affected me in my metaphysical aspect sponsors thoughts of how it would be to journey into a few human bodies in various states of health. I'm sure that the torus of the overall body, and the toroidal energy of the cells, must change considerably. With this thought, I suddenly realise that I am back in my metaphysical body-of-Light.

"Oh . . . I'm me again!"

Many comments surge forward, but I will resist the temptation.

"Pan, do you realise that you are developing a real sense of humour? Is it possible that I'm corrupting you in the best possible way?"

Just in case you take this thought too seriously, be assured that I relate to you in the way that you relate to me, and to life.

"I know that. I find it easier to take life with plenty of humour. I mean . . . a whole race of immortal Beings living as though they are mortal, believing death is the End. Or seven billion people each creating their own reality . . . and doing nothing but blaming each other for it! And the idea that you can fight for peace! Or storing weapons of death in the name of peace. How can I take us seriously? Homo Sapiens . . . wise man . . . it's a joke. We are far too immature for that. We are . . . Homo Infantus. Infants learning to grow in a classroom called Earth. I hope we have our graduation party very soon!"

I suddenly take notice of the Nature that surrounds us.

"Oh, my gosh . . . we went into the planet over the Antarctic, and we have come out somewhere in the tropics. How did that happen?"

We took a short cut.

"Okay . . . ask a stupid question!"

All control of your journey is now yours. I'm retiring for a while. Behave!

"Oh, right! Thank you so much for the experience. Pan . . . you said you are retiring for a while. Does your job description have any retirement plans or holiday benefits?"

No . . . but it does have you.

I am not sure whether to feel immensely flattered, or . . . ?

As usual, I feel the departure of Pan, though to be honest, his presence is always very nebulous. It is not that I *actually feel* Pan go; it is more like a cloud moving in front of the sunshine without creating shade, and the temperature remains the same. Very subtle.

Having had some metaphysical experience with hospitals, this is where I focus. I am not selecting any particular one. We will see what happens. With this thought, I step . . . Between . . .

and out into a large hospital in a very large city. Ah, I have been here before.

In my body-of-Light, I move purposefully into one of the many large buildings. I like this. I definitely prefer to be in my Light-body. I feel much more like me, and less like drifting metaphysical protoplasm. Mind you, if I could feel nauseous as metaphysical protoplasm near the Earth's outer core, I would have been far worse off in my Light-body. Pan knew!

Okay, Michael, pay attention—I am here to seek the human torus in sickness and in health. With this thought, I drift/glide down a corridor packed with people, a bustle of two-way people traffic. I purposefully place an energy screen around me, so that people are no more likely to walk into me than into each other. I have never quite come to terms with people walking through my Light-body, even though it has happened many times. Sometimes the feeling is very pleasant, sometimes it is nasty, but all in all I prefer to choose with whom I exchange energy—for no matter how subtle, this happens. I walk/drift quite slowly, allowing my energy-screen to operate more easily. The hurrying people are not conscious of me at all, but the metaphysical aspect of each person honours my wish for privacy. Metaphysical Beings do not walk through each other any more than physical people deliberately collide. And, as I so often write, first and foremost, people are metaphysical, not physical. Difficult to grasp, huh?

All goes well, and I enter the waiting room that I was heading for. It contains a large group of people, but most are sitting down in a reasonably ordered fashion. As I watch the Chaos/Order ratio, a red of anxiety Chaos is strongly dominant, but that is to be expected in these worrying circumstances. I see a man and a boy sitting, waiting, side by side. Reading the energy-signature of the man, I learn that his wife is in emergency; he is very distraught. His son is very young, maybe three, and he only knows that something is wrong.

I move my Light-body into the man, who is maybe around his mid-thirties. Every cell in his body has become tight and inflexible, while the torus of each cell seems to distort in waves of distress. The cellular torus continues to act in a toroidal fashion, but they are twisted and slightly malformed, losing the flow and cohesion of normality. Looking into the boy, all is very different. There is tension in the cellular structures, but flexibility remains. The torus of each cell is 'doing its thing' in the manner for which it was designed, without any impairment.

I sigh. As adults, we so easily become tense with worry, never realising that we are pushing energy out of us at a high volume. I have said earlier; energetically, we leak. We leak from the moment we wake up in the morning, till we are back in the deep sleep of night; when we recharge. If people could see the vital necessity of the recharge, sleep would receive far more attention than late night entertainment.

In the difference between father and son, I have learned that the torus can become easily corrupted by stress and anxiety. What happens with sickness? Or at the point of death? I move my focus away from father and son toward his wife in the emergency room. As I enter the room, I see that the activity has quietened. She is either dead, or considerably better. Energetically, I see that she is recovering. Good. Already she is past danger, barring a galloping hospital infection like staphylococcus. But at this stage, all is well for a fast and complete recovery. It appears to be a serious kitchen accident with a knife, not a suicide attempt. Nobody would cut themselves so drastically across one side of the ribs as she has. She lost a lot of blood, but her energy-field has nothing of self-attack in it.

Knowing that accidents are unrealised purpose, meaning old trauma reinventing itself, I look into her energy-signature to read her story. Ah, yes. She did in fact suicide under extreme pressure about two incarnations ago, successfully bypassing this in her last incarnation. This time around, still carrying an old deep-seated guilt, she is subconsciously replaying the drama in hopes of a resolution. From her composure and her energy-field, I would say that it is resolved. It seems all she really needed to do was face a life-threatening period of bleeding without terrified hysteria, and without screaming self-blame. And reading her very calm field-of-energy, she has done this admirably. Despite her so-called accident, she is a very capable woman.

Her energy-field changes again as her husband is ushered in with her son. She feels a mild self-retribution at scaring him so badly. But as he lovingly, tenderly and carefully holds her, her energy changes to contentment. On a deep metaphysical level, there is acknowledgement of lesson learned, mission accomplished.

Pleased with her positive outcome, I focus on seriously ill people, drifting upward through a couple of floors to an area of more controlled, quieter bustle. I go into a ward of no more than ten or fifteen men, all of them with serious lung problems. Some have pneumonia, some have emphysema. I say *serious* because these are all hospital cases, not mild cases—albeit unpleasant—that can be treated at home. As I look at their fields-of-energy, I see into their lungs. Nasty! Viral and/or fungal infections have caused serious inflammation in all of them. Some men are fighting to breathe, literally gasping, while a number of them are on oxygen. I do not get an energetic impression that all these men are dying, but several are seriously ill. One older man is definitely struggling to survive, his energy leaking away from him. I am not surprised to see that the energy of the lungs is directly connected with the heart energy. I have no doubt that most, if not all, of these men are having either emotional domestic issues, or emotional issues with themselves. In our bodies, energy connects. No illness is an isolated expression of discord. Just as Love positively connects, so, with negative energy, discord connects. A critical or judgemental attitude to ourselves, or others, affects the heart. What affects the heart, affects the lungs. The effects become known according to which organ is weakest, or most susceptible to the negative energy that is being constantly generated.

I went through my own year of intense grief in losing my late wife. By the end of the year, my lungs were badly congested. The punch of loss to the heart, and the ensuing grief, creates a negative energy which attacks the lungs. I see that a couple of these men have lived through recent bereavements, and their lungs are affected by it. A few of them are asthmatics. Energetically moving into the energy-field of one of these men with emphysema, I feel his dragging efforts to get enough oxygen into his lungs. Sad. What a price for smoking. Another has a similar struggle with asthma. Having never had asthma, I now have a greater empathy for what it must feel like. Scary! The toroidal structures within the cells of his lungs are more distorted than any I have yet seen. I will not attempt descriptions—it is enough to say that they are severely distorted away from normality. Not only are they distorted, but his overall physical body torus reflects this distortion, although definitely not so dramatically as in the cells of the lungs. At one bed a nurse is standing, chatting briefly and soothingly with a man whose every breath is a struggle. I inspect her lungs energetically so I can make a comparison with the men. Gosh, this is how it should be. Her lungs, which are functioning perfectly, have a cellular torus that is almost classical in its beautiful shape and energy flow.

Some of the worst inflammation is in the lungs of men with pneumonia; the torus is quite brutally distorted. Any flow of normal energy is impossible. When the normal flow of energy is hindered or blocked in various ways, inflammation is the result. As the nurse moves from the bed of the man struggling to breathe to check on another, I notice she has the slightest of limps. Energetically, I see she has an elasticated ankle brace for an almost-healed twisted ankle. In her ankle joint I clearly see inflammation. Yet this inflammation is very different from the inflammation in the lungs of the patients. It never occurred to me that inflammation could come in differing energies. The cells in her twisted ankle have a very mild toroidal distortion, but the energy of her ankle distortion is very different from the energy distortion in the patient's lungs.

Okay, so what happens to the torus at the point of death? This must be the very ultimate extreme of toroidal stress.

With a focus on human death, I am drawn toward the men's ward for terminal cancer. Ugh, what an unpleasant way to die. I have been here before, or to a ward very similar. I choose a men's ward because having been through my own forms of suffering, I empathise with them. All illness is caused by a basic depletion in energy. From my observations, I have learned that the body is a complex of differing energies, all designed to flow into one harmonic and holistic expression. *Holistic,* meaning both physical and metaphysical as One. When one of the areas of energy in the body loses its harmonic with the whole, then the whole also loses energy; it is no longer complete. By ignoring, or even denying our spiritual selves, we are immediately denying a holistic life experience, thus physical illness is easier to invoke and should not be unexpected.

We often hear a comment similar to this; "My aunt is the sweetest, kindest woman, but she is dying of cancer and, unless drugged, is in terrible pain. Why is this so?" I know this sounds harsh, but being kind and sweet to others is not rewarded. Too often it is a subconscious restitution based in being strict and unkind to the inner-self. Many people treat others far better than they treat themselves. When I was a young man, I learned from the Church of England that it was a sin to Love yourself. Now that I have left the church and grown in wisdom, I would say the reverse is true—although sin is a concept based in judgement.

In all my metaphysical journeying, I have never found anyone in a hospital, or in their own home, who is dying of terminal Love. Worth thinking about!

I enter the energy-field of a man who is very sick indeed. His energy-signature indicates a lifetime of smoking; a lifetime potential about to be considerably shortened. Smoking is indicative of a person who is seriously into self-attack—and it is very effective! Emphysema is another result, also lethal. The man I am with is not a bad man in any way at all, but his relationship with himself is poor, to put it mildly. How strange that we are a race of Beings where ninety-five percent of us still do not realise that our relationship with ourself is our most important and vital relationship of all. It is the basic relationship that determines our relationship with God, with our lives, our relationship with other people, our relationship with our bodies and health, and our relationship with abundance.

Like I said, this man is not a bad or wrong, and he is loved by a wife and two children, but he dislikes himself, and he is now very close to death. Feeling slightly morbid about my quest to see the torus under these conditions, I nevertheless persist. Energetically, I am in his energy-field, watching the toroidal energy of his cells. He has cancer in his lungs and liver. Actually, it is running rampant at this stage, but the liver, not the lungs, was the target of the earliest onset, and is the most damaged area. In effect, it has reached a stage where all energy is draining from this area—and is not being replaced. The metaphysical torus of each cell is literally collapsing in his liver.

So that is it. As death approaches, the body closes down, and the torus of each cell collapses. Feeling compassion for this poor man, I expand my Love/Light, filling him from within. Under this Love/Light influence, every torus in every functioning cell, for a brief moment, inflates to full perfect energy—then collapses. With a soft contented sigh, he stops breathing.

Knowing that his final moment was peaceful, I step . . . Between . . . and out into my study. I sit for a few moments, feeling moved by the unknown man. How strange that he could have such a good relationship with family and friends, and such a poor one with himself. I have no doubt that if the personal inner critic had been silent, he would have lived a longer and much healthier life.

ELEVEN

THE MYSTERY OF MICHAEL

The rush and bustle of another Christmas has ended, with the entry into the New Year duly celebrated. I have reached an age when I sometimes reflect on the past. Mostly I am as fully engaged in the moment as possible, but Christmas and a New Year are surely times for reflection. As I have earlier said, each year I learn of the passing of a few more friends around my age, and I remember the good times we used to have. Although I have moved far from them, it is not only distance that has created separation between us over the years, it is the spiritual path that I chose. We each walk our paths in life alone. I am more fortunate than most. In my marriage with Treenie we were able to hold hands on our different, separate paths, and now, in my marriage with Carolyn we are able to walk arm-in-arm on our different, but close, paths. I have been, and am, very blessed.

When, as a farmer in the island state of Tasmania, I suddenly stumbled onto my spiritual path, I attempted to get my friends to walk it with me. I was very naive. Under the stimulus of enthusiasm for my new spirituality, I would write reams of poetry. Even though my poems were filled with pain, as my inner hurt and torment poured into my words, I thought they were brilliant! So, being a generous person, I attempted to share them with as many of my friends as possible. I think word went around that the English farmer on top of the hill had gone mad. Printed poems under my arm, I would call on various farming friends, who, mysteriously, were not home. Once, as I walked away from a house, and I turned back to knock again on the door, I saw a curtain quickly pulled back into place. I was devastated. It had never occurred to me that I was probably the biggest bore in the township.

In these ways I learned that the spiritual path is a lonely one. Especially for a farmer whose friends are mostly country folk; they walk their rural paths. It took awhile for me to learn that everyone is walking their own spiritual path: the difference was that I now *consciously* walked mine. As an Aries of high passion and energy, I ran, rather than walked, and this was even more off-putting for many of my friends. We remained friends because I learned that most friendships have boundaries that should not be crossed, so I refrained from imposing my poems and my newfound spirituality on them. Marriage, happily, is a friendship where all borders and boundaries can be dropped. A marriage where they are retained is a marriage that is lacking in closeness, maintaining distance rather than creating intimacy.

Luckily, Treenie's path was similar to mine, so it was probably inevitable that our shared paths eventually took us away from farming in Tasmania, and away from those passing friends who are now the memory which began this reminiscing! As a family of Treenie, myself, and four children, we travelled around Oz with a small caravan (trailer), taking almost a year. We then helped to create a community of what was supposed to be like-minded people. My naivety dies very slowly! I must say, however, that although I still retain some unshakeable naivety, most of it evaporated under the stimulus of a community filled with people of good intentions, but very muddled, angry, and emotionally confused. I include myself.

In that community, however, something extraordinary happened to me.

First, to fill in the background, let me step back to when I was a teenager on my father's farm in East Anglia, England. I left school at fourteen, so I had spent most of my teen years and into my mid-twenties working on my father's farm before his illness and death set Treenie's and my feet on the path of immigration to Oz.

As the 'boy' on the farm, and a very strong one, most of the 'dirty' work was given to me. This is simply the way it was in those days. But much of the dirty work was far dirtier than I ever realised. Each year we would keep some of our own wheat and barley for seed. Unfortunately, barley and wheat seed were often eaten by wireworm (a beetle larva) while they were sprouting in the soil. This could decimate the crop, so it had to be dusted with a poison powder before it was sown. I must have been born naive. I never gave a thought to the content of the poison powder, although in reflection, my father must have known how dangerous it was. Not to his credit that he gave me the job. It should have been sent away to be done under carefully-controlled and supervised conditions.

Thus, I spent a few weeks each year powder-dusting our seed wheat and barley. I could taste the ochre-coloured cloud in which I worked, breathing it in and constantly licking it from my lips. I can still distinctly recollect that flavour. Only many years later did I learn that just two of the deadly components were mercury and cadmium!

As though this was not enough of an assault on my body and health, I would spend many weeks in the grain silos when the moisture in the grain had caused it to go mouldy. When this happened, the grain 'caked' in the affected silos, and it had to be shovelled out. My job! This was an all-too-often repeated scenario.

With a handkerchief tied over my mouth, I worked in a thick cloud of mould dust as I shovelled the grain toward the outlet. For all the good the handkerchief did, I need not have bothered. Again, all this happened with the blessings of my father. I do not blame him for any of this, but today I am amazed by his sheer lack of awareness, or care. Many of the farm workers of my era who did this job on other farms in grain-growing countries long ago died of 'Farmer's Lung'. In some cases mould spores were the direct cause of death, in others the damaged lung tissue was an invitation for other fatal infections.

Okay, still in perfectly good health, let us now jump across to my farm in Tasmania, after having recently emigrated. This was a hill farm, situated on the foothills of Mt. Arthur. Although I could use a tractor on the major portion of the hills, a fair amount was too steep for this. It was on those steep slopes that blackberries grew in thick, luxuriant abundance. I always had more than enough work to do: a single person with one hundred and eighty hectares (four hundred and forty-four acres), one hundred and thirty cows, one hundred of them dairy cows to be milked twice a day, their calves to be hand fed, and about two hundred piga pigs. On our dairy farm we used to separate the milk, feeding the skimmed milk to the pigs, and selling the cream to a cheese factory. Even though Treenie helped enormously, with all the land work on top of that, I did not need to deal with blackberries.

Nevertheless, when the weather was dry and pasture in short supply, I needed the extra hectares of land that the blackberries were growing on, so I began spraying them. Because of the steepness of the land, I had to do this by hand. Looking back, I realise now that my naivety was holding hands with stupidity. The blackberry spray of those years used two ingredients out of the infamous agent orange mix used in Vietnam; these were 2,4-D and 2,4,5-T.

As I sprayed this death mix onto the blackberries, it was often blown back into my face. *Very* often! When my backpack spray container was filled, it usually slopped out of the lid as I walked, running down my back and legs to puddle in my boots. I was often soaked in the mix, especially when I slipped and fell forward on the wet, green, steepness of the slopes.

Enough—let us now return to where I mentioned that something rather extraordinary happened to me in our community. Treenie and I only lived in the community for four years before our path took us away. The extraordinary event was in my third year.

This strange event has come to mind quite often in the last few months. I realise, now, how flippantly I dismissed something that I did not understand, something that left me with a sense of awe. What happened undoubtedly saved my life, yet, at that time, I did not know that my life was at risk. I was forty-three years of age, and totally committed to my spiritual path.

Okay, with the background filled in, we will return to the present.

A few days ago I decided that I would like to go back and metaphysically see more precisely what it was that happened to me during that long-ago extraordinary process.

"Pan . . . you know what happened back then, don't you?"

You really think I sit around watching you?

I am shocked. "Pan! You're overdosing on humour."

As long as you are planning to visit yourself in the past, you will not need me to accompany you. Not even you can meddle and interfere with yourself. Just look and learn.

"I like it when you are with me. I learn more."

If I am truly needed, I will be there.

I chuckle. "Okay . . . you stay at home and practice your humour!"

I really do enjoy the playfulness of Pan, although I recognise it as a reflection of me.

Michael, start at the beginning. Go back to study the energy of the powder dusting and grain mould, as well as the chemical spray later on. Then you can progress to the incident that interests you.

"Oh . . . thank you. I would not have done that. See, just one more reason why you should be with me."

Or, you could think it through first . . . then act.

"Hmm, I thought I had."

You have a disposition toward leaping before looking . . . but it serves you well.

A faint energetic feeling as Pan withdraws. Leaping before looking—*moi!?*

Relaxing, I focus on Michael in his late teen years, when he was powder dusting our seed grain. I am not so sure I want to revisit this brash young man. But, if this is what Pan so clearly recommends, this is what I will do.

I find my thoughts wandering to some of the near-death experiences Michael had around those turbulent years, wondering why there were so many. Was he jinxed?

Dismissing them, I focus into my Light-body.

Taking a step . . . Between . . . I step out onto a field of stubble. What in the world . . . ?

I am standing in a field of wheat stubble on my late father's farm in England, while some way off a young man—Michael—is riding an old motorbike slowly across the field. Young Michael is on a 1927 Sunbeam motorcycle, and he is looking for a hare. The farm in England had a large population of hares, as did most farms in East Anglia. I watch as Michael cruises slowly, his eyes wise to the 'freeze or flight' techniques of hares. In his hands he has an old double-barrelled 12-bore shotgun, fully loaded. I remember this; young and stupid!

All that remains after the wheat has been harvested is stubble. This field would soon be ploughed up once again in the usual winter ritual. I watch the energy of this young Michael, and not surprisingly, I see the red Chaos of his inner excitement. Relaxed he may look, but he is tense, ready to snap into action. Taking my metaphysical vision very close, and into him, I see his toroidal energy is in prime condition. His field-of-energy is very strong and surprisingly large; surprising, even though I already knew this!

Suddenly, in front of the motorbike, a large hare leaps up and away. Instantly, Michael opens up the throttle of the motorbike, rapidly accelerating as he gives chase. Shotgun in his right hand, the other on a handle of the motorcycle, he goes tearing after the hare. Crazy! Just at the moment when the hare was in range of the shotgun and he swings it into a pointing-at-the-hare position, the front wheel of the bike hit a sudden dip in the soil (a plough furrow). It was deep enough that Michael and the shotgun went one way, and the motorbike went another. As Michael hit the ground, there was the loud explosion of a shotgun blast, and the pellets tore up the side of Michael's shirt, without touching his skin.

I watch his field-of-energy as he lay there in shock, slowly looking at the blasted shirt, peering at his ribs, and lying back to stare at the sky in wonder. His field-of-energy opens like an umbrella, then swoops close to his body like an umbrella closing. This happens several times, as he pants for breath from the impact with the hard soil. Watching him on an inner level, I see the torus of each cell do exactly as the umbrella effect had indicated. Each torus opened fully, then closed to a tiny, almost non-existent state; then it stabilised. He was bruised and torn a little bit, but it was nothing. I watch as he reflects on the miracle of being alive. I watch as he decides that this was stupid. I watch as he decides that his angel is looking after him. And as I watch, I see *something* withdraw from the scene.

This really startles me. What was it that ensured his safety? Had it been an angel, I would have easily seen it. I know angels — or at least, on a metaphysical basis. Was it — could it have been

5v.

Pan? No. This does not *feel* right. What I saw was an energy-field, but there was nothing else. Normally, there is a Being, or person, or animal, insect, whatever, within the energy-field. Hmm, this does not make sense. And why am I here? Did my thoughts simply wander into the narrow escapes from death in Michael's late teens, early twenties—or were they gently nudged with a very subtle touch? Alone, huh! This is Pan's compulsion.

I watch Michael as he shakily gets to his feet, staring at the intact shotgun and walking over to the undamaged motorcycle. I hear him mutter about this being the last time he would try hunting in this way. A hare wasn't worth it! I agree! Already his field-of-energy is rapidly calming, the excited, shaken red Chaos giving way to a fairly even black of Order. It is certainly not Balance, but a calm, stable place within himself.

Without any intent or direction from me, I am stepping . . . Between . . . emerging on the cliffs of Whitby, also in England. Okay, what is going on here?

"PAN!" Not a sound or feeling of Pan. Hmm . . . !

Despite my initial confusion, I instantly know why I am here. At least, I do if another close brush with death is what this is all about. And of course it is. Those stray thoughts of close calls with death just as I stepped Between are what this is all about. I know Pan is behind this, but why? What am I supposed to learn? I already know that Michael was a reckless young idiot. Perhaps I need to remember that he was also careless!

I watch as another familiar scene unfolds. Michael is climbing the steps that wind up the steep, grass-covered Whitby Cliffs to get a good view of the shoreline and ocean. With him is Treenie, who Michael has just met for the first time at Robin Hood's Bay. They met on a week-long youth-club holiday. With them are two friends, David and Rosemary, who have also just met. Eventually, as they climb, they came to a large scoop in the sheer cliff face where they could sit on the wild stringy grass and admire the view. And it was hot, very hot in the long dry English summer of 1955.

The scoop in the cliff face could have fitted maybe twelve people at a squeeze, so there was plenty of room for the four of them. As I metaphysically watch the group, they sit in the hot sun chatting. I can see the heat getting to them as they all began to feel ever more drowsy. Soon, Rosemary lay back sleepily. "Just going to close my eyes for a moment," she said, as she fell asleep. Then David lay back and closed his eyes.

"Everyone's getting sleepy," Michael said. "Even me!"

For Michael to sleep during the day generally meant he was ill. But it was *very* hot, a natural sun trap. Treenie lay back and closed her eyes, falling asleep almost instantly.

I watch Michael as he stares at Treenie, completely smitten. He had no idea that they would share the next fifty-one years of their lives; forty-eight of them married.

I watch as Michael falls asleep. He is very close to the edge of the cliff, but facing away from it. Having no fear of heights, he is unconcerned. Okay—careless! Maybe an hour passes.

Michael groans, then, still half-asleep, he begins to roll over onto his other side. As he is halfway over, for a split second, I see a *something* interposed with him, then it is gone. In that instant, Michael opens his eyes—to find that he is staring pop-eyed down the cliff face at the rocks and foaming sea about sixty metres (one hundred and ninety-six feet) below him. Had he kept his eyes closed, he would have finished the roll-over on his long plunge toward a horrific death.

I watch him as he abruptly sits up, clambers to his feet, and gets well back from the edge. He is aware of how close a call it was, but is totally unaware of the *something* that intervened between him and death. He had no idea.

Watching all this, I realise why I am visiting these incidents of near death. Very clearly, I have something to learn.

Abruptly, I am back a couple or so years, still on my father's farm. This is new, stepping Between without my doing so. "Pan . . . why are we doing this?"

As expected, no reply. No suggestion that Pan is even in the neighbourhood.

Oh gosh, this is embarrassing. I am not sure that I should share the gross stupidity that I know is about to unfold. I cringe as I remember this. It seems that shaking hands with death leaves a lasting impression! I am watching a combine harvester. Michael's father is driving it as he and Michael go cutting their way round and round a field of barley. In his defence, Michael is about sixteen, heedless, brash and stupid. To be fair, he was never so much stupid as reckless; the impossible concept of his death a zillion miles away—okay, he was stupid!

In my Light-body, I watch very carefully, hoping to identify the *something* that I now know will be involved. Michael works on a platform on the harvester—this is the 1950s—taking care of the sacks of grain as they fill, dragging each one away to replace with another empty sack. Hard, sweaty, dirty work. The harvester platform held about ten sacks of grain. When the platform was full, the sacks would be dragged off and put on a nearby waiting farm trailer. Michael also has a 12-bore shotgun on the combine harvester, which he used to shoot hares as they ran from the noise and the cutting bar. His excuse was that the hares were either given away or sold for eating. Michael loved his shooting, taking pride in being a good shot. Right now, he is almost out of cartridges.

Here comes the insanity!

I metaphysically watch as a hare comes running out of the barley. Michael sees it only as it is almost out of range. He grabs the shotgun, points and shoots. The hare is hit, but keeps going slowly. As high-energy animals, hares do not die easily. Metaphysically, I see its field-of-energy as it struggles to get away. The raw, red Chaos of pain and terror pumps energy into its body as it struggles to get away, while each cellular torus is rippling and distorting.

Loathe to use another cartridge, and hating to let a wounded animal get away to slowly die, Michael jumps off the harvester and chases after the hare. It has stopped. Running up to it, Michael reverses the shotgun and, raising it high as a club, swings the butt at the hare's head. It moves, he misses—the shotgun snaps in half, firing the last cartridge that tears through his shirt under his left arm without touching his skin. This was actually the first time; the motorcycle the second—and last!

Despite watching carefully, the *something* that interposed itself between Michael and the shotgun as it snapped and fired, vanished in an instant. I watched as Michael's father stopped the harvester. Jumping off, he ran to Michael. He had seen everything, and looked even whiter with shock than Michael. I remember his anger at Michael's stupidity, and his relief that he was not dying from a shotgun blast.

Okay, so I am revisiting Michael's stupidity, and I know that something is protecting him from himself, but I do not have a clue who, or what it is, or what it may be.

"Pan . . . enough! I don't need to see anymore. I know Michael did stupid things . . . and I have seen that *something* saved his life, every time. It's very humbling."

Nothing. Not a hint that Pan has even heard me.

Abruptly, I am again involuntarily stepping . . . Between . . . and out once more. This time I am with that powder dusting machine that I used to turn by hand for a few weeks each year.

Michael is working in the cloud of ochre-coloured dust, with no protection whatsoever.

Pan suggested that I study the energy of this dusting powder and the mould dust in the silos. Hmm, I'm not sure what I should look for.

Naturally, Michael is completely oblivious to my presence. I am a metaphysical field-of-energy; Michael is a field-of-energy operating within a physical foundation. He is busily engaged in turning the handle on the wheel that spins the cylinder in which seed grain and lethal powder are being thoroughly mixed. I can see why Michael quickly grew strong; the dirty jobs were invariably hard work.

However, this brush with death is a very slow-acting one, and I am here to see the energy of the powder. Metaphysically, I focus into it—yikes! I know almost nothing of chemistry, so I do not know what I am looking at on a physical basis, but from an energetic viewpoint, I am seeing death by toxic poisons. The ochre-coloured dust cloud is seething with the red of a very hostile Chaos. This stuff is anti-life! The torus of each cell of the dust particles is a tortured torus. As I look, I realise that if each component were isolated this would not be so, but the mixture of these toxins causes an energetic reaction that, literally, tortures the components.

Fascinated, I look into Michael's field-of-energy. This is not good. The toxins are being inhaled with his every breath, and have spread throughout his body via his bloodstream. I am shocked to see that they are accumulating in his brain and bone marrow. This is *horribly* not good. When heavy metals visit a body, they tend to overstay. This nasty mix of toxins would remain with him for many years to come.

I need shift in time only a fraction to be watching Michael as he shovels mould-caked grain out of the affected silos. In our farm silos the moisture content of the grain should be no more than 12% maximum. This mould develops at 16% and over. A faulty reading on the moisture tester could cause this, but more often it was the rush and hurry of a wet harvest when the grain was put in the silo for just a week or so—and overlooked until too late.

The blue/grey mould dust that billows around Michael is far thicker than the powder dust, but not so purely toxic. It works in a different way. As I zoom in on the mould spores, it is clear that each spore is living, and they continued to live in Michael's lungs as he breathed them in. I shudder. His lungs retain a seething array of living mould in their tissue, but this does not seem to travel in his blood to other parts of his body. The mould spores show the red of Chaos only because they have been disturbed from their place in the damp grain. Even in Michael's lungs the spores show no bad red of Chaos, but obviously this is not a good place to grow them!

Okay, so by the time I emigrated I was walking death, what with heavy metal toxins and a few trillion mould spores residing in my lungs. So, where now?

Nothing happens. No shift Between. No me going anywhere!

I wait. Waiting.

Nothing. More nothing.

A lot more nothing.

"Pan . . . what are we waiting for?"

Nothing! This is ridiculous. Pan said he would not be with me, yet I continue talking to him as though he is. Hmm, brain toxins!

What am I missing? Toxic powder, mould spores, and now I am waiting to be whisked away to see the energetic poison of chemical spray.

Ah ha. Focus on chemical spray, and step Between. I try—nothing.

No Between.

This is getting serious. Carefully I revise all that I have seen. Have I missed something? Have I made an assumption? I revise my thoughts and focus. Maybe my thoughts about emigrating as living death were exaggerated. It's got to be something. Ah, did I see the *something* in the powder and mould dust? No, I did not. Look again.

THE MYSTERY OF MICHAEL

Once more I focus on Michael in the toxic dust, and Michael in the mould dust. I look very, very carefully for a *something*. I do not see it. But as I watch, I notice something that is strange. Michael does not cough, not in either of the two different types of dust. He seems to breathe easily, despite the fact that he should not be able to. I change my way of looking at him, and I see a gossamer thin coating of Light surrounding every cell in his body. It is most especially concentrated in his lungs and brain, but oh, so very nebulous. Even my metaphysical vision struggles to see it. I am having to use metaphysical sensory perception to perceive it, rather than actually see it.

Automatically, I focus on Michael at the time of his emigration. Yes! My deepest sense of metaphysical perception is aware of the Light around every cell. Why? How? Is this normal?

I stare at Treenie, who is with him. Straining my metaphysical sensory perception to its limit, I am unable to perceive any Light coating the cells in her physical body.

The 'why' of my question is obvious. The Light kept Michael alive. Which still leaves—why me? Is this normal? What *is* normal? Normal is a word we use for consensus reality, while this life-preserving Light expresses from a greater reality.

I must have learned what was needed, for suddenly—I am back in action.

I have involuntarily stepped . . . Between . . . and out to Tasmania, on my steep hillside hectares of blackberries.

This is where Michael danced with death: his partners, the deadly 2,4-D and 2,4,5-T.

There he is—the spray in its metal backpack tank, slopping as it usually did, while he doggedly slogs his way up or down the steep slopes to get at the blackberries. Even as I watch, the wet spray is gusting into his face as the breeze eddies and swirls in the gulley. He slips on the wet vegetation, and a copious cupful slops

257

from the loose-fitting cap of the tank to run down his neck. Oh, great! I am obviously here to see him at his careless, stupid worst!

"Okay, Pan. Enough. Point taken."

Remembering that I need to observe the deadly mix metaphysically, I look into it on a cellular level. Oh, my gosh! This is worse than the powder and mould dust combined. This is an odious, seething, anti-natural red Chaos. Reluctantly, I now look into Michael's body on the same cellular level. I see no mixture. All I see is ugly red Chaos spilling through his skin and being inhaled, entering his bloodstream through his skin, lungs, eyes and mouth. And, as before, that scarcely perceived gossamer coating of micro-fine Light over every cell is somehow protecting him from too much physical damage. He had no idea. Although in a different expression, this Light is the *something* that intervened each time Michael was about to do himself physical injury. He was very well protected—but by whom, or what?

Once more, I involuntary step . . . Between . . . and out into a small valley next to the Cotter Dam, close to Canberra in Oz. Why am I here? Abruptly, I know.

This is where Michael was attacked by a madman.

Yikes—I hope Pan is not trolling through all Michael's misadventures. I've had enough. What is to be gained by any of this?

"Pan . . . can you simply lift me out of here? Please! Let's just assume the *something* intervened in this incident also. What can it teach me that I haven't already learned?"

Nothing. "PAAAN!"

Nothing. I sigh. I suppose I'll just have to see this through.

This was 1976, a few months prior to the commencement of the Homeland community. Michael was with a group of his friends at the site of the first 'Back To Earth Festival' in Oz. About ten thousand hippies, New Age folk, musicians and dancers, artists, etc., all came together to celebrate their rising consciousness. Also

attracted were hangers-on, but they were a tiny minority. Oh—
and one madman. Okay, I'll be kind—one seriously deranged
man!

This was Michael's first and only visit to the Cotter. With his
friends, they shared a campsite close to the river running through
the valley. Michael was there for about five days. It was on the
second morning that he met a guy who seemed to want to befriend
him. The man was a weight-lifter, with the appropriate bulky
muscular development. Michael thought he was a bit strange the
times they chatted, but, his naivety intact, he did not take much
notice. The man clearly had anger issues, which Michael rather
unwisely dismissed.

On the fourth day Michael was walking along the riverside
track, when this guy leapt out from the shadows of a huge
boulder, putting a stranglehold on Michael from behind. He was
muttering about saving the children. He was going to kill Michael
because he thought that Michael was planning to kill all the
children. For Michael, the penny dropped—the man was nuts! If
you should ever end up in a gorilla's stranglehold, you will find
that it is painful and scary.

From my metaphysical viewpoint, I am watching as all this
happens. I see the fright on Michael's face, then the following look
of determination. Michael had decided that two of them were
going into the shockingly cold river, and only he was coming out.
Then, before he could lunge sideways to take them both into the
river, I see a flash of *something* interpose itself between Michael
and the man with the stranglehold. Suddenly, holding onto the
strangling arm, Michael drops his bodyweight downward as his
teenage years of judo training kicked in, and with a twist he comes
up, bringing the arm around and up behind the guy's back.

Despite the guy's outburst of swearing, Michael forced the
hand and wrist higher and higher until it was at the back of his
neck, and the man finally pitched forward onto his face. Locking
him into place with his farm-honed core strength, Michael shouted

to a number of people who, with dropped jaws, were watching all this. "Get the police, quick!" Michael held the man's arm in a position that should have broken it, until the police—who were already patrolling the festival grounds—arrived. Watching all this, I see the sweat on the guy, his giant muscles straining as he tried to get free. I see his glaring eyes, his pupils tiny pinpoints of hate and anger.

Michael was thankful when the police took him away. He told them what had happened, and that the man was very dangerous. Michael never saw him again. He heard later that the guy had apparently calmed down very quickly, and seemed so rational and contrite that the police released him. Next day, he had a large drum of petrol on the top of a Landrover, attempting to blow it up. He was screaming that someone was trying to kill the children. Ironic that he was the only person trying! This time the police took him into psychiatric custody.

Watching all this unfold, I now knew why, in an attack where all rationale and logic indicate that Michael should have been convincingly strangled, he was able to reverse the situation. The *something* had intervened.

I still had no idea what that *something* was!

Another involuntary step . . . Between . . . and I am standing in the front garden of our farm house in Tasmania. Okay, I know this one!

"Pan . . . please, I'm fed up with this. Can we speed it up . . . please?"

As I metaphysically watch, (The full story is in *A Glimpse of Something Greater*) Treenie and Michael had two Sunday afternoon visitors. They were admiring the lovely garden when, suddenly, a farm neighbour came marching up to Michael with a rifle—which later proved to be loaded. Pointing the gun at Michael, he accused him of stealing his six thousand dollar stud bull. Treenie had slipped away when they first saw the neighbour approaching with the gun, and phoned the police. It took them nearly an hour to arrive, the whole time of which the agitated and angry neighbour held the gun on Michael. Michael kept talking to hold the neighbour's attention, because their visitors were clearly not enjoying the afternoon's entertainment.

To keep this short, the police arrived and took the neighbour away, not Michael. The police were annoyed with Michael because he refused to press charges against the demented neighbour. He figured the poor man already had enough problems! The six thousand dollar bull turned out to be a borrowed, six hundred dollar bull, which Michael found in one of his paddocks the very next day! The deranged neighbour ended up detained in a psychiatric prison hospital.

As I metaphysically watch this scene unfold, I am looking for the *something*. At first I cannot not see it, but with that extra perceptual extension of my normal metaphysical level of awareness, I finally realise that it is coated over the rifle! This suggests that in some esoteric manner, the gun was no longer under the neighbour's control.

"Pan . . . a question. I get the feeling that, metaphysically, Michael knew he could not be shot. Is this true?"

No reply. Yet, it is true. I *know it*. Michael felt preternaturally calm throughout the whole incident—when he had every reason not to! The visitors were completely freaked out.

I wait for my involuntary step from here . . . to wherever . . . but nothing happens. No involuntary shifts. I wait—and I wait.

"So are we done? Am I in control again now?"

Yikes! What is wrong with me? I keep having a conversation with Pan, and I have yet to see, feel, or perceive any indication that he is with me. Yet he must be. Something keeps on moving me around to its own agenda!

Finally, I realise that I am again in control of my metaphysical journey.

Focussing on the remarkable incident that happened when I was at the Homeland community, I step . . . Between . . . and out into the community.

How the community came about is not important here—that story, along with others, is also in the aforementioned book. Michael named it The Homeland Foundation, Centre of Light, and with an average of around forty 'inmates', he spent a lifetime of four years in his self-made prison. Today, I have no connection with Homeland, but for those four years it was the whole focus and inspiration of Michael's life. It was definitely vital in his developing spirituality and eventual enlightenment. I regard them as years well spent!

I, the metaphysical Mixael, am now watching the unfolding events that happened to the physical Michael at Homeland. The year is 1979.

I intend to take careful note of what happened to Michael, for it was beyond all physical normality. For the previous two years, he had been going through a torrid time, learning lesson after lesson about himself. However—apart from mentioning that the prior two years were spent in the equivalent of a non-stop emotional cement mixer, being thrown, twisted, and pounded through every emotional contortion and confrontation that he had long avoided—this is not the book in which to share such stories or concerns.

Enough to say that Michael was at a crisis point. He knew this, but only on a vague level. He went the usual route of attempting to understand what was happening to him, but he failed. He knew that physically he was quite ill, and that emotionally he was wiped out, but his act was of strong and competent normality. He was not sure if other people believed in it, but rather astonishingly, he did! The term today is—chronic avoidance.

Our main concern here is the crisis point.

One day, which began as normally as community life can begin, Michael consigned himself to work in the garden. All went well until late afternoon, when he began to feel rather strange. Most people at Homeland lived in small or medium-sized caravans (trailers); Michael's and Treenie's was one of the biggest. He walked back to their caravan rather earlier than usual and lay down. Treenie asked him what was wrong, to which he replied that he felt a bit strange, a bit light-headed. He felt unwell enough to undress and get into bed.

Gradually, the strangeness intensified. He began to shiver, *really* shiver. He was freezing in the warm-temperate valley. Then, just as suddenly, he was sweating profusely, *really* sweating. By late evening, Michael could hear himself raving in complete delirium. He heard Treenie say she was going to take his temperature, again. Having raised four children, they had the usual Fahrenheit thermometer of those days, and Treenie was skilled in the common practice of taking temperatures and reading the thermometer. Michael felt the thermometer slide under his tongue, watching her in a very detached way as she took it out. Under a bright light, she read the temperature, frowned, then read it again. She turned white.

"Wassup?" he slurred.

She looked at him. "Your temperature is 106 F."

Michael giggled. "Being pickled." He could hear himself giggling.

"No doctors. I'llll be awlllright."

All that night and halfway through the next day, he alternately sweated and froze. When he shivered, he could not stop his teeth from rattling. When hot, he sweated profusely. His sweat smelled so vile and horrible that Treenie slept in one of the bunk beds.

Within thirty-six hours from the onset of the fever, Michael was recovering. In two days he was fully recovered. What was that all about, they wondered? They read some literature about human temperatures, about how it is supposed to be dangerous to let the body go over 105 F. Most said that 106 F was when the brain could be damaged and the body could die. Michael said they were obviously wrong, but he conceded that he had been in a dangerous temperature zone.

As Mixael, I am taking you through this in a step-by-step account of that time, while I am metaphysically watching it in the way of a fast-forward movie.

No big deal, Michael thought at the time; high temperature, very unpleasant, all over.

He was wrong.

Late one afternoon, about three weeks later, he began to feel shaky, light-headed, and rather strange. Oh no, he thought, not again. The reality was, 'oh yes'. Within an hour, he was again in bed shivering and shaking under nearly all the bedclothes they possessed. Then the sweating began. About five hours later his physical body was sweating profusely, his temperature raging. He was burning up. Treenie took his temperature several times, getting more tight-lipped on each occasion. She did not tell him what the reading was. It was only later she told him that he was nudging well over 106 F. At some point during all this, Michael was forced out of his physical body, moving in his astral-body to a place at the top left corner of the caravan where he could watch both his physical body and Treenie. He spoke to her, telling her not to worry, but she could not hear him. He kept trying to reassure her, forgetting that they were now in different realities.

Not for a moment did Michael fear for his life. It simply did not occur to him, despite all he had read about the danger of body temperatures going too high. The stench that came from his sweat was truly awful, absolutely revolting.

Once again, in about thirty-six hours he was recovering, and in two days was back to normal.

This cycle continued every three weeks for nine months. The worst was yet to come.

Michael and Treenie were staying in Sydney, N S W, with some friends. There was to be a party for Virgos, and as this was Treenie's star sign, they were both going. At four o'clock in the afternoon, Michael knew that he would not be going. He told Treenie that he was very sorry, but 'you know what' is coming back. For some reason they both thought it had ended. Treenie was very frustrated to be missing the party. She told Michael with some fervour that he should wait until they got home in a couple more days. *Then* he could be ill!

Nevertheless, the fever took hold again, and in about four hours Michael was raving. Treenie had the thermometer—just in case!—and duly recorded his temperature. This time it was 107 F. Treenie went white with shock and anxiety. Luckily, their hosts had already gone to the party, reassured by Treenie that Michael's fever was just a little passing flu! What she later described as Michael's raving was very different from his reality. He was attempting to tell her what he was seeing. In their bedroom he saw four Beings-of-Light, one at each corner. Their focus was on Treenie, not him! He thought that seemed unfair, considering! Between them, in perpetual flight without going anywhere, was a white dove with a banner trailing daintily behind it. On the banner were the words 'Remember the Golden Dawn'. By now, much to Michael's distress, Treenie was lying on a spare mattress on the floor, frightened, and softly crying.

As Michael watched, a shaft of white Light came down through the ceiling onto Treenie, and she immediately fell asleep. He knew that she would be okay. The Light-Beings then turned toward Michael. They did not speak aloud, but he clearly inner-heard a message for him to just endure, that all was well no matter how high his temperature, and that this process would last for as long as it took for the purification of his physical body.

Treenie was cheerful enough the next day, apologising to Michael for being annoyed with him in his state of distress. He was still going through raging, stinking fever, and bouts of shocking chill, but it was good for him to hear. They agreed; no doctors. Michael told her what he had inner-heard. Maybe they were the words two naive adults needed to hear, but they trusted this inner-guidance implicitly.

Three weeks later, back in the community, the fever struck again. Michael had reached the stage where he knew a couple of hours before the first symptoms that the fever was visiting again. And so this continued for nine months. Later, Michael could not help but attempt to correlate his nine months of fevers with a human pregnancy. But what was going to be birthed?

The last time Michael had the raging fever was one of the times of complete delirium. His temperature was again nudging over 106 F, but he was striding over the planet Earth in boots that allowed him to take giant strides; ten kilometres and increasingly becoming more gigantic. As he got used to it, he was crossing countries and continents in huge, giant strides. He tried to share this with Treenie as he strode along, but the words and meaning, which were clear to him, were total gibberish to her.

Over the years, Michael has often looked back and marvelled that Treenie never called in a doctor. She knew he did not want one, but under that sort of pressure . . . ! It quickly became obvious that Michael had been through a massive detox of a very intense nature. Fever is the tool of a healing crisis, but he had not been aware that he needed healing—or from what.

As I, Mixael, share the physical story of what I see, I am also observing its metaphysical counterpart. I say counterpart, but in truth, counterparts are equal to each other. The metaphysical and physical are considered counterparts, but the metaphysical is immortal while the physical is mortal. That hardly rates as equal!

As I metaphysically observe the fever periods that Michael endured, I am obviously looking to see where and how the *something* is involved. I am struggling to attain the necessary metaphysical state of perceiving the gossamer layer of Light coating the cells of his body. It is when looking at Michael just before the fevers begin that I get my first clue. I see that the Light coating is far less at the onset of the nine months of fevers than when I perceived it in his teenage years. As I move in closer, magnifying the energy of his cells, I see that the Light is not so much wearing thin, but is fading in intensity. Michael is now about forty-two years of age, and has had that film of Light coating the cells of his body since he was in his late teens.

I now see that, prior to the fevers, Michael's body was struggling to maintain its cellular integrity with the diminishing coating of Light. The truth is simple; without the healing crisis of raging fevers, Michael would have physically died. Watching on a cellular level while one of his fevers is raging, I see the toroidal energy of each cell going through an inside-out distortion. I gasp. The fever was a metaphysical cleansing. The physical body and the metaphysical body were working in tandem as a healing team. First the metaphysical cleansing, then the physical went through the same process. Fever is not possible in the metaphysical body, but the physical counterpart could not avoid it. Michael's natural body Intelligence was the overseer of the process, and the moment his physical body reached its absolute limit in feverish temperature, then the temperature would plunge down into the even more distressing chills. In many ways, his physical body was part of an orchestra, with the body Intelligence as the conductor. Without medical intervention, this played out brilliantly. His brain was not damaged as some medical literature said would happen at or above 106 F, nor did he die. In fact, I have often surmised that this was the point when Michael began to tap into Intelligences above and beyond the normal human contact. Michael's body was not only cleansed and healed, but his energetic vibration was lifted and enhanced.

As I watch the *something* under the conductorship of Michael's body Intelligence, waxing and waning at the most brilliantly appropriate moments during each healing crisis, I realise that the *something* could not indefinitely shield Michael from death by self-inflicted violence, or from the mercury and cadmium in the powder, or from the mould-laden spores, or the terrible toxins of 2,4-D and 2,4,5-T without the *something* jeopardising itself. I now metaphysically see that not only the metaphysical and the physical bodies were being repaired and healed, but the *something* was also being healed. But—I still do not know what it is.

"Pan, I know you are here. What is this *something*? It is time for me to know."

I am surprised you do not know.

"What is obvious to you remains mystery to me. You tricked me. Go alone, you said. I was never alone . . . and I thank you."

You so often perform better under pressure. One more journey and you will have the answer. Go back to the scene of your greatest violence.

I know exactly what he means. Another story in that aforementioned excellent book!

Focussing on the scene, I step . . . Between . . . stepping out into a field of spoilt cut hay.

Oh, dear God—now I know.

"Pan, do I have to go through with this. I absolutely know."

It would be wise to see it through to deepen your insight.

Not wishing to bore the readers who may have already read this story, I will keep it short and simple. It was early summer in England. The hay had been cut and it had rained. The hay was turned over, and it rained. Repeat this two or three more times, and the hay was almost ruined. Today was sunny, a beautiful day. At nineteen years of age, Michael was out in the field turning the hay with a pitchfork, with its two long, slightly curved tines. With him was an older man, Stan, a man filled with hate for the class system in a very class-conscious England. It is ironic, for to Michael, class did not exist. Nevertheless, Stan took his spite out on Michael. He would move into a monologue of stories, lies and half-truths about the past history of Michael's family. Michael called it his 'Litany of Spite'.

Michael had a rage problem. He was a difficult, forceps delivery and born in a rage. At school he had nearly killed another boy in a fight. Michael was afraid of his rage, afraid of what he might do. Temper is hot, and brief: his rage was icy cold, implacable. So he bore Stan's victimisation stoically, never telling his father, who was Stan's employer. Michael pushed his rage deep down, enduring the spite and torment for five years.

On this beautiful sunny morning, using the pitchforks, Stan and Michael were gently turning the hay by hand. Michael was loving it, enjoying physical labour. After an hour or so of silent work, Stan suddenly began his 'Litany of Spite' from his position behind Michael. In an uncontrollable instant, Michael's rage came to the surface. He turned, stared at Stan, and taking a step toward him, drew the suddenly deadly pitchfork back, ready to ram it into him. With a look of horror frozen on his face, Stan's eyes bulged as he knew what was about to happen. He knew Michael's strength and he knew of his rage, although he had never seen it.

Michael drew back the fork, every muscle fully tensed, ready to smash it into Stan. Just at the instant he was about to slam the pitchfork forward, an incredibly powerful wave of Love swept through him. Every cell tingling with Love energy, he felt he was glowing. Stan was still locked in place, frozen, waiting for his dreadful end, when Michael lowered the fork. In utter bewilderment, he heard himself say, "You will never be able to do 'that' to me again. I Love you." Michael was very deeply embarrassed. By 'that', he meant 'victimise', but he had never heard of the word in his youth.

Michael walked over to the other side of the field and, as the day and work continued, he was aware of the Love energy gradually fading. That dramatic moment changed his life. Stan was never able to victimise Michael again, and his class hatred dwindled away. Michael decided that his guardian angel had saved him yet again, for he attributed all his narrow escapes to her. (An angel had to be a *she* for a lusty young male!)

Many years later, when Michael Awakened, he walked his timeline, simultaneously experiencing every moment of the lifetime he was about to walk-out from. I say *simultaneously* because he entered every frame in the movie of his life in the same moment. You can do that when you are no longer in linear time.

It was not a guardian angel who had saved Michael from life imprisonment; it was the Awake and enlightened Michael himself.

Newly enlightened, and in his timeless Light-body, Michael placed his hand on the shoulder of teenage Michael, allowing him to feel the Love/Light of Self. Flooded with Love—the moment was changed. Michael then followed the path that would take him to enlightenment, which in turn allowed him to step back and change that terrible moment—which allowed him to follow the path which would take him to enlightenment . . . allowing him to step . . . !

This I had previously learned. Now, however—on entering this reality-frame, I had instantly known exactly what the *something* was in each incident I have mentioned—there were more! The *something* was Michael—or to be accurate, his Love/Light energy. An enlightened Michael was protecting the younger Michael on his path to enlightenment. Enlightened Michael was keeping Michael alive so that he could follow the path of his greatest probability, reaching the probable moment of his conscious enlightenment. You have to agree—this gives a whole new depth and meaning to holistic!

Only after Michael had simultaneously walked his timeline and created the probability changes in his own current lifetime, did Michael walk-out.

And I—Mixael—walk-in.

All of which begs a few questions.

"Pan, does this, or can this happen to other people?"

*This was **not** a special selection for a special person by a special committee of Light Beings; this was the result of Michael becoming spiritually enlightened. The enlightened Michael went down his lifeline* *to his own birth. From that point, he made all the probabilities favour him to reach the moment of enlightenment.*

"But that sounds incredibly . . . unfair!"

Life is not a competition. You know this. You also know that each person creates their own reality. When Michael stepped into his own timeline, he was living each moment of his life simultaneously — metaphysically and physically — thus he was able to influence the choices that confronted him. He created this for himself. This is no privilege that took place. He was not a chosen one. He exercised his creative power as an enlightened man.

"So . . . does this mean that anyone who becomes spiritually enlightened can then ensure that their past is re-created to lead to the perfect outcome in their future?"

Michael . . . focus. What you call 're-created' is not the past being changed; it is creation in the moment of creation. All time occupies the same space.

"Oh . . . my . . . gosh! Of course. I just never realised that timelessness could be turned into such a personal metaphysical triumph. When I take timelessness into this context, it all makes perfect holistic sense. It even expands my view of holistic!"

Sensible holistic creation must surely make perfect holistic sense!

Yes, it certainly does. Hopefully, as Mixael, I am no longer making and compounding a buildup of linear errors. I like to think that I am more fully synchronised in the moment of creation; that which we call life.

"Thank you, Pan, for not being with me while you were with me. I told you I learn more when you are with me, even if you are not with me."

Focussing on my study, I step . . . Between . . . and home once more.

Because I relate to myself in everyday physical life as Michael, this has been an amazing journey into self-discovery. It was also rather tricky to write, clarifying which me is me. When metaphysically journeying I relate to myself as Mixael, so looking at the past of Michael was quite challenging inasmuch as keeping the identities separate, when, so far as the physical world is concerned, they are one and the same.

In my life now, I am steadily moving toward being the soul-Being I truly am—Mixael.

TWELVE

Exploring Dimensional Shifts

I heard recently on an Internet YouTube that there are now more hits on the Internet concerning 2012 than there are on pornography. What criteria for comparison! Having no interest in sexual deviation, I am not really sure what this indicates, but it suggests that people who are hung up on sex are now able to get hung up on fear. And it is the fear of the unknown that drives this need to know what *might* happen. The other big YouTube attraction now is dimensional shifts—namely from three-dimensional reality into fifth-dimensional reality, plus plenty of catastrophic Earth Changes. Much of what I have listened to on the Internet is purely trite speculation. Some is based in religious fervour, and there are more than a few manic theories, but I concede that there are those who say it close to the way the course of probabilities indicate.

There are a few people on the Internet who claim to have heard directly from a divine source, and are stating *this is how it will be.* This is biased and unwise, for it will decide the course and actions of many people who may take this as divine guidance. It is definitely not my experience. Nothing is set and fixed about the future. If it is, then we are no more than puppets with no control over our destiny. The opposite is true; the way we live determines our destiny.

I concede that the many people of a consensus reality will most probably have a consensual experience of Change/dimensional shift, but first and foremost, each person will continue to create their own reality. If five or six billion people create the same consensual reality, so be it, but it will be a reality manufactured from *old reactions* rather than *new choices*.

The probability of a dimensional shift is a strong one. But when I listen to some of the speculation about the third and fifth dimensions, I get the impression that these people see dimensions in the way of a high-rise building. We live on the third floor, and the fifth floor is just above us. All we have to do is go up two flights of stairs and we are in a higher dimension. The fourth dimension seems to be a floor that nobody lives on!

I am not mocking this. When Earth Changes visit or dimensional shifts take place, I honestly do not think there will be much to mock. Okay, people like me—and there are many of us—may well feel an inner rejoicing, because we happen to believe that an upliftment in human consciousness is vital for our future. But in the full flux of Change, we are all very much on our own; we will need our own clear-headed or heart-felt insight. Internet guidance based in pure sensibility would be valuable and appropriate, rather than rigid statements of what *will* happen. Such statements are so often biased speculation or prejudiced channeling. I think it was after I heard that we will all be picked up by a fleet of spacecraft that I quit the Internet. I do concede that I only browsed a few of the endless links on the Internet about the issues of Change, and I accept there may be some very good guidance available. Nevertheless, my advice is to follow *your* heart feeling/knowing, rather than someone else's cerebral or channeled speculation.

I also heard on an Internet YouTube that there will be a day of darkness during the period of the dimensional shift. Another person said there will be two days of darkness, and yet another that there will be three days of darkness. The probability is high that one of them will be correct. Although whether it is one, two or three days of darkness hardly matters. Add to this no electricity anywhere on the planet, and darkness takes on another meaning. Then add to this no moon or starlight, and the darkness is no longer our normal night darkness. It is absolute pitch darkness; a form of sensory deprivation. Three days of this would be an interesting dynamic to see where we are at, both individually and collectively.

These were my thoughts after browsing the Internet. I had been looking for some clear and capable person who might share from an unbiased 'probability' viewpoint. But all that I found were statements of *this is what will happen*, or *this is how it will be*. Sorry, I do not buy that. While I fully accept that what these people speak of are definite *probabilities*, they are not the *certainties* in the way that they are stated. It eventually occurred to me that having offered my experiences of Earth Change probabilities, maybe I could investigate the repercussions of a dimensional shift. Maybe I could offer my insights in the closing of this book. At the very least it would do no harm, while at best it may clarify insights, alleviate fears, and offer a heart direction for some people.

I turn my thoughts toward my beloved teacher.

"My intentions are always known to you. Where do I go to learn more about dimensions and dimensional shifts?"

I would think your family in a fifth-dimensional reality would be the obvious choice.

I sigh. "Why didn't I think of that? You're right . . . it was just too obvious."

Another journey for you on your lonesome.

"Yeah . . . right. Every time I think I'm alone, you are pulling my strings."

Be fair. Only when they need pulling. I am quite sure that Cardifer and Carienne will keep you out of any meddling.

"Pan, I do **not** meddle. I get involved. And I do **not** need a chaperone. Your and their companionship is very welcome, but not as old mother hens looking after a chick."

I inner-feel Pan chuckle. *Enjoy your journey.*

It is considerably later before I am settled in my study and ready for metaphysical journeying. I have spent some of the time keeping Cardifer and Carienne in my thoughts so they will be expecting me.

Relaxing, and moving into the altered state of consciousness where I engage my Light-body, I step . . . Between . . . and out into the garden of Carienne and Cardifer's home. I glance around in surprise; the garden has changed.

Hello, Mixael. With these words, Carienne runs up to me, embracing my Light-body in such a loving way that I feel it as a touch of warmth. *Welcome my friend,* Cardifer says, very gently hugging my Light-body.

We have picked up enough of your mental broadcast that we are reasonably sure we know why you are here, Carienne says.

You want to chat about dimensions, eh? Cardifer adds. *But come along inside, our chairs remember you and are waiting.*

"Remember me?"

Why of course. You have an energy-field that goes into their memory storage. Once you have engaged their comfort and they know your energy, they remember you.

"Wow! That's amazing."

Actually, it is a fifth-dimensional creation.

"You said 'chairs', but I always sat in the same one. You mean they communicate?"

Cardifer laughs. *They share information.*

Once inside their remarkable home, I choose a different chair, and recline in its luxury.

"Gosh, smart chairs. So . . . what can you tell me about fifth-dimensional reality? It is assumed—with good reason—that we may be going through a dimensional shift this year, 2012, and I would like to know more about it."

Carienne, who is sitting close to me, speaks, *Mixael, this is one of the prime factors behind your decision to walk-in to Michael's body in the 20ᵗʰ century. The idea was to bring your emotional body to a state of completeness while you integrated into that period. Then you would be able to contribute your wisdom and consciousness during the period of change. From our viewpoint many probabilities are still in place. Some of the most frightening probabilities have been either erased or greatly reduced by the growing consciousness of the more aware percentage of your people.*

"That's really good to know. So the probability of serious disasters is reduced?"

I did not say that. The probability of disasters through earthquakes, tsunamis, cyclones, and the like, which are related to Earth Changes are reduced, because the consciousness of the more aware people connects with the planet itself. The consciousness of the masses is connected to such things as nuclear power stations, huge dams, the inner workings of cities, electricity, finances, electronic communications and such. All these, and more, are created by people.

"That makes sense. I had not seen the distinction. So while the probability of Earth-based disaster has lessened, the human-based disasters remain. How do we reduce them?"

You know the answer to this. If the greater percentage of the population raises their consciousness toward Love, compassion and care for humanity . . . everything changes.

"Carienne . . . you are talking about consensus reality change. Consensus reality is the more-of-the-same type, the stuck-in-the-mud mentality, the old consciousness of die-hards."

Then my dear, there is a probability they will die hard!

"Oh! Then I'll draw comfort from the fact there is no real death, and that we each create our own realities. This is certainly going to be a time of *epic* growth potential. I say 'going to be', but the reality is we are already in it. The financial system is collapsing, despite all efforts to correct it, or the pretence that it will improve, and everything will be as it was. 'If' or 'when' it finally crashes will contain a growth potential in itself. This turmoil is stemming from the new expressions of human consciousness clashing with the old."

Which brings us back to the dimensional shift.

I chuckle. "I got distracted."

No, it all connects. Everything your frame-of-reality faces is connected to consciousness.

"Yes, absolutely. So, tell me about fifth-dimensional reality."

Mixael . . . why don't you tell us?

"Huh? I came here to learn from you."

My dear, you are lapsing toward being the former Michael. And, I may add, Michael is no longer the former Michael. He, too, is an enlightened soul. Mixael, you left a fifth-dimensional reality to walk-in to a third-dimensional reality, but you remain a fifth-dimensional person. Do you honestly believe that you could be here now, talking with us in your metaphysical body, if you were living a three-dimensional reality? How many people of third, fourth or even fifth dimensions do you encounter during your mystical journeys? As we told you on your previous visit, few of our people can manage to do what you so effortlessly do.

Carienne's words hit me like a soft and loving punch in my heart; a punch with impact. I feel something shift, as though a hidden shadow is pulled aside, and suddenly an inner sun is shining—a sun that I know, I had known—that somehow I lost my connection with. I take a deep breath as a wave of some higher emotion sweeps through me. Tears trickle down my physical cheeks, but it is of pure joy as some deep, long-contained, inner-knowing is released.

I look deep into her eyes. "Carienne . . . from my heart, I thank you."

You are very welcome. I have to say that I cannot comprehend what it must be like to make the journey back into a lower dimensional reality in the way that you have.

"It is like stepping into a prison, locking the door, and joining everyone else in prison. But because nobody knows they are imprisoned, we all live an illusion of what we think is freedom . . . but it is not freedom. Add to that, it is like stepping into a dream and joining everyone else in the dream, but because nobody realises that we are dream-living in a dream, we all dream different versions of the same dream . . . versions of unimaginable loss."

Carienne gives a little shudder. *I find it difficult to comprehend. So my dear, give us a summary of what you remember of fifth-dimensional reality.*

I take another deep breath. As I have mentioned before, this is not about breathing; it is a human reflex to do with relaxing — an inner releasing, a letting go.

I take a timeless moment to focus within myself, within Mixael. I intend to tap into the quintessential self that for so long has been submerged in my three-dimensional reality. Mixael's talents have not been unused, obviously, and increasingly they have become apparent, but never have they been fully released. And even now that release will be a gentle, ongoing process.

"I'll probably ramble a bit as I pull it together, so be patient. Dimensions are basically about consciousness. I think that most people look on dimensions as structure and form, but this is only part of the story. I'll keep this really simple. If you make a wafer-thin pencil line on a flat piece of paper, the line represents a one-dimensional reality; length. Flatland life would be *very* contained in this reality. If you fuse the pencil line with the piece of paper as one, it represents a two-dimensional reality; length and width. Now Flatland life could move forward and backward, and side to side. A bit better! If you crumple the paper with the pencil line, you now have a three-dimensional reality; length, width, and height. No longer Flatland, life can now move up and down, forward and backward, and from side to side. That's us . . . although dolphins physically do it better than we do. So . . . this takes care of the physical aspect. Am I making sense?"

Carienne laughs. *It's a novel way to describe it.*

"Obviously the consciousness of a three-dimensional person would be unable to properly express in a one- or two-dimensional reality, but the reverse is also true. A one- or two-dimensional person would be overwhelmed and horrified by a three-dimensional reality. So with the structure of a three-dimensional reality in place, the next few dimensions are about the consciousness of whoever is growing in the dimensional realities. In our three-dimensional world, we have a wide range of human consciousness. Each level of consciousness has its own frequency. A person of low consciousness and low frequency has a different experience of life in a three-dimensional reality than a person with a higher frequency from a raised consciousness. Consciousness is not like a weed; it does not just grow, regardless. More like a cultivated plant, it has to be fed and nurtured to grow. The basic fertiliser for the growth of human consciousness is pure, divine Love. How am I doing? Any corrections?"

Cardifer smiles. *Quite the opposite. I'm impressed. Please continue.*

"In my reality we are in the throes of a dimensional shift. It's happening. This is creating a greater polarising of people than ever before. Anger, rage and violence are growing in the lower frequency, while compassion, care and Love are growing in the higher frequency. The lower frequency people have fixed and rigid beliefs; they cling to habits and want a structured life with little change in it. None of this is bad or wrong, I am simply indicating that people are moving into one frequency or the other—polarising. We are now reaching the pivotal point where the lower and higher levels of consciousness will be compelled to move in different directions. They will each move toward their own. A bit like 'birds of a feather flock together'. Consideration, care and compassion no longer need to be bullied by blame, rage and anger. This compulsion to move apart involves a fourth-dimensional reality, because a fourth-dimensional reality is the result of progressive steps toward expressing a higher consciousness.

"The core of our planet Earth is solid, probably rock and metals, spinning in a huge outer core of molten liquid rock. Enormous pockets of polarity deep within the Earth are now moving and shifting, particularly in the northern regions. I am over-simplifying, but as this occurs, it affects both the gravitational pull toward the centre of the Earth and the Earth's magnetic field. All this, in effect, creates a fourth-dimensional reality opportunity interacting within a physical three-dimensional reality. In turn, this opens avenues of opportunity for the people who express a higher consciousness. For the lower frequency people, the very idea is a joke. For higher frequency people, it offers the opportunity for telepathy with other dimensional Beings. It creates the opportunity to attune with our own bodies and heal ourselves by directed Loving focus. It allows for self-empowerment of a higher calibre. It means that thought and emotion directed from a higher consciousness are more empowered to create or heal whatever they focus on."

I pause. *You are on a roll,* Carienne says, laughing. *It's fascinating.*

"Hmm, I'm pleasantly surprising myself. To continue; generally, the basic focus of lower consciousness is about each person saying, "What's wrong with my life? Who is to blame for it? I want more." And so on and so on; always more of the same. For them, this will be their creation. On the higher consciousness level, a fourth-dimensional reality is already operating in our third-dimensional reality. A great number of people have inadvertently connected with this higher frequency and are using it to help lift the consciousness of the masses. Interestingly, our

Internet, which has long offered the dregs of human depravity, is now also a medium for the very opposite. *Avaaz* is a global civic Internet organisation giving a voice to tens of millions of people who wish to protest against tyranny, greed and oppression, while encouraging loving care and compassion. Through *Avaaz*, a rapidly growing wave of aware and caring people finally have the means and voice to take some form of action, and protest against global domination by the powerful corrupt and degenerate cabals. But . . . I digress.

"As best as I can say it, the fourth dimension offers us the opportunity to fine-tune and master our mental faculties, and use them for a higher purpose. Many people are doing this, most are not. It is becoming obvious that all mental and emotional baggage will need to be dealt with in the fourth-dimensional reality for a person to progress onward. Fourth-dimensional reality, used with a focus of loving care and attention to the thoughts, is the bridge to a fifth-dimensional reality. *Avaaz* is a perfect example of fourth-dimensional reality being used as a step toward the peace and goodwill that a fifth-dimensional reality holds.

"This brings up another factor. In a three-dimensional reality, the big majority of people are left-brain dominant. This produces the typical subconscious, clever-holding-hands-with-stupid people who move into positions of authority. The left-brain dominant people worship at the altar of the intellect. As a generalisation, these people grow intellectually, but do not grow in consciousness. This is not implied criticism; this is what is actually happening. And, of course, there are many exceptions to this.

"Okay, now for a step into a fifth-dimensional reality. This is different again. In our third and fourth-dimensional realities, we live in linear time. We have clocks to mark the progression of seconds, minutes and hours. We have yesterday, today and tomorrow. We have a calendar to mark the progression of linear days and weeks and months and years. We are hugely oriented toward linear time. In fairness, we have needed it . . . and we still do in the way that the world works for us, or the way we have created it to work.

"It's an interesting aside that the indigenous peoples measured time by sunrise, noon, and sunset. They measured it by the seasons, by the migration of animals and birds, and by the flowering and seeding of their food plants. While they were not subjugated by time in the way that we are, they did have their own measures. I guess what I am saying is that linear time and a three-dimensional reality go hand-in-hand. Unrealised, we use linear time to bridge the emptiness of separation that we have created. In your fifth-dimensional reality you have gone beyond the third-dimensional belief that all life is separate, so you do not have to use linear time to bridge the illusion of separation.

"Anyway, the point I'm getting at is that in a fifth-dimensional reality the relationship with linear time is very changed. In a fifth-dimensional reality, we live in the moment. Of course, the paradox is that in a three-dimensional reality we also live in the moment, but we are not conscious of it. We think *ceaselessly*, and our thinking takes us out of the moment. We cannot think our way into the moment, only away from it. Most people have still not figured this out. And we never really stop thinking . . . not even while sleeping. So, our relationship is with linear time, not the conscious moment. And there is an absolutely humongous difference between them! Fifth-dimensional reality means living fully in the consciousness of the moment. Consciously living in and with immediacy."

Hence your Mayan prophecy. Linear time ends during the period of the dimensional shift.

"Gosh! I'm surprised that you know about such things. I'm also surprised that everything I came to learn from you, I'm finding within myself."

It was just waiting to emerge. If needed, we will fine-tune it when you have finished.

"Thank you, I welcome that. I think I'm going to need help soon, but one interesting aspect is that people in a fifth-dimensional reality are whole-brain. I'm right-brain dominant, and I have to say I like this. Right-brain people are very heart connected. I love the fact that the whole-brain people of a fifth dimension use conscious intelligence rather than subconscious intellect as most of us do. Your people live fully conscious all the time. In my book, *The Magic Formula*, I wrote that we need to be *more of who we are, and less of who we are not.* Sadly, in a three-dimensional reality, most people live more of who they are not, while here, in a fifth dimension, you live far more of who you are. There is a huge difference.

"I have a question. You once told me that because you have a different relationship with time in the fifth dimension, your parents are still living, appearing little older than you. Could you expand on this?"

Cardifer and Carienne look at each other, then laugh. *We were each waiting for the other,* Carienne says, smiling. *We age very slowly. This is not because we are physically superior to your people, we are not. Although I should say that when all inner conflict is ended, finished, then the physical body reflects it.*

"Excuse me for interrupting, but I disagree. You are far superior to us physically. You literally radiate health and vitality, all of you."

I will rephrase my words. We do not have bodies that are genetically superior to yours. Our bodies are superior only because we live in harmony with ourselves. When the mental and emotional bodies are in harmony, the physical body is in harmony.

"But your DNA must be more switched-on than ours. We have sixty-four codons in the double helix spiral of our DNA, but apparently only twenty are switched on. This is the current thinking. I have a slightly different theory. While we remain bogged down in three-dimensional logic and reason, dogma and beliefs, anger and blame, etc., we are unable to utilise more of our brain. The way we each use our brain is connected to the codons of the DNA. A right-brain dominant person uses their brain in a very different way from their left-brain counterpart. Right brain has a relationship more with conscious intelligence, while left brain is more with subconscious intellect. Okay, I know I have already said this, but here is my point: we cannot use *conscious intelligence* subconsciously . . . obviously! We use the intellect without knowing the difference. It is only by utilising conscious intelligence that we grow in consciousness. As we grow in consciousness, more of the codons are switched on, and more of the whole brain is available. The body is One organism, not a collection of parts. I should also add that there is now evidence that about one percent of our children are apparently immune to all disease. They appear to have four more codons switched on than the mass of humanity. Even some adults are showing this. This suggests that a new human Being is already living in our dimension, waiting for the dimensional shift. Anyway, your having many more switched-on codons in your bodies than we have in ours means that your bodies actually are superior to ours. By living in a state of harmony—body, mind, emotions and soul—you are living the potential that awaits us."

Well stated. I concur. It becomes obvious that when you are living in constant harmony with yourself, the dynamics of the body change. Add to this a focused, loving awareness consciously directed at the body, and the body thrives. The cells of our bodies reproduce far more slowly than in your reality because they become exhausted far more slowly. In turn, this means we age very slowly. Also, in the fifth dimension we have a completely different relationship with time. For us, time is holistic. We do not measure linear time. We live in the moment, the meeting place of the past, the present, and the future. When you consciously live in the moment, the probability future is One with the probability past.

I laugh. "Probability past?"

Mixael, be in the moment with me and our energy will merge, clarifying meaning. As you live in the moment fully conscious, you are living at the point of creation. All time occupies the same space . . . you know this! This means that as the future is in constant flux, so also is the past, for they occupy the same moment.

"Yes . . . of course. It was the way you used your words that threw me. I teach that the past is not set and fixed, and that we can change it. I used to teach how. But I never quite saw the past as the constant dynamic of a probability. In our three-dimensional reality we get caught up in the habitual illusion that the past is fixed and finished. I know it is not, but you have given me a whole new perspective. I now see that the past did not need to be changed, because the only fixture it had was in the structure of a three-dimensional reality belief. But then again, because of that belief structure, changing the past did, in fact, change the person's relationship with it. It set them free from a structure that was unacceptable by creating a structure that was much more serviceable. Gosh . . . all illusions. All three-dimensional games . . . and yet, for all that, they were creative and constructive, with positive outcomes.

"By the way, I smiled when you said, *Be in the moment with me and our energy will merge, clarifying meaning.* So simple, yet this is a fifth-dimensional reality. We could do this in our three-dimensional reality, but we don't. We don't even listen. We can hear a person talking, but we are not truly listening because we are too busy thinking. We can *hear* and think, but we cannot *listen* and think. True listening *is the actual merging of energy* that you mentioned. So in this way we misunderstand each other all the time. And we don't even know it is happening. We very rarely merge consciousness to get absolute clarity.

"Anyway, if you don't mind, let's return to your people's slow ageing."

Certainly. One other factor about our age is that we have no relationship with ageing. We do not have a language of age, about how old I am, or any reference to retired people, or to retirement villages, or about old age homes where people go while they wait to die. Carienne paused reflectively. *What a sad way to live. As our people live in the moment, they grow in wisdom, insight, and perception. After very long lives, people here do die, eventually leaving their bodies, but this is generally when great age and choice induces them to take the long sleep. In this gentle conscious process, they leave their physical bodies prior to another incarnation. Thus, we too grow in consciousness, eventually reaching the moment when we are able to either ascend, or incarnate into a higher dimensional reality.*

"Gosh, another higher dimensional reality. Actually, I do have some insight into a sixth- dimensional reality. At this higher frequency, a person's mental, emotional and spiritual bodies become fused, as One. In the fifth-dimensional reality, the mental and emotional bodies are . . . fine-tuned, brought into the most perfect harmony possible. The next step with such balance is full integration of the bodies. The physical frequency becomes high enough that it can fully combine with the mental, emotional and spiritual. This must be a *very* holistic Being."

Well said, Mixael. Your memories are returning. Just a little applied stimulus is all that it required.

"Which is why you suggested that 'I' tell 'you' about a fifth-dimensional reality!"

Cardifer gets to his feet. *Very impressive, Mixael. Now I suggest we go outside and see if we can stimulate your memories regarding the way our buildings are created.*

"I like that suggestion."

We walk out of their home, and I turn around to look at it. Houses in this dimensional reality are nothing like ours. There are no bricks and mortar, nor are there any houses that are square, or even rectangular. These houses are all flowing contours, with one wall flowing into another with no corners and seldom any truly straight lines. To look at it their home is fairy-like, almost bubble-like compared with ours. It looks as though a good storm would blow it away, yet the *feeling* is contrary to this; it *feels* powerful. Not so much strong as powerful.

Touch it, Mixael, Cardifer says. *I think you will be able to connect with it despite your being metaphysical. The fact that you can recline in our chairs suggests this.*

To look at their home is to see a flowing shape somewhat similar to ours, but there all similarity ends. This has a translucent appearance, even though I cannot see into it.

"It looks translucent, but I can't see into it. Are you able to?"

People cannot see into it, but we can see out of it if we so choose.

"Hmm, that's neat. You can see who is knocking on the door for a social visit!"

Cardifer chuckles. *This is a joke, right? We do not knock on doors for social visits. We connect telepathically, and if, or when, we visit—which happens often—our home opens itself to the visitor.*

"The house opens the door, or the door opens the house, or the house opens itself?"

Cardifer laughs. *Okay, enough jokes. Just place your hand on our home and connect energetically. Then you can tell us as much about house construction as is triggered in your consciousness.*

I reach out and place the flat of my hand on a section along the side of the home. Oh! My first impression is of a friendly state of consciousness. I did not expect that. Even as I speculate on whether the building is conscious or not, I know that it is. Even as I wonder if it can move, I know that it cannot. As I wonder if this is a type of artificial intelligence, I know that it is a fusion of human consciousness, Nature consciousness, and the consciousness of—emotion!

This is a surprise. "How can emotion be a state of consciousness?"

Carienne smiles at me. *How could it not be?*

I stare at her, stunned. And like a rising sun, my hand still on the house, Light shines into me—and I see the consciousness of emotion. I am filled with clarity and knowing. Of course, this is the way it has always been. How could I have forgotten this? I know that in a sixth- dimensional reality the physical, mental, emotional, and spiritual bodies all merge into One state of consciousness. How could emotion merge into consciousness if it is not consciousness? I shake my head in sheer amazement. How could I have forgotten this?

By living in a three-dimensional reality, my dear. By taking on a body of that dense vibrational dimension. Emotion is not recognised as a state of consciousness in your frame-of-reality. Carienne smiles in apology. *You were broadcasting!*

Holding my hand on their home, I let it feel my gratitude and appreciation for the inner revelation I have just received. Although I am still feeling shock as the implications of my realisation sink into me, I am aware that the house is registering wellness. Not pleasure at what happened, but a feeling of increased wellness as it shares and integrates my energy. I feel our energy more strongly mixing and merging. As this happens, I inner-see a group of people standing in a circle, holding hands at the place where this home now stands before it was created. Cardifer and Carienne are with her parents, two close friends, and three other people. The energy of the other three indicates that they specialise in home building, utilising energy fusion. They have qualities in their energy-fields that I have never seen before. One has a very strong heart connection with the consciousness of Nature, while another holds a strong empathic connection with the consciousness of human emotion combined with, and channelled through, powerfully focused imagination. The third has a strong ethereal connection with the elemental forces within an etheric dimension. When I say a *strong connection*, I should add that they have a clarity and knowing of their conscious connection that is *very* focused and *very* powerful. Not a shred of doubt or confusion about this exists in them; they have a focus and concentration on the task at hand, which is almost absolute. These three people are specialists. This is definitely not three- dimensional stuff!

They all stand holding hands, eyes closed, for several timeless hours of pure and focused visualisation in Nature, imagination with emotion, and heart intention via the higher etheric. Not for a micro-moment does their attention waver. Then, as an awareness of this procedure slowly unfolds within me, I see the gossamer thin, ghostly outline of the house emerging from an etheric dimension to very slowly take shape where it is now situated. It seems to grow out of the Earth and air. After another long period of no-time, the people open their eyes, smiling at each other. Then, one by one, Carienne, Cardifer, the family and friends stand back, leaving the woman with the elemental connection to now place one hand on the silken-like building as it continues to emerge from an etheric dimension, while she has her other hand open and facing toward the sky.

After a long period, she bows to the building, then respectfully steps back. Next, the man with the Nature connection steps to the house and, kneeling down, he places one hand on the house and the other hand on the Earth. Again, a long period of timelessness passes, and he too gets to his feet, bows, and steps back. The third, a woman, steps forward; one hand is placed on the house, with the other over her solar plexus. Again, the long period of no-time, and she too bows and steps back. All in all, this procedure has taken from sunrise to sunset—even though this is not quite the same as ours in this fifth-dimensional reality.

At this stage, the whole group disperses back to their homes. I watch as over the next few days—they don't measure days as we do; I use it to communicate—the home gradually and gently consolidates. It is rather like watching a flower bud very slowly unfold into the beautiful blossom that awaits, for this home is truly beautiful. Colours of the rainbow flow over the translucence in accordance with the feelings and emotions of those who look at it. At this stage, it is registering the colours of the emotions and consciousness of its creators. During this period it is regularly visited by Cardifer and Carienne as they develop and affirm their relationship with this incredible conscious structure of blended and synchronised human emotion, Nature, and the etheric realms of creation; their home.

I have no idea how long I am standing with my hand on the house as all this insight and vision unfolds within me, but I eventually turn to my dear friends. "Oh my gosh! That was incredible. What an utterly amazing creation."

We realise that you were seeing it created, and we too are astonished by this. You have exceeded all our expectations. We expected you to have some conscious recall, not a full inner-vision of its actual creation.

"I also realise that the consciousness of the home is always linked to the people within it, or energetically connected with it."

This also is correct.

"Are you able to tell me anything about a dimensional shift? I mean, from our three- dimensional reality to your fifth-dimensional reality. I realise that this will not place us here, but it seems to me that Mother Earth herself deserves to experience a higher frequency."

As you know, Mixael, this depends on a complex variation of probabilities. We are not able to make predictions about your reality. We can say that the waxing and waning movements of human consciousness in your reality impinge on ours, rather than affect it, but this only indicates whether your people are accepting and growing, or denying and stagnating. Basic things like this. Beyond that we would be speculating on the probabilities.

"Hmm, I guess my question was a shot in the dark!"

*What is **your** speculation?* Cardifer asks. *How do **you** see the outcome, or the most probable outcome? You are far better placed than we are. You are living in that reality, and while we are not very far away in consciousness, we are far away in the divine and loving principles of everyday living.*

"Which is a higher consciousness! In truth, you are a long way ahead of us."

Cardifer and Carienne both shrug, smiling a touch ruefully.

We walk into the Nature of their garden. When I say their 'garden', it is simply a reference with which we are familiar. Here, they have no gardens, as such. The beautiful translucent home has a relationship with the land on which it stands, drawing energy from the Earth, the etheric realms, and the balanced emotions of the inhabitants. It then returns this energy, combined and fused into one unique energy combination that is of, and more than, the original indrawn energy. Because of this process, the 'garden' is not tamed and cultivated. Each of these incredible, conscious homes stands on an area which for us would be around a hectare. In a way, all this belongs to the consciousness of the home. Except there is no belonging! The conscious home has a relationship with all the surrounding area of a conscious Nature. Knowing the consciousness of its inhabitants, the home organises the Nature of the area to grow and present itself in the way that is most pleasing and fulfilling to the people who live there. They, in turn, love and appreciate the surroundings. This love and appreciation feeds their conscious energy back into that of the home and Nature, which creates a perfect natural cycle of ever-growing consciousness.

In this 'garden' it is clear that naturalness obviously pleases Carienne and Cardifer. It is not wild Nature that surrounds them, neither is it tamed. Birds and animals abound, very similar to what we might see in our more remote gardens. The area in which they live appears as though the spirits of Nature have created a landscape easy to walk in, easy to see through, yet it somehow appears as though to be untouched by any landscaping. About three centuries ago, the Japanese developed a way to fasten a purse to their kimono sash with a netsuke. This netsuke was carved from some odd-looking stone, or a piece of twisted wood, or misshapen seedpod, etc., but always something from Nature. The art was to bring the greatest expression out of the object with the very least human interference and input possible. Some of the netsukes that collectors own are incredible works of art. My point is that the area around the conscious home is rather like this. It is changed without any sign that it has been changed. Utterly beautiful, awe-inspiring, and, as with the netsukes, energetically enhanced.

All this simply comes back to me as we walk in the area of the home/Nature energy. And, as usual, I am broadcasting my unfolding inner knowing and clarity.

Your conscious recall is really quite astonishing.

"You earlier mentioned that your relationship with time is different from ours. But we did not follow through on this aspect of fifth-dimensional life."

Again, Mixael, focus on your inner knowing of this.

I do so—and knowing is there! In this reality they have time in the way we do, even though they live in the consciousness of spherical time, but they do not create time linear in the way that we do. If they have an agreement to meet a friend in—three weeks, our time!—a specified future moment, this is imprinted in their consciousness. They do not forget, because this is not about memory; it is about the conscious moment. If we have a reminder pop up on our computer screen, we do not have to remember every birthday in the family. For the people in this reality, once the appointment is imprinted, it will pop up in their consciousness in perfect, appropriate timing. They do have a past and a future for reference, but they consciously live in the conscious moment. For us, the very idea that the *moment* is conscious is unheard of— but the moment *is* conscious. The moment is the only place for the full expression of consciousness, and this could not happen if the moment was not conscious within itself. The moment is pure consciousness, receiving and expressing consciousness. Sorry, you either get this or you do not!

I speak to Cardifer and Carienne. "You are correct again; the essence of time has come back to me. But it's rather tricky to explain. I do have another question that you may need to answer. As I look at your home, I see that it is more than three dimensional, but I don't have a language for what that 'more' is. To me, I see a toroidal shape in the house, which is taken beyond any three-dimensional torus that I have ever seen. Can you elaborate on this?"

Cardifer chuckles. *I can use words and descriptions that are not in your language, and you may even know what I mean, but how will you communicate it in your reality? However, to keep this as simple as possible, let me state it this way. Whenever you use the higher etheric or higher astral energies as a means of conscious creation, then you are stepping beyond the ordinary three-dimensional structure with which we are all familiar. You see the result of using our focused emotional energy, along with a higher etheric energy in the creation of our home. If we were to go into one of our cities, you would see what happens when you add the higher astral aspect to this.*

I should add here that cities in this fifth-dimension reality are nothing like our cities. Because transport is personal, without limits and almost instantaneous, the cities are spread out within Nature, and also grown from it. Thus, their cities embody that vital creative relationship between the buildings, Nature, directed emotional imagery, and the higher etheric and astral energies, all in a harmonious dynamic. Although the cities are not densely populated, they have the most incredible buildings which—to us—defy all laws of gravity. For us, their towering spires of creation would be pure fantasy. Gravity, too, is different here! In this reality, they harness gravity in a way that allows them to create geometric shapes that would be impossible without controlled gravity. They use controlled gravity as a means to stabilise their creations.

This is wonderful, Mixael. It is all coming back so easily.

"This has been a truly wonderful visit for me. I came specifically to ask you a whole heap of questions about fifth-dimensional reality, and you have shown me that it is all within my own state of consciousness. This is the big thing you have given me. I have tried to remember my Mixael knowledge in my daily life, but it always seemed to evade me. Now I know that it is not based in memory, so it cannot be remembered. It is all within my consciousness, just waiting for me to recognise it. I cannot put into words how grateful I am to both of you, my very dear friends, and your wondrous and beautiful home."

It has been our great pleasure. As you now return, we know that within your consciousness all you need will be there as you need it. As you would say . . . trust!

We share hugs of Love/Light, and I step . . . Between . . . and out into my study.

I am instantly connected with Pan.

Did you get the answers to your questions?

"You know perfectly well what happened!"

In fact, you got far more than you expected. You have learned more about consciousness. Just as the **knowing** *is within you, so also it is in all people. Different levels of knowing, maybe, but far more is available to each person than questions will manage to uncover. This was why some of those devoted to their spiritual paths used to practice contemplation. Today, many people practice meditation, but very few follow the path of contemplation.*

"I'm not sure that many people would know how, or even what contemplation is."

How would you explain it?

I smile. "I should be good at this by now. Let me first explain the difference between meditation and contemplation. Meditation is about reaching silence; no thought, no mind, just pure Beingness. Contemplation is about taking a thought, concept, or idea—time, for example—and focusing on it. . . then letting it go . . . while holding it within your attention. You do not think about it, nor question it, nor seek understanding or explanation . . . nothing. You simply hold it within your attention and observe whatever flows into your awareness. Eventually, with practice, you deeply connect with the essence and energy of time. And in perfect timing, it will reveal itself to you. Good pun, huh?"

I feel the delightful inner smile of Pan. *A good explanation. Now you should be ready to follow the suggestion of Cardifer. What is the most probable outcome of the planetary changes that you face?*

"You probably know exactly what will probably happen, because you, my most beloved of non-physical teachers, are the principle God of Nature."

And if it is probable that I probably do . . . ?

"I know . . . you are simply getting me to dig into my overworked consciousness once more. Okay . . . the question: In my exceedingly humble speculation, which is the most probable of the probabilities facing us during the big Change?

Do not answer to me. Speak/write your answer to the people who will read your book.

"Hmm, that's a good idea. Thank you, beloved Pan. See you later."

※   ※   ※

After all I have been through, I do have a unique insight into this time of major Change. But be aware, Dear Reader, that all this is no more than my selection of three of the most probable of the continually changing probabilities. The more people choosing Love during this period, the more profound will be the affect on the overall outcome. I cannot highlight this enough.

I would also like to emphasise that a humanity ensnared in more-of-the-same is the very worst possible scenario for our future. Change *is* taking place, but this is still with the minority of people. If the mass human consciousness continues into another cycle of repetition, this will lead us to the very worst possible outcome. Do not fear major Change—welcome it.

Before I offer my selection, I wish to make a clear, strong statement. It matters not at all whether any of my selection come about, or not . . . *we are going to experience major global Change.* This is not a probability, it is a certainty. It is impossible for our planet to sustain a continuation of our consumer driven society. Our human population increases by two hundred thousand people daily, and we are already consuming the resources of one and a half earth planets to sustain our western greed. If the world's population was to consume the same as the U.S. is today, it would require nine earth planets to provide the resources. And this is the direction we are heading. We are a human population tottering on the brink of mass 'unsanity'—not insane, but definitely not sane! Poverty is becoming rampant. I state for a certainty that the world's economy is close to *total* collapse; this means the closure of all banks. And this is *very* close. It may happen before you read this.

Our oceans will soon be so drastically depleted that they will no longer be a food source. Our world's fresh water is rapidly becoming increasingly scarce. Our forests are being depleted at a horrific speed. We have a huge and dramatic increase in human malnutrition, suicides, starvation and diseases, along with unprecedented mental and emotional illnesses. For our very survival, within the next two *decades* our way of living will be compelled to change more than during any two *centuries* of change in human history. There is not a person who will not face major Change in our coming years.

You may ask, "Why is it so? Why can't we create voluntary change?" The answer is simple and brief. We have created the problems because our human consciousness has not grown, only the human intellect. We let go of 'wisdom' and embraced 'clever'. We forgot that 'clever' holds hands with 'stupid'! I will say it one more time; by relying on our intellect and living subconsciously, we do not grow in consciousness. Only by constantly using conscious intelligence do we consciously grow. Watch or read the media for proof! In clear and simple terms, humanity will be compelled to grow in consciousness. Those who are open to newness will be able to help build a new world, those who cling to more-of-the-same will not be here.

So, having said this, I will define my selection in three leading categories of Change. Let me say also that these categories are not separate, for each will act upon and affect the others. I have separated them simply for the sake of my presentation; they are not in any particular order.

1 . . . The human consciousness: mostly metaphysical.
2 . . . The Chaos rising factor: mostly physical.
3 . . . The dimensional shift: metaphysical and physical.

The human consciousness:
Mostly metaphysical, this will be the most preferred choice on offer!

Throughout the past millennium we have all had endless opportunities to either grow in consciousness, or stagnate. Generally, we have all grown intellectually, but at the cost of our basic intelligence, our common sense. As I have often stated, growing intellectually does not necessarily mean growing in consciousness, although this can and does happen for very many people. Nevertheless spiritual concepts are *not* spirituality, they are the intellectualism of spirituality.

We have reached the place in this human cycle where each person falls into one of two basic types; the 'more-of-the-same' mass of people, or the fewer 'newness and openness' people. The huge majority of people cling to the old, the repetition, the safe and secure, while the minority encourage and propagate newness in their lives. Of course, there are subcategories in this; those people who cling to sameness, yet are kind-hearted and loving, and those people who welcome newness, yet are mean-hearted and spiteful. We *are* a complicated race of Beings!

As you will note, this summary is *hugely* over-simplified.

A strong probability is that as we continue deeper into the currently happening shift in human consciousness, nothing will appear to change. The many predictions will be seen as a big joke, the flop of the century, and people like me will be open to ridicule. In this probability, however, as each person reaches the end of their physical life—whether by some accident, or illness, or natural causes, or whatever—each person will eventually incarnate into the continuing reality expression of the last few millennia of their many lifetimes.

Some of the 'more-of-the-same' types will incarnate into the relatively peaceful times of the hunter/gatherers, while those with major aggression issues will probably incarnate into times of prolonged and violent warfare. But each will be in the reality that most perfectly fits the state of consciousness which they have created and in which they have lived. In the 'open to newness' classification, the probability is most of the people will incarnate into a Golden Age

Certainly, those 'more-of-the-same' people who are kind and compassionate will incarnate into a reality expressing this, while those few people of 'newness' who have remained poor in spirit will incarnate into their own reality expression. For whatever type of person I very loosely describe, each will be in the reality of their own expression and creation.

And no person will ever know that this has all happened before!

The Chaos rising factor:
Mostly physical, this probability will probably be on everyone's hit list!

The simple reality is that Chaos *is* rising—fast. The sun is becoming ever more active as vast cosmic winds blow closer to it than at any time in our history. These are not winds such as we experience; these are winds blasting at millions of kilometres per hour. Solar flares can be immense beyond imagining; bigger than Earth! The sun changed its polarity a few years ago, and now, with increasing sun activity, the electromagnetic field of our Earth is becoming increasingly destabilised. Add to this our wandering North Pole, the shifting pockets of polarity, and subtle gravitational changes, and we have the ingredients to seriously destabilise our planet. The result: volcanic activity, earthquakes and tsunamis. Despite this, I have seen a probability where just the vast sun flares are enough to erase our global electricity supply. I am no electrician, but I do know that it does not take much to cause a power outage or power cuts!

With the probability of the world's electrical power erased, the resulting probabilities are not pleasant to contemplate. It suggests that every nuclear power plant on the planet is now a threat to us because of overheating; meaning—meltdown. With Europe liberally dotted with outdated and vulnerable nuclear power plants, this suggests holocaust conditions. It is the same scenario along the West Coast of America, and with other nuclear power plants all over the world.

To this probable global devastation, add no communication, no moving vehicles, no heat, no water, no food, no lights, no hospitals or medication, and a global population almost insane with fear. This probability is one of violent and massive Earth Change. It is one where Earth plates may shift suddenly and violently. It is a probability that savagely and drastically reduces the human population. And it has happened before! Even without any destructive Earth changes, we would most probably destroy ourselves! It is certainly a probability that will define our personal levels of consciousness. There will be many who, without a qualm, will kill to survive. If our cities become bloody killing fields, we will rudely learn that although some of us live in a sophisticated and high-tech world, this should never imply that it is a civilised one. The hunter/gatherers were *far* more civilised than we are.

In this probability, we join with the probabilities of the human consciousness. If any of us kill to survive, our eventual death will place us in our own personal hell. If we attempt to help others, not deserting our Love and compassion, and we get killed, we will be in our own personal heaven. I repeat once again: death is purely physical. We are immortal Beings living in mortal bodies. We are soul Beings and as souls we continue, no matter what happens to the body or the planet. I could write more of this probability, but you already get the point of this. We, each one of us, are the creators of our own life-paths; we create their direction, we create their content, we create their destination.

The dimensional shift:
Metaphysical and physical, this probability sounds quite mild — it is not!

It is probable that we will experience a polar shift. The Poles are unstable, particularly the North Pole. It is not by accident that over ninety percent of our population lives in the northern hemisphere where the polarity is intensifying, and is already *unstable*. Add to this, we are an unstable humanity. We need to remember that everything on our planet that is happening is connected to everything on our planet that is happening. And I mean exactly this! Consider also the fact that, particularly in the north, immense pockets of polarity deep in the planet are shifting. The effects of the increasingly powerful polarity energy are affecting humanity. Everybody is energetically being polarised: we are either moving more strongly to the negative, or more strongly to the positive, of human nature. Everyone's 'stuff' is coming up — everyone's! How we each resolve it during this present time period will depend on which way we are polarising our energy. This 'polarity balancing' is entirely our own, individual responsibility.

Okay, add to this equation the dimensional shift that is already taking place. Ergo, those people who move with a positive polarisation of their energy-fields are now shifting into a fourth- dimensional reality. Those who move with the negative polarisation of the human energy-fields will stay embedded in the three-dimensional reality. None of this is right or wrong; it is the outcome of the growth or the non-growth in our personal expressions of consciousness. It is probable that as the polarity intensifies, so the dimensional pull will intensify, compelling us toward one side of the fence, or the other. There will be no fence sitting!

When we reach the crucial point where all humanity has moved into the frequency of their polarity field — it gets interesting. When this happens, it is probable that we will get a period of *total* darkness. Let me speculate here. Imagine we had three days of absolute darkness. No stars, no moon, no glimmer of light on the planet or in the sky. Three days where nothing that uses an electrical charge will work . . . including flashlights. Candles, yes; a flame is an element of Nature, but even the light of a flame will be determined by our polarity. So, three days of total can't-see-a-hand-in-front-of-us darkness. Add to this the probability of the Mayan prediction of the ending of linear time. The probability here is again affected by our state of consciousness: the period of *total* darkness could feel like an endless nightmare, or it could be experienced as mere moments of rapture.

During this period of total darkness, of timeless no-time, a full dimensional shift takes place. For each and every one of us, this means a period of complete energetic transition into 'more-of-the-same' or, into a 'reality of Newness'.

On the fourth day a renewed sun shines new Light on a transformed planet Earth.

We are now in a fifth-dimensional reality — a Golden Age is born.

The planet is new, revitalised. All pollution is gone; the rivers and lakes are now pure sparkling water, the atmosphere clean and clear, the oceans regenerated. Gradually, people realise that only one type of person remains on the New Earth. The people with a positive, loving polarity. It is the end of all war. The end of all tyranny. The end of base human negativity. The end of police, of law enforcement, of force. Instead, it is a humanity of Love, of newness, of new creation. A humanity of responsibility, of compassion, of freedom. New, powerful free energy sources are now available to the people of a higher consciousness.

We make the shift from one in seven people living with daily hunger to one in seven people spiritually enlightened. Everything . . . *everything* changes.

What happens to all the other people? They will probably be living in the continuing reality of the life they knew. They will say, "Those idiots were wrong, nothing happened." They may even ask, "Where did so many people go?" But they will very quickly forget us. We will not ask, we will know.

Okay . . . all this is a definite probability with a little personal speculation based on my metaphysical experiences and insights.

Can we make this our reality? Yes, we can. In every moment of your life, in every situation in your life, in every confrontation in your life, in the face of every fear in your life, with every person in your life, with every tiny aspect in your life, with the *self* of your life . . . always, always, always . . . choose Love.

Love is not something you have, or can intellectualise. Love is the living, creative energy of the Being you are. You *are* Love and Light. But you have to consciously live that Love.

Choose Love. Live Love. Be Love.

Choose . . . live . . . be . . . divine, absolute, unconditional LOVE.

See you in a New and Golden Age.

AFTERWORD

Four and a half months have elapsed since I finished this manuscript. Carolyn and I have been on my annual tour of spiritual teaching, consequently expanding my view of world events during our visits to twelve other countries. During this time the e-book version of this book has been made available. Now, before publishing the printed version, I wish to add a few more words regarding my perceived changes in the probability of major Change.

This is not based in my metaphysical travels with Pan, but rather in my own insights and intuition regarding the overall movements in human consciousness. My feeling is that the people who are choosing Love are rapidly decreasing the probability of catastrophic and damaging Earth Changes. No power is greater than the power of Love, and no power can bring a more positive potential for Change than Love. While we have the apparent dichotomy of a far greater percentage of people taking a negative approach to life, their negative energy has nowhere near the effect as the energy of those people expressing the power of Love. We have reached the time when the few have a far greater influence over our future than the many.

Those choosing and living Love are expressing in a fourth-dimensional reality, while those moving in the direction of fear are becoming more deeply embedded in our third-dimensional reality. The year 2012 is a pivotal time in our human history. The indication is that the far greater creative power of a higher dimension will swing the balance away from a huge scale of catastrophic disasters to more of an apocalypse . . . not meaning global destruction as in the Bible, but taking the original Old English and ecclesiastical Latin meaning of *uncovering and revealing* the truth. By this I mean the truth about the mass manipulation, repression, and exploitation of the people of the world by the cabals of the Illuminati.

I know that we are not alone in this universe, nor in this galaxy; my metaphysical travels have clearly verified this. I also know that what affects one cell in a human body affects the whole body. Equally, what affects one planet in the galaxy affects the whole galaxy. I am convinced that the cabal thugs have had negative help from those in the galaxy who specialise in the exploitation of other Beings. I am equally certain that we will have galactic intervention from those far more powerful, Love-based Beings who have a concern for our future welfare. We are living in the time of a major flux of Change. If this Change was catastrophic— as in the loss of the world's electricity and the consequent meltdown of the world's nuclear power stations—it would be an event which would eventually kill billions. I intuitively feel that this will not happen. It would achieve nothing in consciousness. Galactic intervention could easily neutralise our nuclear weapons and power plants with their far superior technology, and my heart and my intuition embrace this probability.

The key to Change is simple. Those who choose the positive power of Love will be moved toward a positive and loving reality future, while those who negatively react with fear, blame, and aggression will be moved toward a future reflecting this consciousness.

I can only repeat my mantra . . . Choose Love.

About the Author

The deep wisdom contained in Michael's spiritual Enlightenment and his inner-experience of unconditional Love is the basis for his 5-Day Intensives, seminars and books, currently in thirteen languages. Michael's public speaking tours have included invitations to Australia, New Zealand, Norfolk Island, South Africa, The Netherlands, Italy, Switzerland, Austria, Belgium, Germany, France, UK, Denmark, Sweden, Norway, West Indies, U.S.A., Canada and Japan.

An extraordinarily gifted communicator, Michael imparts and conveys unconditional Love heart-to-heart, far beyond the reach of words, creating the space to awaken from a dream . . . to ignite the Love that exists within each person.

Michael's 5-Day Intensives are based in Unconditional Love and emotional completeness.

For information on Michael's international events, tour schedule, books, CDs, free audio downloads and much more, please visit:

www.michaelroads.com

RoadsLight pty ltd
PO Box 778
Nambour, QLD 4560
Australia

info@michaelroads.com

CPSIA information can be obtained at www.ICGtesting.com
Printed in the USA
BVOW04s2202180615

405303BV00001B/16/P